ChauceR POET OF MIRTH AND MORALITY

HELEN STORM CORSA

———————

chaucer

POET OF MIRTH AND MORALITY

———————

UNIVERSITY OF NOTRE DAME PRESS

By permission, all textual references
are to *The Works of Geoffrey Chaucer*,
edited by F. N. Robinson, second edition,
1957, published by Houghton Mifflin
Company, Boston, Massachusetts

Publication of this book was
aided by a grant from the Ford Foundation

pREfatORy notE

There are many reasons for the continued enjoyment of Chaucer's poetry. One of the most important of these is, of course, the comic vision one participates in. The centuries that have passed since his death in 1400 have in no way diminished the quality of the joy his poetry arouses. It is a joy manifested in many ways, all the way from a quiet sense of well-being to the open and spontaneous laugh.

This study is an exploration of some of the ways Chaucer's vision of life and of the human condition is comic. Its governing thesis is that his poetry provokes joy because his philosophical and theological view of life confirms some of man's most treasured dreams. Indeed, it affirmed, and continues to affirm, in its artistic complexity, the possible realization into actuality of some of man's most essential wishes. In short, his mirth reveals his moral premises. It proclaims an Order, both in this world and the next, even as it celebrates the struggle of the individual to maintain equilibrium in spite of obstacles both within and without the self. All his poetry, whether elegy, tragedy, romance, saint's legend, or fabliau attests to his acceptance of the complexities inherent in coexistence, dynamic and dramatic, of two potentially warring elements: the assertion of the self and that of what he called the "common profit." His mirth is moral and his morality is mirthful. It is this that keeps him perpetually fresh in his comedy.

I have incurred, as any interpreter must, so many debts from the accumulated treasury of Chaucerian criticism and commentary that I do not know how to begin the task of acknowledging them. It is a debt accruing from the words of his earliest critics to the words of those who have continued to illuminate his poetry in our own day. What is one's own in the blur of memory formed by many years of familiarity with the works of the poet and of his critics is not possible to designate. What insight is coincidentally another's, what particular suggestion created for me some new insight into the text at some time or other, are matters I am not able to recognize, regardless of how much I would like to. To many of my students I owe much. Their ready interest, their quick perception and frank enthusiasm, were the most important incentives for this study.

To those who have read this exploration of Chaucer's comic art and have made suggestions I am very grateful. Especially to Professors Mary Ruth Michael and Naomi Diamond, colleagues of mine, must I "doon some observaunce." They never pleaded "the diversity of thinges" academic as a way out of examining and criticizing. To Howard Rollin Patch, "worthy friend" of Chaucer, I owe special thanks. Like "Affrycan" in *The House of Fame,* he was always cheerfully intent upon pointing out the error but never ceased to attend upon the good "aventure." His recent death has diminished the ranks of medieval scholars to a degree that cannot be measured.

For the year's leave of absence which gave me the opportunity to finish this study, I thank the President and the Trustees of Wellesley College. To all those who endured the writing of it I dedicate "this bok of which I make mencioun." I hope that "if ther be any thyng that displese hem . . . they arrette it to the defaute of myn unkonnynge, and nat to my wyl, that wolde ful fayn have seyd bettre, if I hadde had konnynge."

Wellesley, Massachusetts
August, 1963

contents

part one

---

the early poems

chapter 1

THE EARLY POEMS:
PRELUDES TO COMEDY

The four poems, *The Book of the Duchess, The House of Fame, The Parliament of Fowls,* and *The Legend of Good Women,* usually called "Early" in the Chaucer canon, in comparison to *Troilus and Criseyde* and *The Canterbury Tales* are minor achievements. They are nevertheless important preludes to the major achievements and contain within them not only thematic concerns and narrative techniques that will be characteristic of the greater poems, but also intimations as to the particular nature of Chaucer's comedy.

Exactly in what order the four poems were composed has not been settled conclusively. It is certain, however, that *The Book of the Duchess* is the earliest, and for the interpreter of Chaucer's art this is fortunate. Although a poem of a fairly young poet, it is a complex and sophisticated one, revealing a "maker" already sensitive to the significance of form, already skilled in the control and projection of content. That there are awkwardnesses in the making of rhymes or that there is a monotony in the verse form are observations that do not detract from the validity of the conclusions one can draw, conclusions that provide reliable criteria for the study of the companion poems. To put it briefly, this poem confirms one of the essential premises of this book: Chaucer knew what he was about, and an understanding of what he was clearly about is a welcome guide to the study of all poetry that follows *The Book of the Duchess.*

Although owing nothing to the form or to the traditions of the classical elegy and resembling in no way the elegiac poems of the Middle Ages, *The Book of the Duchess* can be called "an elegy." The happy fact about occasional poems is that the interpreter need not apologize for talking about the poet's intention. Whether commissioned by John of Gaunt or offered to him by Chaucer upon the death of Blanche in 1369, the poem was intended to commemorate and to console. This it does in ways that are graceful, in ways that convey ultimately a joy that transcends the particular grief. Bereavement and loss, sorrow and loneliness, the undeniable fact of death, are the subject matter of this poem and are never minimized; yet because of the way Chaucer shapes and formulates his matter the poem, in the very act of lamenting, becomes a poem in praise of the love that had been between John of Gaunt and his duchess, a celebration of life.

For the scheme of his elegy Chaucer chose that of the Love or Dream Vision, a form popular throughout the Middle Ages. The choice was an apt one. The form by its nature was dramatic as much as it was narrative. Its convention that made of the poet a dreamer as well as a visionary gave Chaucer a chance to create a small drama with settings, entrances and exits, two characters, a miniature plot with suspense and climax and resolution. And the small drama made it possible for him to offer consolation in a way so indirect as to avoid the pitfalls of sentimentality and easy piety, yet so clear as to translate the desolation of loss into a peaceful acceptance. The poetic talent that made the most of the dramatic properties in the convention of the Dream Vision, that made out of the fact of loss an affirmation of the fact of love is the same poetic talent that made out of the contentions and exigencies of life the comedy of the Canterbury pilgrimage.

Of the two characters in the poem the narrator appears first and holds the center of attention for the first four hundred and forty-five lines. It is he who is the protagonist, the one to whom something happens. It is he who hears the story of the life, the love, and the loss experienced by "the man in black" and who grows from callow imperception in the course of the dream into a kind of imaginative and emotional maturity. Though he only dimly senses that something important has happened to him, his organization of the dream into an account of it reveals that an understanding of the full significance is not far from him. It does not matter whether the narrator is identified as Chaucer or as a character created for the part. What matters is what kind of man he is before he meets with the man in black in the dream and what happens to him as he begins slowly, somewhat obtusely, to take in what it is that is being told him. Even at the moment of awakening he is aware that so "queynt a sweven" is full of import. In due course of time he will put it in rhyme "as I kan best." In the meantime the recounting of the "sweven" as it happened to him must suffice. The poem, of course, reveals exactly what it is that the dream has done to him, and what it reveals is that in the encounter with the fact of love and the fact of death, the narrator-poet has been made aware of the degrees of the felt reality of both. His growth, from the literary and artificial understanding of love and death to the sense of what they really are, makes of the particular loss suffered by John of Gaunt an experience that becomes universalized. Some of the quality of the graciousness of this elegy is created by this universalization.

The lines that open the poem seem upon casual reading to be straight narrative, accomplishing the usual things that must be accomplished before anything of importance can happen. What they actually achieve is of far greater significance than this. Although there is to be no reference to death or to loss for some time, the narrator is in a mood that is explicitly "melancholy." The minor key of the poem is sounded immediately, the key that, with the exception of a significant shift to the relative major, will remain the key of the whole poem. Sleepless in the melancholy, he has what is almost a sense of the loss of self, an awareness of emptiness, even a haunting moment when he feels meaningless:

> I have gret wonder, be this lyght,
> How that I lyve, for day ne nyght
> I may nat slepe wel nygh noght,
> I have so many an ydel thoght,
> Purely for defaute of slep,
> That, by my trouthe, I take no kep
> Of nothing, how hyt cometh or gooth,
> Ne me nys nothyng leef nor looth.
> Al is ylyche good to me—
> Joye or sorowe, wherso hyt be—
> For I have felynge in nothyng,
> But, as yt were, a mased thyng,
> Alway in poynt to falle a-doun;
> For sorwful ymaginacioun
> Ys alway hooly in my mynde.
>
> (1-15)

His spirit "sleyn . . . of quyknesse" so that he has lost "al lustyhede" makes him "fear for to dye." The effects of the "sorwful ymaginacioun," of the felt depression, he can describe precisely; about the cause of it he is unclear. The suggestion is that he has been suffering unrequited or unacknowledged or unproclaimed love "this eight yeer,/ And yet my boote is never the ner." It is the depression itself that matters, not the cause; it is the feeling that nothing is dear or hateful to him, that "al is ylyche good," that preoccupies him. Sad and melancholy "by the book," causelessly unhappy at the beginning, the adventure of the dream will show him the nature of real sorrow and will leave him almost aware at the moment of awaking of the difference between real anguish and the gentle sadness he has taken to be the "real thing."

With apparent indirection and irrelevance Chaucer leads his narrator by two stages into the important experience that is the significant matter of the poem. In the first stage he is awake and in his restless search for release from his woe and sleeplessness he calls for a book to distract him. In the book that "spak . . ./ Of quenes lives, and kinges" he reads of the death of the "king Seys" and the lament of Alcione, the queen. In the second stage he is asleep and dreams of meeting a "man in black" who tells him of the death of his lady and laments his loss. The two accounts of love and loss in death are closely related though not clearly so to the poet-dreamer. His recounting of both the tale he found in the book and the experience of the dream shows him to be somewhat puzzled about the meaning of them. He does indeed speak of what he does not really understand. As the man in black says to him at significant moments, "thow wost ful lytel what thow menest." Thus it is that in spite of our awareness of his melancholy, we are also given a view of him in his gentlemanly obtuseness that is a comic view. The figure of the poet-dreamer is from the beginning an amusing one, yet the humor created by our understanding of him never detracts from the grave simplicity or from the sad dignity of his reporting of the tale and the dream.

The poet-dreamer is a man of literal as well as literary mind. He retells the story of Seys and Alcione with economy, each detail important in ways that he does not consciously recognize. But the tale has clear importance for Chaucer's elegiac intention and its retelling says much to John of Gaunt about the way to accept the fact of death. In miniature it is what the drama of the whole poem in honor of the Duchess will tell: that love *is* and death *is* in existential reality, and that the acceptance of the fact of death is the only consolation possible in existential reality. Before the confrontation in the dream of the poet-narrator with the fact of the particular death of Blanche, he encounters the fact of death in an artifact; the particular experience is prepared for by the literary experience and before it is undergone is thus already part of universal human experience.

Like the lovers of the dream, Seys and Alcione are man and wife, though in the "romaunce" it is the husband, Seys, who dies, not the wife. Alcione's fear of loss and the quality of her love are conveyed in very few lines, but they are intimations of the great anguish in the loss of his love felt by "the man in black." " 'Alas' quoth shee, 'that I was wrought!/ And wher my lord, my love, be deed?' " (90-91). To the account of the un-happiness of the queen the poet responds with real feeling, his initial

mood that held all joy and sorrow to be "ylyche good" and thus in-
distinguishable now lessening:

> Such sorowe this lady to her tok
> That trewly I, which made this book,
> Had such pittee and such rowthe
> To rede hir sorwe, that, by my trowthe,
> I ferde the worse al the morwe
> Aftir, to thenken on hir sorwe.
>
> (95-100)

That he can take to heart the distress of a lady of literary legend but is
so reluctant to believe in the loss of a real lady creates an irony that is
more comic than tragic, but at the same time promises well for his final
response to the "man in black" when it comes in its full conviction.

The recounting of the tale continues to work its multiple purpose, revealing the character of the reader, laying a basis for the irony to come,
and offering in prefatory form, consolation to John of Gaunt. Alcione cries
out in her sorrow for a dream in which the fate of her husband will be
revealed, for "som certeyn sweven/ Wherthourgh that I may knowen
even/ Whether my lord be quyk or ded" (119-121). The popular belief
that dreams can be revelations of truth functions importantly here: it
warns the narrator that he should be aware of the clear significance of
his dream that is to come and at the same time it says to John of Gaunt
that what the dream is to say about the quality of his love for Blanche
and the pain of his loss is in the nature of a revelation granted as a kind
of grace. The prayer of Alcione is granted. The moment is a comic one.
The agitated busyness of Juno in sending her messenger to Morpheus,
"the god of slep," to request that he "go faste into the grete se,/ . . . take
up Seys body the kyng,/ That lyeth ful pale and nothyng rody" (140,
142-143); the recounting of the arrival of the messenger at the ear of
Morpheus, crying "O, ho! awake anoon," threatens the solemnity of the
tale. But it is the way in which the story of Seys and Alcione is concluded
that resolves the sorrow not into banal piety but into the relief that knowing and accepting reality can bring. Standing at the foot of the bed on
which lay the woeful Alcione, uncertain of the fate of her husband,
Morpheus in the appearance of the drowned Seys "called hir ryght as
she het/ By name." And his words constitute the climax of the tale in
its function in the elegy:

> "My swete wyf,
> Awake! let be your sorwful lyf!
> For in your sorwe there lyth no red,

For, certes, swete, I nam but ded;
Ye shul me never on lyve yse.
But, goode swete herte, that ye
Bury my body, for such a tyde
Ye mowe hyt fynde the see besyde;
And farewel, swete, my worldes blysse!
I praye God youre sorwe lysse.
To lytel while oure blysse lasteth!"
                                    (201-211)

"For certes, swete, I nam but ded" is an assertion of such simplicity that it places the fact of death in a perspective allowing neither for an exaggeration of its importance nor for a diminution of its sadness. And in the reminder that "To lytel while oure blysse lasteth" lies the hint that sorrow also is not eternal. In the conclusion of the retold story Chaucer offers to John of Gaunt his first real consolation, an offer all the more effective and graceful in its dramatic indirectness, made without the conscious awareness of the poet-narrator, freed of all the clumsiness and awkwardness of direct statement.

What the poet-narrator now wants is sleep, an escape from the sorrow he has been in as well as a refreshment for his weary body, for it is "agaynes kynde/ . . . to lyven in thys wyse;/ For nature wolde nat suffyse/ To noon erthly creature/ Nat longe tyme to endure/ Withoute slep and be in sorwe" (16-21). His common sense is but another evidence of his somewhat practical and literal mind and points up his figure as an amusing one. But at the same time the words indirectly and gently admonish John of Gaunt. Half in jest, half in earnest, impressed by the account in the "romaunce" of the effectiveness of prayers to Morpheus, the "god of slep," the poet-narrator makes his own prayer. Ironically, the tale of death has left him gayer in spirits than he had been. The relish with which he details his offerings to the god "or hys goddesse, dame Juno,/ Or som wight elles" if sleep will come to him creates a passage of transition not only from the state of being awake to the state of sleeping and dreaming, but also a movement from the melancholy of the opening of the poem to the joyousness of the beginning of the dream. From the moment the poet promises in semi-jest, gifts in return for the gift of sleep to the moment he meets, in his dream, the figure of the "man in black," the mood of the poem is gay.

The promise "in game" of a feather-bed "Of down of pure dowves white/ . . . Rayed with gold, and ryght wel cled/ In fyn blak satyn doutremer," of many a pillow "of cloth of Reynes," of painting the god's halls "with pure gold" and tapestrying them "many fold" to his surprise wins him sleep: "sodeynly, I nyste how,/ Such a lust anoon me took/ To slepe, that ryght upon my book/ Y fil aslepe" (250-275). And the sleep brings the dream, so wondrous and so sweet, "Y trowe no man had the wyt/ To konne wel my sweven rede" (278-279). The gaiety of the dream is the context within which sorrow is described and made real; ironically again, the elegy becomes more joyous than sad while never reducing the quality of sorrow that is being immortalized.

Death, love, loss, sorrow seem far removed from the mind of the poet and from the intention of the poem as the dream begins. Faithful to medieval convention, it opens as all good dream-vision poems opened: "Hyt was May." The poet, now asleep, dreams that he awakens, as indeed he is shortly to awaken to realities he had been asleep to at the beginning of the poem. The joyous brightness he finds around him fills him with gladness. The "smale foules" that had roused him "thorgh noyse and swetnesse of her song" sat on the tiles above his "chambre"

> And songen, everych in hys wyse,
> The moste solempne servise
> By noote, that ever man, y trowe,
> Had herd; for som of hem song lowe,
> Som high, and al of oon acord.
> To telle shortly, att oo word,
> Was never herd so swete a steven,—
> But hyt had be a thyng of heven,—
> So mery a soun, so swete entewnes,
> That certes, for the toun of Tewnes,
> I nolde but I had herd hem synge;
> For al my chambre gan to rynge
> Thurgh syngynge of her armonye.
>   (301-313)

"The mery . . . soun" fills the room with a gaiety matched only by the bright loveliness of the wall paintings and of the glass in the windows "that to beholde hyt was gret joye." With affection the Dreamer gives some particulars about the pictures, listing the stories that were so popular in his day: the story of Troy, of Hector, of Medea and Jason, and "bothe text and glose,/ Of al the Romaunce of the Rose." The list seems to have little relevance for the central fact of the whole poem, and its inclusion can be judged to be "mere convention." Actually it sounds the note in the far distance of the theme of loss and of love.

Joy permeates the whole atmosphere of the poem and seems almost to possess the poet-dreamer in a kind of ecstasy. "My wyndowes were shette echon," he relates,

> And throgh the glas the sonne shon
> Upon my bed with bryghte bemes,
> With many glade gilde stremes;
> And eke the welkin was so fair,—
> Blew, bryght, clere was the ayr,
> And ful attempre for sothe hyt was;
> For nother to cold nor hoot yt nas;
> Ne in al the welken was no clowde.
>
> > (336-343)

Into this sunlit clarity, matching it in brilliance, comes the sound of a horn being tested by a hunter "for to knowe/ Whether hyt were clere or hors of soun." All that matters to the dreamer is to respond to the vital joy of the moment. His melancholy far in his waking past, he takes his own horse and joins the hunt that is clattering into action outside his "chambre." Except for the hint that the hunt is a hunt to "slee the hert with strengthe," the mind of the dreamer and the concern of the poem are, apparently, more removed from the fact of death than ever. The hunt is a dream-hunt, its detail vivid and specific, its logic the logic of fantasy. There is a great rout of people, "oon" of whom the Dreamer questions: "Say, felowe, who shal hunte here?" At the reply "th'emperour Octovyen" the Dreamer and the "felawe" are off together, "fot-hot" in the hustle and bustle and excitement of the chase. There is a moment when the poem's concern with loss is touched upon, when the hunt in the dream is related retrospectively to the story of the death of Seys and preparatively to the encounter with the "man in black," for the "hert" so long chased "staal away/ Fro alle the houndes a privy way." The "hert" that is pursued and lost, the resignation to the loss by the hunter who "wonder faste/ Blew a forloyn at the laste" (386) echo the purport of the Ovid story, though not in the conscious recognition of the Dreamer. For him, the loss of the hart means the loss of the hunt, for as suddenly as it had come the hunt and all its gay confusion are gone. Then there appears to the poet-dreamer the famous puppy: "A whelp, that fauned me as I stood,/ That hadde yfolowed, and koude no good" he reports, as charmed by his puppyness as readers have been since the day he came "and crepte . . . as lowe"

> Ryght as hyt hadde me yknowe,
> Helde doun hys hed and joyned hys eres,
> And leyde al smothe doun hys heres.
>
> > (392-394)

Animals as guides into the world of adventure, spiritual or otherwise, were familiar props in medieval literature; but nowhere is there a puppy of the essence of puppyhood like this one. The poet-dreamer's enchantment with him leads him through a meadow into a wood. The whole mood of bright joy that has characterized the dream is reaffirmed in the quick dart and dash of the pursuit of the puppy: "I wolde have kaught hyt, and anoon/ Hyt fledde, and was fro me goon;/ And I hym folwed, and hyt forth wente/ Doun by a floury grene wente" (395-398).

"Floures fele," sweet grass thickly carpeting the meadow make it a place almost rivaling heaven, "for hit was, on to beholde/ As thogh the erthe envye wolde/ To be gayer than the heven/ To have moo floures, swiche seven,/ As in the welken sterres bee" (405-409). The poet-dreamer is conscious that in this spot he is far removed from sadness, from the haunting melancholy that had preoccupied him, from the death of things in the world of man and the world of nature:

> Hyt had forgete the povertee
> That wynter, thorgh hys colde morwes,
> Had mad hyt suffre, and his sorwes,
> All was forgeten, and that was sene.
> For al the woode was waxen grene;
> Swetnesse of dew had mad hyt wax.
>   (410-415)

The exact description of the forest, each tree standing by itself, ten or twelve feet apart, each tree huge, "clene withoute bowgh or stikke" except at the top where the broad, thick branches are not an inch asunder, is effective even when its close similarity to other literary forests is recognized, for it conveys the impression of the precise detail of a dream-scene. Its fantasy-clarity is full of living things: fawns, does, roes, squirrels "that sete/ Ful high upon the trees and ete," and other "bestes" too many to count. It is in this forest that the Dreamer, surely by now almost bemused by the gay fantasy and the joyous brilliance of the dream, encounters "a man in blak,/ That sat, and had yturned his bak/ To an ook, an huge tree" (445-447). With a suddenness that precludes any real adjustment the Dreamer is moved from the brightly living world of the dream's beginning to an encounter with grief and with death. It is no wonder that he is slow to recognize the reality of the nature of the sorrow he meets. Had he ears ready to hear he would have heard that the "man in black" is lamenting the death of a loved one. But he has not ears to hear anything except what could have been "a complaint" as unreal in its motivation as the fantasy of the rest of the dream.

> I stalked even unto hys bak,
> And there I stood as stille as ought,
> That, soth to saye, he saw me nought;
> For-why he heng hys hed adoun,
> And with a dedly sorwful soun
> He made of rym ten vers or twelve
> Of a compleynte to hymselve,
> The moste pitee, the moste rowthe,
> That ever I herde; for, by my trowthe,
> Hit was gret wonder that Nature
> Myght suffre any creature
> To have such sorwe, and be nat ded.
>
> (458-469)

The "compleynte" works all its charm on the narrator-dreamer and arouses his sympathetic response:

> 'Ful pitous pale, and nothyng red
> He sayd a lay, a maner song,
> Withoute noote, withoute song;
> And was thys, for ful wel I kan
> Reherse hyt; ryght thus hyt began:
>   "I have of sorwe so gret won
> That joye gete I never non,
> Now that I see my lady bryght,
> Which I have loved with al my myght,
> Is fro me ded and ys agoon.
>   Allas, deth, what ayleth the,
> That thou noldest have taken me,
> Whan thou toke my lady swete,
> That was so fair, so fresh, so fre,
> So good, that men may wel se
> Of al goodnesse she had no mete!"
>
> (470-486)

And in his response to the great sadness he apprehends to be in the figure before him, the Dreamer, gently, courteously, moves to offer some relief. His polite address to the "man in black" confirms the impression of him as more self-conscious than not, as aware of form and of rank, as considerate of sorrow; his first important words to the grieving knight reveal that he is still in the mood and the spirit of the experience of the hunt:

> "Sir," quod I, "this game is doon.
> I holde that this hert be goon;
> These huntes konne hym nowher see."
>   (539-541)

Again the attitude of the figure of Seys toward "his" death—"I nam but ded"—is recalled to the mind of John of Gaunt as well as to us, the readers. The king Seys is dead, the hart so happily pursued in the hunt is gone, the "man in black" is not to mourn—"this game is doon." The tale from Ovid, the opening incident of the dream, the serious concern of the poem are all here chordally united.

The opening question the poet-dreamer asks of the knight marks the moment when the poem becomes a dialogue that is almost a small play upon a minute stage, and it reveals the degree of selective inattention that is to be characteristic of the questioner throughout the interchange, an inattention that is to be gradually broken down in the course of the dialogue.

> "By oure Lord," quod I, "y trow yow wel;
> Ryght so me thinketh by youre chere.
> But, sir, oo thyng wol ye here?
> Me thynketh in gret sorowe I yow see.
> But certes, sire, yf that yee
> Wolde ought discure me youre woo,
> I wolde, as wys God helpe me soo,
> Amende hyt, yif I kan or may.
> Ye mowe preve hyt be assay;
> For, by my trouthe, to make yow hool,
> I wol do al my power hool.
> And telleth me of your sorwes smerte;
> Paraunter hyt may ese youre herte,
> That semeth ful sek under your syde."
>   (544-557)

It is at this point in the poem that the protagonist, the poet-dreamer, becomes a figure for criticism, judged to be an object for ridicule, or a medieval version of the psychotherapist. He is neither of these. He is the same man who was in melancholy woe at the beginning of the poem, the same who read the sad tale of Seys and Alcione, the same who responded with joy to the birds, the brilliance, the gaiety of the hunt, and the willfulness of the puppy, egocentric yet empathetic—a figure who continues to amuse but who does not cease to be serious. His questions that follow from this initial one, tactless and maladroit as they undoubtedly are, are in character. But in our irritation with them we are led to listen to the replies given by the "man in black" as if we could supply the questioner with the ears he lacks. And the care with which we listen creates in us an acceptance of the intensity of the sorrow that is being related in spite of the somewhat conventional terms it is related in. In this oblique way, in this apparently devious fashion Chaucer can put into the words of the man who both is not and is John of Gaunt the words that describe his grief, praise the loveliness and belovedness of the lady he has lost, and make totally convincing the protestations of love he has felt for Blanche.

The "man in black" replying to the first question, "Telleth me of youre sorwes smerte" describes his sorrow. Gently he denies that the poet-dreamer can help him in any way: "No man may my sorwe glade,/ That maketh my hewe to falle and fade,/ And hath myn understongynge lorn,/ That me ys wo that I was born!" (563-566). No longer centering our attention on the poet-dreamer and his experience we move to a perspective that lets us see both characters together. It is a perspective that makes us apprehend the actuality of the Knight's loss even as we understand the uncomprehending attentiveness of the dreamer. From this perspective we hear the lyrical description of the sorrow that more immediately and directly heard might well be sentimental and conventional, so that when the line "For y am sorwe, and sorwe ys y" sounds forth, we are convinced that the grief is real, not literary. The language is conventional; clearly the facts of loss and sorrow are not. The poet-dreamer's assumption that the lament he hears is formal and literary is surely reconfirmed by the Knight's use of the chess game metaphor. It is literary language familiar to the ears of the poet-dreamer whose pre-dream moments have been preoccupied with ways to verbalize about, and respond to love's anguish and loss. But to us, and to John of Gaunt, the lament upon "Fals Fortune" rings with meaning that transcends convention:

> "The false thef! what hath she doo,
> Trowest thou? By oure Lord I wol the seye.
> At the ches with me she gan to pleye;
> With hir false draughtes dyvers
> She staal on me, and tok my fers.
> And whan I sawgh my fers awaye,
> Allas! I kouthe no lenger playe,
> But seyde, 'Farewel, swete, ywys,
> And farewel al that ever ther ys.'"
> (650-658)

To our minds come the words of the drowned king, Seys, "And farewel, swete, my worldes blysse!/ . . . To lytel while oure blysse lasteth," and to our ears the sound of the horn lamenting the escape of the hart, its tone caught in the word "forloyn" that signals the recall of the hounds.

The poet-dreamer is somewhat annoyed at the reference to Fortune: Socrates, after all, counted "nat thre strees/ Of nought that Fortune koude doo," and with a tactless jocularity he reminds the grieving knight of the absurdity of dying for the loss of a loved one: ". . . ther is no man alyve her/ Wolde for a fers make this woo!" (740-741). Hyt ys nat soo" protests the man in black, stung by the joviality that is almost callous:

> "Thou wost ful lytel what thou menest;
> I have lost more than thow wenest."
> (743-744)

This poignant phrase, repeated at crucial moments throughout the rest of the dream, forms an important part of the climax, and speaks to John of Gaunt and to us of the central theme of the poem, reminding us and him of the elegiac intent that is its chief motivation. But the poet-dreamer's failure to understand is still an issue and continues to keep him from us at a "comic" distance.

The next question put to the knight, its persistent good nature suggesting also a growing unease and curiosity, brings forth a recounting in somewhat general terms of the facts of his life as a young, courtly lover, a man devoted to Love with will, body, heart, "and al," and describes his first sight of the lady who is to be the object of his love. The details of this section of the poem are perhaps more of the courtly love convention than are any others and may well be thought to bemuse the poet-dreamer even more. That the qualities listed as those of the lady were or were not those of the real Blanche is a question quite irrelevant. Idealized as the abstractions are, they are also by now, quite plausibly the characteristics of a real person. Like no other lady she was " as the someres sonne bryght," "Debonaire, goode, glade, and sadde,/ Symple, of good mochel, noght to wyde"; her face "whit, rody, fressh, and lyvely hewed,/ And every day hir beaute newed"; her speech "softe," "friendly," "wel ygrounded,/ Up al resoun . . . wel yfounded" (821; 860; 905; 919-922). Unlike the ladies of courtly romance she was not cruel: "Hyr lust to holde no wyght in honde,/ Ne, be thou siker, she wolde not fonde/ To holde no wyght in balaunce/ By half word ne by countenaunce,/ But if men wolde upon hir lye" (1019-1023). His praise of her, his loving description of every notable quality is climaxed in a moment of intense and lyrical declaration:

> "But wherefore that y telle my tale?
> Ryght on thys same, as I have seyd,
> Was hooly al my love leyd;
> For certes she was, that swete wif,
> My suffisaunce, my lust, my lyf,
> Myn hap, myn hele, and al my blesse,
> My worldes welfare, and my goddesse,
> And I hooly hires and everydel."
>   (1034-1041)

The Dreamer's interruption at this moment of emotional intensity shocks us by its imperception: "By oure Lord," quod I, "y trowe yow wel!/ Hardely, your love was wel beset;/ I not how ye myght have do bet" (1042-1044). Yet, at the same time, the exclamation crude as it is, is not surprising; the Dreamer's failure to comprehend the actuality of what he is hearing is still inevitable for the very quality of the knight's words can only sustain the impression that the experience is a literary one. He even betrays some impatience as he fears the knight will not move on to something else than this lyrical romanticism: "Now, goode syre, . . ./ Ye han wel told me herebefore,/ Hyt is no nede to reherse it more,/ How ye sawe hir first, and where" (1126-1129). What he wants to know now is "the manere/ To hire which was youre firste speche;/ . . . And how she knewe first your thoght,/ Whether ye loved hir or noght" (1130-1134). The "man in black's" response, "thow nost what thow menest;/ I have lost more than thou wenest" (1137-1138), revealing his almost infinite patience in the face of his clumsy though well meaning questioner, seems to strike the ear of the Dreamer for the first time with some meaning. For the first time he picks up the word "los"— " 'What los ys that?' quod I thoo" (1139). Still in the world of literature and the love lament his mind can understand only in terms of the literary convention: loss means desertion, perhaps?

> "Nyl she not love yow? ys hyt soo?
> Or have ye oght doon amys,
> That she hath left yow? ys hyt this?
> For Goddes love, telle me al."
>   (1140-1143)

And the knight now begins the last section of the small drama, describing in ways more particular than he has yet, his approach to the lady, his anguish and joy in love, and the kind of love that in time he won from her. The translation of the literary conventions once more into particular terms says over again that the love and the loss are "real."

But what makes for the degree of the felt sorrow as the poem approaches its dream-climax is the degree to which this section rises into joy. The pain of the loss is measured by the quality of the happiness that had been. The lament that had begun in woe for a moment becomes a paean in honor of mutually felt love:

> "So whan my lady knew al this,
> My lady yaf me al hooly
> The noble yifte of hir mercy,
> Savynge hir worship, by al weyes,—
> Dredles, I mene noon other weyes.
> And therwith she yaf me a ryng;
> I trowe hyt was the firste thyng;
> But if myn herte was ywaxe
> Glad, that is no nede to axe!
> As helpe me God, I was as blyve
> Reysed, as fro deth to lyve,
> Of al happes the alderbeste,
> The gladdest, and the moste at reste.
> For trewely that swete wyght,
> Whan I had wrong and she the ryght,
> She wolde alway so goodly
> Foryeve me so debonairly.
> In al my yowthe, in al chaunce,
> She took me in hir governaunce.
> Therwyth she was always so trewe,
> Oure joye was ever ylyche newe;
> Oure hertes wern so evene a payre,
> That never nas that oon contrayre
> To that other, for no woo.
> For sothe, ylyche they suffred thoo
> Oo blysse, and eke oo sorwe bothe;
> Ylyche they were bothe glad and wrothe;
> Al was us oon, withoute were.
> And thus we lyved ful many a yere
> So wel, I kan nat telle how."
>   (1268-1297)

There is one question left. The poet-dreamer asks it with all the bluntness that is in his nature, the simplicity of it perhaps betraying his own sense that he should really know what he thinks he does not know. "Sir . . . where is she now?" The "man in black" delays briefly, then speaks:

> "Now?" quod he, and stynte anoon.
> Therwith he wax as ded as stoon,
> And seyde, "Allas, that I was bore!
> That was the los that here-before
> I tolde the that I hadde lorn."
>   (1299-1303)

That he is apprehensive of the Dreamer's readiness to understand is clear:

> "Bethenke how I seyde here-beforn,
> 'Thow wost ful lytel what thow menest;
> I have lost more than thow wenest'—
> God wot, allas! ryght that was she!"
>   (1304-1307)

Between the dreamer and the reality there is no longer the illusion of the literary metaphor, of the artifact situation; the moment of illumination is upon him, and his grasp of the truth is almost immediate:

> "Allas, sir, how? what may that be?"
> "She ys ded!" "Nay!" "Yis, be my trouthe!"
> "Is that youre los? Be God, hyt ys routhe!"
>   (1308-1310)

"With that word ryght anoon" says Chaucer, "they gan to strake forth; al was doon,/ For that tyme, the hert-hunting" (1312-1313).

Nothing remains for Chaucer except to awaken his sleeper in as natural a way as possible. In the last moments of the poem the dream fades as the dreamer watches the man in black disappear into a white castle. And the transition between the world of the sleeper and the real world is made by the poet-dreamer's hearing the castle bell "as hyt hadde smyten houres twelve":

> Therwyth I awook myselve
> And fond me lyinge in my bed;
> And the book that I hadde red,
> Of Alcione and Seys the kyng,
> And of the goddes of slepyng,
> I fond hyt in myn hond ful even.
>   (1324-1329)

The poem ends with the dreamer once more the center of attention.

In the dream he has learned something about the nature of real love and real loss. He is, in a sense, "reysed as fro deth to lyve," awakened from the experience with death into continuing life. His questions so persistently directed at the grieving knight in the dream have not helped in the easing of the sorrow of the Knight; that is the same at the end as it had been at its first utterance. The man in black has shown no evidence of change. He is the one who has been in possession of the incontrovertible fact of death. But to the dreamer something significant has happened. It is not merely the figure of the man in black that contains the consolation of the elegy; it is the whole complex of the poem. That death is final and that the loss of the loved one is absolutely irrevocable are never evaded, nor are they denied their full pain in the present world by being translated into promises of cessation in the next world. But there has been joy in the love, enriched and heightened in the context of the loss. She is "but ded," the "hert rused and slipped away"; death is bearable, containable, in the form of the poem where the prevailing atmosphere is one of experienced happiness, the dominant memory one of "bright joy." The poem that consoles by immortalizing the tale of the love between John of Gaunt and Blanche, his duchess, compliments also in saying that in the experience within the dream, the poet-dreamer has come for the first time face to face with the nature of Reality in death, and more importantly, with the nature of Actuality in love. Though every moment in the poem has to do with loss, with sorrow, with death, at the same time it has to do with winning and gaining, with life, with love, and with joy. There is no instant when that which is woe is not in the process of being transformed into joy, when that which is death is not being turned into something living. And the whole poem becomes in the course of its development an affirmation of the fact of gladness in love even as it memorializes the fact of loss.

THE PARLIAMENT OF FOWLS

Of the other early poems *The Parliament of Fowls* is the only one that is an artistic whole. Exactly when it was written is not known; perhaps ten years after *The Book of the Duchess*, just before the writing of *Troilus and Criseyde* and after the apparently unfinished *House of Fame*. Since the exact date is barely conjecturable, and since the study of Chaucer's development as a poet is not primarily the point of this book, to look at *The Parliament of Fowls* after *The Book of the Duchess*, as a prelude to the greater comedy of *The Canterbury Tales*, is possible.

Death and Love have been the subjects of *The Book of the Duchess*; Love is the subject of *The Parliament of Fowls*. Whether this is an

occasional poem or not is still a disputed question. But there seems to
be no quarrel with the interpretation of it as a poem that is an extended
definition of Love: Love in the harmony of the spheres, Love as pictured
by allegory and literature, Love as formalized in the courtly tradition,
and Love as physical enjoyment—ruled by Nature, joyously praised in
the roundel that ends the poem on a lyrical moment that is rare in
Chaucer:

> "Now welcome, somer, with thy sonne softe,
> That hast this wintres wedres overshake,
> And driven away the longe nyghtes blake!
>
> "Saynt Valentyn, that art ful hy on-lofte,
> Thus syngen smale foules for thy sake:
> Now welcome, somer, with thy sonne softe,
> That hast this wintres wedres overshake.
>
> "Wel han they cause for to gladen ofte,
> Sith ech of hem recovered hath hys make,
> Ful blissful mowe they synge when they wake:
> Now welcome, somer, with thy sonne softe,
> That hast this wintres wedres overshake,
> And driven away the longe nyghtes blake!"
>   (683-692)

The key struck in *The Book of the Duchess* was minor although its
development was never dirge-like; indeed, the ultimate effect was one
of "gladnesse." The tonal quality of *The Parliament*, although having its
moments of solemnity, is gay; its movement *con brio;* its conclusion
con amore. It is a poem much more obviously "comic" in its subject, if
we accept the conventional view that comedy on the simplest of levels
is "happy" in tone and subject. It is a poem "of good aventure," joyous
in its celebration of natural beauty, affectionately tolerant of the impossible ideal and the probable real in the concepts of love it describes,
and dramatically vivid in its moment of high farce in the give-and-take
among the common birds during the Parliament.

Once more Chaucer makes use of the schema of the dream-vision, and
as in *The Book of the Duchess*, his choice is an effective one. The
dreamer here is not specifically identified. His role is not as important
as it was in the earlier poem, since he is almost entirely an observer,
his participation in the action he dreams of limited by the very character
he gives himself. He is, after all, one unacquainted with love, therefore
he can only be a spectator of it. So far as the birds are concerned he

does not exist. He stands unnoticed among them as a reporter, jostled and crowded by the throng:

> For this was on seynt Valentynes day
> Whan every foul cometh there to chese his make,
> Of every kynde that men thynke may,
> And that so huge a noyse gan they make
> That erthe, and eyr, and tre, and every lake
> So ful was, that unethe was there space
> For me to stonde, so ful was al the place.
> (309-315)

Sad because he has not experienced love—"For al be that I knowe nat Love in dede,/ Ne wot how that he quiteth folk here hyre" (8-9), he can, nevertheless, dream quite clearly about its nature. His knowledge, like that of the poet-dreamer, has come from books, and the dream reveals to him that he also knows more accurately than he realizes when awake. But the experience of the dream, since it has no active place for him in its world, leaves him where he was when he entered it:

> And with the shoutyng, whan the song was do
> That foules maden at here flyght awey,
> I wok, and othere bokes tok me to,
> To reede upon, and yit I rede alwey.
> I hope, ywis, to rede so som day
> That I shal mete som thyng for to fare
> The bet, and thus to rede I nyl nat spare.
> (693-699)

His distance from the action of the Parliament, his human figure standing unnoticed in the noisy bird-world make of him a figure of comic irony, a man of letters whose subject is love, which he understands vicariously, albeit fully. It is not what he does not know that keeps the attention, but what he does know as he sees it take place around him.

The dreamer's ineptness in love is more than a little caused by his reluctance to love, by his fear of its pain: "The lyf so short, the craft so long to lerne,/ Th'assay so hard, so sharp the conquerynge,/ The dredful joye, alwey that slit so yerne:/ Al this mene I by Love" (1-4), he begins. And his fear makes him visibly timid even in the comforting protection of his dream-guide, "Affrycan." Whatever bliss Cytherea may in theory promise, he is not at all convinced, and before the gate into the garden of Venus he hesitates, frightened. The "vers iwriten" above the gate does indeed promise joy, but conjoining the golden half of the gate, written in black are words that promise quite the opposite, and he does not know whether to enter or to leave. What comforts him after he has been shoved into the garden by Scipio is the promise that he is safe from the effects of love. "It stondeth writen in thy face,/ Thyn errour, though thow telle it not to me," says "Affrycan." And offers the reassurance:

> "But dred the not to come into this place,
> For this writyng nys nothyng ment bi the,
> Ne by non, but he Loves servaunt be:
> For thow of love hast lost thy tast, I gesse,
> As sek man hath of swete and bytternesse.
>
> "But natheles, although that thow be dul,
> Yit that thow canst not do, yit mayst thow se.
> For many a man that may nat stonde a pul,
> It liketh hym at the wrastlyng for to be,
> And demeth yit wher he do bet or he.
> And if thow haddest connyng for t'endite,
> A shal the shewe mater of to wryte."
>   (155-168)

With this injunction the dreamer is released from any responsibility to feel emotionally about the subject of love, and the poem is safe from the danger of subjective sentiment. "With that myn hand in his he tok anon,/ Of which I confort caughte, and wente in faste," says the dreamer, leaving behind the self of the waking world, willing now to be merely a viewer, ready to respond objectively to what he is to see. "But, Lord, so I was glad and wel begoon!/ . . . For overal where that I myn eyen caste/ Were treës clad with leves that ay shal laste,/ Ech in his kynde, of colour fresh and greene/ As emeraude, that joye was to seene" (171-175).

All that the dreamer sees and hears once he is beyond the gate corroborates his initial impression. From the moment he finds himself in the "gardyn . . . ful of blosmy bowes/ Upon a ryver, in a grene mede" to the moment he awakens from his dream there is little that is not joyous and happy. The "sorweful were" promised so ominously by the black words on the gate never really materializes, except in the squabble of the birds at the Parliament. Nor does the romantic idealization of love that has been promised by the golden words become actual. What the poet within the dream realizes is the possible, even probable, cooexistence of both concepts of love, each concept modifying the other and thereby creating a greater realism.

In allegorical fashion the garden of Venus into which the dreamer enters first, tells him something about the nature of Love. Cupid, and Desire, and "Plesaunce . . . Aray . . . Lust, and Curteysie"; "Delyt, that stod with Gentilesse"; "Beute . . . and Youthe, . . . Foolhardynesse," Priapus, Bacchus, and Ceres people this world as if met together from all mythology, the *Romaunt of the Rose,* and the collective poetic imagination. All around is sound and movement, the feel of air that "so attempre was/ That nevere was ther grevaunce of hot ne cold," confirming that, in the terms of literature at least, the habitation of Love is a blysful place/ Of hertes hele and dedly woundes cure," where "grene and lusty May shal evere endure" (127-128; 130).

Full of the literary vision of Love he goes to the meadow, solitary, meditative, walking alone "myselven to solace." And he enters into the second stage of the dream, the stage where he will observe what Love is like in actual life: romantic and vulgar, contentious and joyous, essentially physical, and ultimately a union, the last stanza before the singing of the rounde̊ that awakens him offering to the dreamer almost a summation of the definition he has seen enacted:

> And whan this werk al brought was to an ende,
> To every foul Nature yaf his make
> By evene acord, and on here way they wende.
> And, Lord, the blisse and joye that they make!
> For ech of hem gan other in wynges take.
> And with here nekkes ech gan other wynde,
> Thankynge alwey the noble goddesse of kynde.
>
> (666-672)

It is Nature, the "noble goddesse of kynde," who presides over the gathering of birds, "a queene,/ That, as of lyght the somer sonne shene/ Passeth the sterre, right so over mesure/ She fayer was than any creature" (298-301). Under her benevolent and wise auspices the highly comic parliament convenes, its subject for discussion the winning and taking of mates. Except for the second book of *The House of Fame* this is Chaucer's most obvious comedy until the *Canterbury Tales,* and it is the most complex of the early poems. The Parliament of birds is, in miniature, what the journey of the pilgrims will be: an assembly of highly individualized natures, gathered for a specific purpose, willing to wait with a reasonable amount of patience the fulfilment of the intention, but soon in contention, bristling into argument, and restored to peace by the presiding "goddesse," as the pilgrims will be kept in relative harmony by the Host.

What the Dreamer sees before him is a small drama, a brief comedy of character, over with in a matter of minutes, full of sound and movement, debate and chatter, order and confusion. The fact that the contenders and squabblers are birds adds much, of course, to the comic effect of the scene. Whether the birds are Chaucer's satiric comments on real people, whether a contemporary situation is being parodied are questions that do not enrich in any significant way the effect of the comedy taking place. What is funny is to hear birds sounding like human beings while never once ceasing to be birds. And the comic conclusion is, that under Nature, the concept Love, blurred in its abstraction, is in the concrete the act of mating, whatever multitude of romantic guises it assumes.

The small drama begins in an orderly enough fashion. First there is the presentation of the formel eagle, "of shap the gentilleste/ . . . the moste benygne and the goodlieste," to be wooed by the three tersels. With courtly grace the royal birds offer their homage and plead their case. For them, Love is to be won in romantic and poetic fashion, its physical essence not so much disguised as ennobled by the graceful and elegant circumlocutions convention demands. The first eagle, "with hed enclyned and with ful humble cheere," approaches the formel with words that honor the French origin of the courtly tradition, beseeching her "of merci and of grace" that she make of him her servant, "to do me lyve or sterve":

> "For certes, longe may I nat lyve in payne,
> For in myn herte is korven every veyne.
> >   (424-425)
>
> , ...
>
> And if that I to hyre be founde untrewe,
> Disobeysaunt, or wilful necligent,
> Avauntour, or in proces love a newe,
> I preye to yow this be my jugement,
> That with these foules I be al torent."
> >   (428-432)

For one delicately comic moment the Dreamer's eyes take in the face of the "formel egle":

> Ryght as the freshe, rede rose newe
> Ayeyn that somer sonne coloured is,
> Ryght so for shame al wexen gan the hewe
> Of this formel, whan she herde al this:
> She neyther answerde wel, ne seyde amys,
> So sore abasht was she, tyl that Nature
> Seyde, "Doughter, diede yow nought, I yow assure."
> >   (442-448)

The second wooer speaks as an Englishman, his words clearly those of an Anglo-Saxon, but his attitude toward Love as much of the courtly tradition as that of his predecessor. "That shal nat be!" he protests. "I love hire bet than ye don, by seint John,/ Or at the leste I love hire as wel as ye,/ And lenger have served hire in my degre,/ And if she shulde have loved for long lovynge,/ To me ful-longe hadde be the guerdonynge" (450-455). The third eagle is courtly neither in word nor attitude, his practical common sense rousing him to some impatience at the parliamentary delay, his somewhat bourgeois nature irritated by all the romantic flimflam:

> "Now sires, ye seen the lytel leyser heere;
> For every foul cryeth out to ben ago
> Forth with his make, or with his lady deere;
> And ek Nature hireself ne wol not heere,
> For taryinge here, not half that I wolde seye,
> And but I speke, I mot for sorwe deye.
>
> "Of long servyse avaunte I me nothing;
> But as possible is me to deye to-day
> For wo as he that hath ben languysshyng
> This twenty wynter, and wel happen may,
> A man may serven bet and more to pay
> In half a yer, although it were no moore,
> Than som man doth that hath served ful yoore.
>
> "I seye not this by me, for I ne can
> Don no servyse that may my lady plese;
> But I dar seyn, I am hire treweste man
> As to my dom, and faynest wolde hire ese.
> At shorte wordes, til that deth me sese,
> I wol ben heres, whether I wake or wynke,
> And trewe in al that herte may bethynke."
>
> (464-483)

His words signal the end of the respectful silence maintained by the common birds; "the noyse . . . so loude rong, 'Have don, and lat us wende'" that, says the Dreamer, "wende I the wode hadde al toshyvered" (492-493). Disorder threatens the Parliament:

> The goos, the cokkow, and the doke also
> So cryede, "Kek kek! kokkow; quek quek!" hye,
> That thourgh myne eres the noyse wente tho.

The goos seyde, "Al this nys not worth a flye!
But I can shape herof a remedie,
And I wol seye my verdit fayre and swythe
For water-foul, whoso be wroth or blythe!"
(498-504)

The goose's assumption of authority sets up a frenzy of protest among the other birds, and promises complete chaos until Nature, "which that alwey hadde an ere/ To murmur of the lewednesse behynde," calls for order, decreeing there shall be a "counsey!" to help the modest formel to choose him who is the worthiest.

The Dreamer's explicit awareness of all that is going on, his response that evidences no astonishment at the scene, reminds us that he is on the scene of the Parliament even though his presence is a matter of no concern to the birds. The earnest preoccupation of the fowls does not strike him as amusing, but his mute attendance, his almost deadpan reporting makes him, for the reader, part of the comic richness of the dream.

The "counseyl" that follows, though never again really chaotic, has hilarious moments of threatened disorder. Argument and counterargument, "laughter . . . of gentil foules alle," pleas that are sometimes sentimental, sometimes crudely vulgar, fill the meadow. There is the cuckoo's outburst that seems about to turn the whole meeting into a fight. "So I . . . may have my make in pes" he shouts, "I reche nat how longe that ye stryve." "Ye, have the glotoun fild inow his paunche,/ Thanne are we wel!" replies the "merlioun," his hostility evident in his vitriolic conclusion: "Thou mortherere of the heysoge on the braunche/ That broughte the forth, thow [rewtheless] glotoun!/ Lyve thow soleyn, wormes corupcioun!/ For no fors is of lak of thy nature—/ Go, lewed by thow whil the world may dure!" (610-616).

Nature, aware that the Parliament is no nearer formulating a reasonable solution to the problem of the formel eagle than it was at the beginning, calls a halt to the "counseyl" at this critical moment: "Now pes . . . I comaunde heer!/ For I have herd al youre opynyoun,/ And in effect yit be we nevere the neer" (617-619). It is she who provides the sensible decree—that there shall be the year's respite requested by the formel, after which she shall be granted her own choice "al fre." "Now, syn it may non otherwise betyde" acknowledges Nature, "heere is no more to seye," and she dismisses the birds, "each with his make," in "blisse and joye."

The comedy of the dream is over. What it has illustrated for the Dreamer is that the Love that had been so confounding to him "with his wonderful werkynge" at the beginning is both a poetic emotion and a sexual relationship. Neither one without the other is a true manifestation. The courtly without the vulgar makes of love a "sentiment" merely; the vulgar without the courtly makes of love, sexuality and lust. The noble birds and the common birds in their contention that is never resolved in favor of one or the other, coexist, and together generate a tension that describes the probable reality. That Love is something continuing in spite of the passing of the moment, that it has in it a kind of endurance that is in defiance of the temporal is suggested by the two stages of the dream. It is preserved in literature, specifically in the garden of Venus where "no man . . . waxe sek ne old"; it is also observable in nature where, since the particular choice for the formel eagle is still to be made, one Saint Valentine's Day will be followed by yet another Saint Valentine's Day.

That Chaucer was concerned with the question of the relationship between the temporal and the eternal is clear from the evidence of the device he used to get his dreamer into the dream. Between the opening lament that speaks of his ineptness in love and the dream that describes the nature of love as men have experienced it, the "I" of the poem reads of another kind of love that is necessary for the winning of eternal joy. It is here that the artistic success of the poem is most questionable, and notable defenses of the section still do not entirely satisfy.

It is in his reading "Tulluyus of the Drem of Scipioun,/ Chapitres sevene . . . of hevene and helle/ Of erthe, and soules that therinne dwelle" that he meets with "*Affrycan*" who is to be the guide at the beginning of his dream. African's role in the *Somnium Scipionis*, as the poet-reader learns, is that of a guide in a dream-vision. Appearing to the sleeping Scipio he shows him Carthage "from a sterry place" and describes the life that follows upon death—for "oure present worldes lyves space/Nis but a maner deth." In a moment of comprehensive vision Scipio is shown "the lytel erthe," the nine spheres, and hears the "melodye . . . that cometh of thilke speres thryes thre,/ That welle is of musik and melodye/ In this world here, and cause of armonye" (57-63). African solemnly defines for Scipio the conditions for attaining eternal "blysse" after the brief moment of life is over: "Know thyself first immortal/ And loke ay besyly thow werche and wysse/ To commune profit, and thow shalt not mysse/ To comen swiftly to that place deere/ That ful of blysse is and of soules cleere" (73-77). "Brekers of the lawe" and "likerous folk" shall also, in time, be released from the pain they must temporarily endure: "Than shul they come into this blysful place,/ To which to comen God the sende his grace" (82-84).

To assume that this brief account of Scipio's vision of the world of man *sub specie aeternitatis* is important in Chaucer's poetic exploration of the concepts contained in the word "love" is valid; but to argue that it is successfully fused into the poem is, it seems to me, open to question. It is true that the concept of "commune profit" is a significant one for one seeking to define, expositorially and dramatically, the general concept, Love. It is true that in prefacing the dream of the poem by a reminder of the finitude of man in the eye of infinity, Chaucer creates the context wherein human and temporal love is seen in all its illusions of continuance and permanence. The world of the dream becomes a passing one before it even materializes. The illusion that the garden of Venus will endure, its temperate air, its "joye more than a thousandfold," its promise that there man shall never "waxe sek ne old" is revealed for what it is—a fantasy. And thus all the dream the poet has is made comically ironic, the intense preoccupations of both literary figures and quarreling birds made humorous in the light of the infinity they ignore. But neither by explicit statement, nor by implicit formal coherence does the Scipio passage become an organic part of the poem's concern with Love; it comes too early in the poem. Chaucer will remind his audience of "the lytel erthe that here is . . . ful of torment and of harde grace" at the end of *Troilus and Criseyde* and turn his tragedy into something that is no longer tragic. And he will end his *Canterbury Tales* by recalling for us that all coming to and fro is but a passing through a world of woe, thus translating the earthly comedy into something more than earthly. In both instances artistic effects are achieved that are more noteworthy than that created by the Scipio passage.

Although not successfully an organic part of the Dream of the poet that is to make him witness to the enacted definition of Love, the dream of Scipio is important for the subject of Order, which runs synchronistically with the subject of Love. The Harmony that is in the "nyne speres" is reflected in the harmonious coexistence in the Garden of Venus of apparently disparate elements: tree, and bird, "delyt and Gentilesse, Plesaunce and Curteysie," Venus and devotees of "Dyane the chaste"; and the world ruled by Nature is one where there is respect for social order, where every fowl is sure of his "owene place," where argument and debate occur, and individualism asserts itself in no uncertain terms, under the watchful eye of Nature, "the vicaire of the almyghty Lord,/ That hot, cold, hevy, lyght, moyst, and dreye/ Hath knyt by evene noumbres of acord" (379-381).

But all the pleading for the artistic success of the Scipio dream remains special. Chaucer's interest in the problem of Order, and in the relatedness of the universal and the temporal, in the tension between Order and Disorder, in the coexistence of apparent opposites has not yet found ways for the expression of its inherent complexity. Although there is much that is potentially more complex about the *Parliament of Fowls* than there was in the *Book of the Duchess*, it is a poem that is more brilliant and charming than it is deeply meaningful. Chaucer seems almost to admit to this judgment in the last lines, aware that more is demanded of his genius than this small, finely wrought piece:

> And with the shoutyng, whan the song was do
> That foules maden at here flyght awey,
> I wok, and othere bokes tok me to,
> To reede upon, and yit I rede alwey.
> I hope, ywis, to rede so som day
> That I shal mete som thyng for to fare
> The bet, and thus to rede I nyl nat spare.
>   (693-699)

THE HOUSE OF FAME and
THE LEGEND OF GOOD WOMEN

Regardless of when it may be conjectured *The House of Fame* and *The Legend of Good Women* were written, they can be looked at together for what they reveal about the nature of Chaucer's comedy. Both are fragments, though to state this about the *House of Fame* is bound to stir up protests among scholars and critics; both poems seem to have been begun because of some personal slight, real or fancied; both show the poet's interest in "the matter of antiquity"—in the stories of Dido and Aeneas, and in the legends of ladies more or less faithful in love; both have as narrator the figure of the poet who, as in the two other early poems, is concerned with attempting to understand the nature of Love.

It is, of course, impossible to know why Chaucer did not finish these two poems which, even in their fragmented states, seem to have been begun ambitiously. Increased involvement in public affairs, problems in his own personal life that distracted him, some temporary but strongly felt disappointment in the reception of his efforts as a poet, all these may have made it difficult for him to finish either poem. Of the two, only the *House of Fame* ever becomes touched into life, though *The Legend* has moments of lyric charm that are noteworthy. Only the second book of the former has evidence of comic power; only the slightest tonal indications can be heard in the Prologue to the latter.

The House of Fame is perhaps the most controversial poem in the Chaucer canon. What it is all about is still a question that arouses heated argument and counter-argument. The solution is as far from satisfactorily proposed as any suggested by the fowls in *The Parliament*. And the continuing attempts at determining its meaning only attest to its very real confusion. After all the scholarly examinations of this poem are taken into account, the questions remain: is it an occasional poem, and if so, for what kind of occasion? is its subject Love, married or betrayed Love? is its theme some statement about the perversity of Fame? is it a versified lesson in medieval physics? is it to be about "tidings of Love, or such thynges glade"? The only possible answer is that it is about all these things but that for some reason they have not been united in all their disparateness into an organic whole. Whatever relation might have been made between these subjects was not found, and Chaucer arrived at what is clearly a moment of climax in the third book with nothing to make the moment climactic. The tidings the man of "auctorite" is to bring are no more clear in spite of his dramatic appearance than they were when hinted at by the eagle in the second book, and how they were to make significant the incidents that they climax is not intimated.

The House of Fame reveals also Chaucer's uncertainty about what narrative method to use. Or at least, each of its books tries a different one, the fact suggesting either an interest in experimenting or a groping for the most meaningful way of telling whatever it was he wanted to tell. The first book is a combination of the autobiographical introduction of the dreamer and a description of the beginning of the dream that is largely a retelling of the story of Dido and Aeneas; the second book is a dramatic adventure with the eagle; the third book is a descriptive account of the Houses of Fame and Rumor, where the dreamer is, as he is in *The Parliament of Fowls*, more observer than participator. The expository, the dramatic, and the descriptive are all tried, but how they were meant to fuse is not clear.

It is true that Chaucer, the "I" of the poem, is the central figure, and it is true that he has certain qualities as a character in the dream. The self-image he proposes is like that of his narrator-dreamers in *The Book of the Duchess* and *The Parliament of Fowls*: he is preoccupied with Love, he is a little naïve, he is given to reading about life more than he is given to living it. But in this poem he is also somewhat petulant, especially in the opening moments of the first book where the long discourse on the nature of dreams leads him to invoke a comic curse upon all those who misjudge this dream as badly as they have his poetry:

> pray I Jesus God
> That (dreme he barefot, dreme he shod),
> That every harm that any man
> Hath had, syth the world began,
> Befalle hym thereof, or he sterve,
> And graunte he mote hit ful deserve,
> Lo, with such a conclusion
> As had of his avision

Cresus, that was kyng of Lyde,
That high upon a gebet dyde!
This prayer shal he have of me;
I am no bet in charyte!
(97-108)

The petulant tone recurs in the third book, when Chaucer, addressed
by the stranger who will lead him from the vision of the House of Fame
to the vision of the House of Rumor, replies in words that echo those of
the opening lines. "Artow come hider to han fame?" asks the man:

"Nay, for sothe, frend," quod y;
"I cam noght hyder, graunt mercy,
For no such cause, by my hed!
Sufficeth me, as I were ded
That no wight have my name in honde.
I wot myself best how y stonde;
For what I drye, or what I thynke,
I wil myselven al hyt drynke,
Certeyn, for the more part,
As fer forth as I kan myn art."
(1873-1882)

But the suggestion of some sort of disgruntlement, added to the per-
sonality-characteristics already made familiar in the other poems where
the dreamer is one of the actors in the dream, has no perceptible significance for the dream itself, and gives no hint as to the essential meaning of the poem. It is only in the second book that the figure of the poet-
dreamer becomes dramatically important, his meeting with the eagle
like that of the dreamer with the "man in black," one between the
knowledgeable and the ignorant, the knower and the unknower. And it
is in this book that *The House of Fame* has its only real comedy,
and its most noteworthy vitality.

It is the eagle in Book II that is comic even more than the situation,
though the vision of the large poet subjected in mid-air to a lecture
on physics is wonderfully funny. Chaucer is there as a captive audience
and has the chance to say little; the giant eagle dominates in his
exuberant monologue and is Chaucer's first full-length comic portrait.

Whatever Chaucer may have thought was "wonderful" about the
dream he describes in Book I of *The House of Fame* does not appear in
the retelling of it. Perhaps he was hampered by his respect for the Virgil
story he was paraphrasing, perhaps he was unsure what use he was to
make of it; at any rate, his recitation of the story of Dido and Aeneas,

while more economical than those of his contemporaries, lacks vitality. Then suddenly, at the end of the first book, the dream does become "wonderful." It is as if outside the confines of the Temple of Glass where he had seen the Virgil story recorded he is freed of the restrictions literature had placed upon him. From observer he becomes participant, responsive to the experience the dream is giving him in ways that for the first time are emotionally believable.

"When I had seen al this syghte/ In this noble temple thus" he says, he is full of admiration and wonder. And he is also curious as to where he is, even a little apprehensive:

> "But now wol I goo out and see,
> Ryght at the wiket, yf y kan
> See owhere any stiryng man,
> That may me telle where I am."
>   (476-479)

Out of the literary confines of the Temple of Glass Chaucer is suddenly conscious of loneliness, perhaps intimidated at the emptiness he sees around him:

> When I out at the dores cam,
> I faste aboute me beheld.
> Then sawgh I but a large feld,
> As fer as that I myghte see,
> Withouten toun, or hous, or tree,
> Or bush, or grass, or eryd lond;
> For al the feld nas but of sond
> As smal as man may se yet lye
> In the desert of Lybye;
> Ne no maner creature
> That ys yformed by Nature
> Ne sawgh I, me to rede or wisse.
> "O Crist!" thoughte I, "that art in blysse,
> Fro fantome and illusion
> Me save!" and with devocion
> Myn eyen to the hevene I caste.
>   (480-495)

Whatever this desolate place may be—whether symbolic of an inner state or a literary convention merely—is difficult to say, for the dreamer makes little of it except as a moment of transition from that which has been intellectually perceived to that which will be emotionally experienced. What comes to him with all the great sweep of a miraculous answer to the prayer is the golden eagle, no mere guide to the heart of the dream, but an important figure in it in his own right. If Chaucer is here following the conventional dream-vision poem in its providing of a guide to the dreamer, he is forgetting that no guide should be of as great a figure as the one who is being guided. Chaucer's almost mute and helpless captivity in the talons of his overwhelmingly kind "frend," points attention entirely to the eagle.

The small scene that takes place between Chaucer and the eagle and makes up the second book of this poem is delightfully funny. Because the dreamer becomes something of an actor in his own dream, there is established for the first time in the poem a perspective, like those in the other early poems, by which he is seen from a distance even as the action he is taking part in is seen. And because he is an actor in the poem for the first time, what happens to him, though it happens in a dream, becomes a matter of vital import. The dream-fact makes the eagle a figure to awaken awe even as the vision of Chaucer in his claws, held "as lyghtly as [he] were a larke," arouses laughter. His fatherly concern for the well-being of the poet-dreamer, his professorial pomposity as he bears Chaucer away "in a swap" become credible in the world of the dream. He never loses an essential "eagleness" in the journey or in the manner of his discourse with his weighty burden; and when he reappears in the third book, his essential eagleness is what is reassuring. Chaucer's discovery of him "perched hye upon a stoon" in the midst of the bewildering agitation of the twirling house of Rumor is a welcome one. It is the discovery of an old and familiar friend and Chaucer's relief is understandable. "He ryght anoon/ Hente me up bytweene hys toon/ And at a wyndowe yn me broghte" remarks the happy poet (1990-1991; 2027-2029).

The comedy in the portrayal of the eagle is fairly simple, even obvious in the way it is created. There seems to be nothing but good spirits at work here. The eagle's comic being says nothing of any sort about the concern of the poem, whatever that concern may be. His presence gives no satisfactory clue to Chaucer's intention in writing *The House of Fame*. His function, he tells the poet, is to obey the command of Jupiter, who wishes to reward "Geffry" for serving Love so long without "guerdon ever yit"; it is not, as Chaucer fears, to "stelefy" him. "And therfore Joves . . ./ Wol that I bere the to a place/ Which that hight the Hous of Fame,/ To do the som disport and game,/ In som recompensacion/ Of labour and devocion" he explains (661-666).

The genial consideration the eagle has for "Geffry" whom he has so suddenly snatched into the air, his sense of his mission, his relish in explaining in a wonderfully careful way subjects that interest him all make of him a more than ordinary guide. Nor is he a mere pompous fool; his is not the comic bombast of the buffoon. About those things which interest him he knows much. His understanding of the theories of the movement of air currently held in Chaucer's day is, apparently, accurate, and his description of the theory is made in some of Chaucer's most exciting verse. The passage is too long to quote, and should really be read aloud (729-852). A silent reading is apt to miss the rise and fall, the sweep upward and the sudden drop downward of the lines as they tell of the movement of sound in the air, "Lyght thing upward, and dounward charge"; or the spiralling effect of the lines that conveys exactly the circling of air when it is broken by sound, even as a stone thrown upon the water will "make anoon/ A litel roundell as a sercle,/ Paraunter brod as a covercle." Whatever sense of order *The House of Fame* as a poem may lack, Chaucer's eagle does not lack it. For him all things are related "in kynde" and he takes enormous pleasure in explaining it to Chaucer, his "leve brother." "Telle me this now feythfully," he asks of his captive student like the kindly professor he is, "Have y not preved thus symply,/ Withoute any subtilite/ Of speche, or gret prolixite/ Of terms of philosophie,/ Of figures of poetrie,/ Or colours of rethorike?/ Pardee, hit oughte the to lyke!/ For hard langage and hard matere/ Ys encombrous for to here/ Attones; wost thou not wel this?" (853-863). To this definition of good teaching Chaucer responds for all generations of students for all time to come: "Yis." The eagle's joy in his success is infectious:

> "A ha!" quod he, "lo, so I can
> Lewedly to a lewed man
> Speke, and shewe hym swyche skiles
> That he may shake hem be the biles,
> So palpable they shulden be."
>   (865-869)

Never does Chaucer's guide lose consideration for his charge, even though he cannot refrain from doing all the talking. As the two approach the House of Fame, the great sound "that rumbleth up and doun/ . . . ful of tydynges,/ Bothe of feir speche and chidynges" like a "grete swogh" fills the poet with fear. But the eagle is ready to reassure. "Nay, dred the not therof," he says: "Hyt is nothing will byten the;/ Thou shalt non harm have trewely."

> And with this word both he and y
> As nygh the place arryved were
> As men may casten with a spere.

Y nyste how, but in a strete
He sette me fair on my fete
And seyde, "Walke forth a pas,
And tak thy aventure or cas,
That thou shalt fynde in Fames place."
                            (1046-1053)

The episode, the most vital in the poem, is over. With the departure of the eagle comedy, good spirits, even a kind of meaningfulness, goes from the poem. For a brief moment Order has been extolled and the "Knower" has revealed some manner of truth to the "Unknower," though what the relevance is to the whole is as obscure as ever.

The Legend of Good Women offers little that is fruitful for a study of the nature of Chaucer's comedy. Written after the *Troilus,* it does not rightfully belong to the "early poems," though it does, apparently, precede the composition of the greater part of the *Canterbury Tales.* Yet its attempt to return to the dream-vision form of the earlier poems and to the poet as character and dreamer, whose ignorance about the true nature of faithful love is the point of the dream, is important to note because of its failure.

The Prologue, in both the original and the revision, begins in some gaiety and good spirits. With gentle irony the opening lines protest the poet's willingness to believe what books tell him is so, even if he has never experienced it in life: "Men shal not wenen every thyng a lye/ But yf himself yt seeth, or elles dooth;/ . . . Bernard the monk ne saugh nat all, pardee!" (Text F, 12-16). Once more Chaucer suggests that his understanding of life has come to him through the written word, and that he is a little stupid about it all:

> And as for me, though that I konne but lyte,
> On bokes for to rede I me delyte,
> And to hem yive I feyth and ful credence,
> And in myn herte have hem in reverence
> So hertely, that ther is game noon
> That fro my bokes maketh me to goon,
> But yt be seldom on the holyday,
> Save, certeynly, whan that the month of May
> Is comen, and that I here the foules synge,
> And that the floures gynnen for to sprynge,
> Farewel my bok, and my devocioun!
>   (Text F, 29-39)

Joy characterizes his love of nature, and is focussed on one flower, the daisy. If this narrator is in love with anything, it is with "thise floures white and rede":

> To hem have I so gret affeccioun,
> As I seyde erst, whanne comen is the May,
> That in my bed ther daweth me no day
> That I nam up and walkyng in the mede
> To seen this flour ayein the sonne sprede,
> Whan it upryseth erly by the morwe.
>   (Text F, 44-49)

It is interesting to see that in what may have been the revision of the Prologue, known as Text G, Chaucer has felt that much of his earlier exuberance needed some correction. Repetitious though they are, the lines in Text F, that say again and again how much he loves the daisy, charge this part of the poem with a spirit that is unabashedly happy. "So glad am I," says the poet, that when he sees the flower all sorrow goes;

> And I love it, and ever ylike newe,
> And evere shal, til that myn herte dye.
> Al swere I nat, of this I wol nat lye;
> Ther loved no wight hotter in his lyve.
> And whan that hit ys eve, I renne blyve,
> As sone as evere the sonne gynneth weste,
> To seen this flour, how it wol go to reste,
> For fere of nyght, so hateth she derknesse.
> Hire chere is pleynly sprad in the brightnesse
> Of the sonne, for ther yt wol unclose.
> Allas, that I ne had Englyssh, ryme or prose,
> Suffisant this flour to preyse aryght!
>   (Text F, 56-67)

It is the worship of the daisy, and it matters not whether the daisy is a daisy or a figure for some lady, that brings him to his dream and the encounter with the God of Love and Alceste, and the composition of the legends of good women that make up the rest of the poem.

The scene of the meeting with the "myghty god of Love" and the "quene . . . clad in real habit grene . . . for al the world ryght as a dayesye" has all the potential for dramatic vitality, and yet it never comes to life, except perhaps in the one moment when the god of Love "gan smyle" (F, 498) and gave some comfort in light of the severe penance asked for by Alceste. Why the poem fails to realize its potential cannot even be conjectured. The poet, standing humble before the accusation that he has been the god of Love's "mortal fo" for having translated the "Romauns of the Rose" and for having "mad in Englysh ek the bok/ How that Crisseyde Troylus forsok" should have had comic possibilities, but he does not. No perspective is established, and the task set him for his penance, the "makynge of a glorious legende/ Of goode woman, maydenes and wyves,/ That were trewe in lovynge al here lyves" depends for its carrying out on so serious an oversimplification of the complex reality inherent in "true loving" that the poet's interest was bound to be unrealizable even before he can begin to comply. It seems as if the theme of the poem contained within it its own inevitable failure for Chaucer. Since it precludes the creation of opposing aspects of truth, it rules out any real tension. And the uncritical way the poet-dreamer accepts the assumption allows for no discovery, for no arrival at some kind of knowledge through the working out of the poem. By now, surely it is clear that these are the motifs Chaucer likes to work with, and when they are not present in the initial conception of a poem, the poem fails.

The struggle to fulfill the penance is gallant, and entirely unconvincing. The legends of the nine ladies, Cleopatra, Thisbe, Dido, Hypsiphyle and Medea, Lucrece, Ariadne, Philomela, Phyllis, and Hypermnestra, all faithful in love (according to the understanding of the period), all deserted by "false men that hem betrayed," are lifeless dischargings of an assignment. Some of the ladies seem to interest him more than others, Dido for instance. But time after time he ignores the opportunity history or legend give him for dramatic treatment, and in explicit terms he states his reluctance to recount more than the minimum. "I coude folwe, word for word, Virgile" he says of the story of Dido, "but it wolde lasten al to longe while" (1002-1003). And he concludes the legend of Hypsiphyle and Medea wearily with: "Wel can Ovyde hire letter in vers endyte,/ Which were as now to long for me to wryte" (1678-1679). Demaphon, the betrayer of Phyllis disgusts him:

> Me lyste nat vouche-sauf on hym to swynke,
> Ne spende on hym a penne ful of ynke,
> For fals in love was he, ryght as his syre.
> The devil sette here soules bothe afyre!
>   (2490-2493)

And the last legend, that of Hypermnestra, simply stops at the end of a couplet, not at the end of the story. Perhaps the words at the beginning "The Wirdes, that we clepen Destine,/ Hath shapen hire that she mot nedes be/ Pyëtous, sad, wis, and trewe as stel" (2580-2582), finally discouraged him from writing any more. At any rate, the poem stops, its interest for the critic more in the evidence of what it lacks that the other poems of Chaucer have, than in its moments of lyricism and gay spirits.

❖   ❖   ❖

All the dream-vision poems of Chaucer are in some way poems of discovery: even *The Legend* seems to promise to be. And they are all dramatic in method. Unlike the dreamers of poems such as *The Pearl*, or *Piers Plowman*, other dream-visions of the period, the poet-dreamer is given the qualities of a "character." The dreamer of the Pearl poem slips from the world of loss into a dream about the lost; the dreamer of the fair field of folk observes with critical and satirical eye the corruption and decadence of the dream world that corroborates his view of the real world. None of the other dreamers has much potential for comedy, none of them exists in the middle distance as a figure of interest in his own right. What makes Chaucer's dreamers essentially comic is their purblindness, which is not, I think, in the situation of the dream, merely a pose. They are neither figures to be laughed at, nor figures who laugh, but are ones in possession of partial knowledge who arrive at full knowledge in the course of the dream-experience, or at some awareness of the degree of their purblindness. What that full knowledge is, is never hidden from the reader; indeed, it is that which gives meaningful form to the structure of the dream itself. That the Duchess is dead is clear from the moment the "man in black" speaks; that the Dreamer must find out that this is really so provides the dramatic movement of the poem. That Love is many things is proclaimed in the opening lines of *The Parliament;* the dreamer's vision of the actuality of the fact is the action of the poem.

Why the discovery of truth is, in these poems of Chaucer, comic and not tragic, or at least "non-comic," is difficult to answer in any simple way. Certainly, the discovery of truth is not, *per se,* comic; indeed, it is also the process of tragedy. Objectively critical terms fail at this point, and one must resort to a statement that is frankly subjective. In every instance what the Dreamer discovers in Chaucer's poems is something of happy import. Though the knight has lost, he has loved greatly; though Fame is fickle and unjust, she is sometimes just; though contention and strife threaten order and harmony, they are never a fatal threat. And all those values that please us in the contemplation—order, harmony, reward, love—become translated into possible reality through the complex workings of the poems. Such a simple observation that literature is not nearly as interesting as life, for instance, becomes a pleasing reality in each of these poems, though ironically the world of the book is the waking world, the world of life is the dream world. And always there is the perspective established between us and the action of the poem, as our somewhat superior view of the dreamer and his experience gives us the right and the power to understand the two together.

chapter 2

TROILUS AND CRISEYDE: COMEDY'S PART IN THE CREATION OF TRAGEDY

It has long been a commonplace of Chaucerian criticism to pay tribute of some sort to the influence of Boethius' *Consolation of Philosophy* on *Troilus and Criseyde.* And like most commonplaces this one is true in ways that are even more complex in the exploration than seem to be so at first sight. It seems possible to say that it is Chaucer's absorption in Boethius that makes his retelling of Boccaccio's *Il Filostrato* a transformation of romance into tragedy, that gives to his vision of life already evidenced in the "early poems," an authority that brings to maturity almost all his powers as creator, and brings to the Italian love poem a significantly informing thesis that is moral in nature.

In whatever version Chaucer knew *Il Filostrato*, the original Italian of Boccaccio or a French version of it, or whether he turned to earlier accounts, meager as they were, to compare them with the Italian romance, he found in the story something so compelling that he had to retell it as meaningfully as possible. He had done translations before; both the *Romance of the Rose* and the *Consolation of Philosophy* reveal, in the care with which they are put into English, great respect and even affection. But the account of Troilo and his betrayal by Criseida seems to have asked for something more than translation. Although following in outline and in almost all detail the action of Boccaccio's poem, Chaucer's *Troilus* is so much more rich in its essence as to turn those details of the Italian poem into accidentals. What it was that compelled his interest in the story cannot be known; perhaps it reflected his concern with the nature of Love; perhaps the reading of it coincided with his apparent enthusiasm for things Italian; perhaps its characters aroused his curiosity. But something happened that brought together the poetic concerns of the past, the philosophic interest in Boethius, and the attraction to a tale of betrayed love that generated the imaginative energy and vision that produced *Troilus and Criseyde.*

Troilus and Criseyde differs from *Il Filostrato* for three significant reasons: it has meaningful form, it has comedy in it, and it has a narrator whose role is clearly defined. It is the combined force of these three things that make of Chaucer's poem a tragedy, a drama of character, a philosophical construct. It is the coaction of these three that turn the episodic narration of the love between the courtly Troilo and the sensuous Criseida into a poem about the transitoriness of love, about the mutability of joy, about the poignancy of human blindness. And each of these three things could have come to Chaucer from his reading of Boethius.

Chaucer was perfectly aware that in his retelling of the Italian story he was writing tragedy. He knew from his translating of the *Consolation* the definition of the form Boethius gives, a definition that is clearly a simplification of Aristotle's: "Tragedye is to seyn a dite of a prosperite for a tyme, that endeth in wrecchidnesse" (Book II, Prosa 2). "Go, litel bok, go, litel myn tragedye" he writes at the end of Troilus, praying that it will win for him the grace to write comedy, "er that he dye." And his tale is not only of one but of three who fall from "prosperite" to "wrecchidnesse." But what makes this poem tragic in the most complex meaning of the word is not its apt illustration of the definition, not its portrayal of the happiness of Troilus and Criseyde, and Pandarus, her uncle and their fall into woe; it is Chaucer's insight into the nature of human blindness, his awareness of the sometimes impenetrable curtain that lies between the known and the unknown, his understanding of the complicated inter-relationships of the human world: it is all these encompassed by a view that sees the finite and the infinite, the timeless and the timed.

Three persons are important in *The Consolation of Philosophy:* Boethius, the prisoner; Philosophy, the consoler; and Fortune, who is not "on stage," but whose person is called to mind as Philosophy defines her nature. Chaucer's knowledge of the work was so thorough that almost every aspect of it permeated his whole poem. I do not like suggesting any *quid pro quo* schematization of the Boethius in *Troilus* for this would falsify and oversimplify what the poem really is. Yet such a suggestion is useful, provided it is not rigidly held to, to make clear how the divinely comic philosophy of this favorite philosopher of the poet generated Chaucer's one tragedy. Briefly, then, it can be proposed that the figure of Philosophy is Chaucer, the narrator; that Boethius, the questioner, who is also the representative of Man protesting his human condition, is Troilus; and Fortune is Fortune in the poem, "off stage," yet dominant in the mind of the hero. The poem, *Troilus and Criseyde*, is the poetical-dramatic illustration of what the Consolation is all about. It is interesting to note that Chaucer divided and reassembled the nine cantos of the Boccaccio into five books, even as the *Consolation* is divided, and that he, too, made of each book a significant unit within the whole poem. But more important is the effect of Chaucer's use of the figure of Fortune in his structuring of the story. However successful his evolving of the significant form for *The Book of the Duchess* or for *The Parliament of Fowls* may have been, the Boethian and common medieval personification of circumstances in the image of Fortune and her Wheel gave him a way of working out the tragedy that enriches the meaning of the tragedy itself.

The poem in its five books is not only an *exemplum* of the moving Wheel of Fortune, it is the Wheel itself. Inevitably, the iconographical presentations of the concept come to mind as one passes in review, briefly and simply, the course of the story, book by book. Troilus, in Book I, is first in false happiness because he thinks he is safe from the woes of love, then he is plunged into sorrow when he falls in love with Criseyde, because he assumes his love must go unrequited. The Wheel begins thus, with its figured hero at the bottom of the turn. In Book II, because Pandarus goes to work to win Criseyde for his friend, the Wheel begins to mount. It is the attainment of Criseyde that will signify the attainment of joy, and "prosperite," even as the gold and silver chalices in the hand of the iconographical hero mean the winning of earthly and spiritual happiness. In Book III, the Wheel has brought its charge to the top, to a joy and an ecstasy that has the illusion of enduring eternally. In the fourth book, the Wheel begins its descending turn. Ironically, each move that had made the mounting turn possible, proves to be responsible for the falling turn. And in the fifth book, Troilus is thrown from the Wheel, his joy turned to woe, his "wrecchidnesse" ended only by death. The solemn words of Fortune that Philosophy quotes to the suffering Boethius ring in our ears: "I torne the whirlynge wheel with the turnynge sercle; I am glad to chaungen the loweste to the heyeste, and the heyeste to the loweste" (Book II, Prosa 2, 51 ff.).

Fortune is not in Chaucer's mind synonymous with Fate or Destiny. Nor is it in Troilus' mind, though he seems at moments to think of himself as victimized by "her." To both the poet and his hero, Fortune is but a way of personifying change or mutability, alteration and the process of ceasing to be, as well as the process of becoming. Book IV is dedicated to her, and the recounting of change is the concern of the book:

But al to litel, weylaway the whyle,
Lasteth swich joie, ythonked be Fortune,
That semeth trewest whan she wol bygyle,
And kan to fooles so hire song entune,
That she hem hent and blent, traitour comune!
And whan a wight is from hire whiel ythrowe,
Than laugheth she, and maketh hym the mowe.
(IV, 1-7)

In miniature the fourth book repeats the three books that have preceded it, as if to show how change leads to further change, how the joys that were given are exactly the ones to be taken away. "From Troilus" Fortune "gan hire brighte face/ Awey to writhe, And tok of hym non heede,/ And caste hym clene out of his lady grace" (IV, 8-10). The prophetic knowledge that sent Criseyde's father Calkas from Troy to the camp of the Greeks, is the same knowledge that leads him to ask the Greeks to arrange for her to be brought away from Troy and Troilus. The character of Troilus, somewhat meditative, given to easy submission to circumstances, that made of him in Book I a courtly lover by his very nature as well as by the books, is the character that will plunge him into despair immediately upon hearing the decree of the Trojan parliament to exchange Criseyde for Antenor, held captive by the Greeks. Unable to see any course of action he retreats into sorrow once more, to be prodded out of it again by Pandarus. It is Pandarus, the same "worthy em," here as in Book II, who brings the lovers into each other's arms, and the ecstasy that marked the meeting of Troilus and Criseyde in Book III rises once more to lyric splendor, though now charged with pain. Book IV ends in sorrow, the Wheel beginning its turn downward. Troilus' departure from Criseyde, so lighthearted at the end of Book III, is heavy with melancholy in spite of her cheerful promise to return "in ten days time":

For mannes hed ymagynen ne kan,
N'entendement considere, ne tonge telle
The cruele peynes of this sorwful man,
That passen every torment down in helle.
For whan he saugh that she ne myghte dwelle,
Which that his soule out of his herte rente,
Withouten more, out of the chaumbre he wente.
(IV, 1695-1701)

So in brief, the fourth book repeats the significant moments of the first three and makes clear that the turns of the Wheel that raised

Troilus to his great joy are the same turns that bring him to woe, as if each spoke that moved his figure upwards was the same spoke that moved him downwards.

The fact of change in itself is neither a tragic nor a comic fact to contemplate. Fortune is not like Fate or Destiny, something that is irremediably ordained nor something to be fulfilled or worked out. As the Wheel image makes clear, that which is good may give way to that which is not good, but the turning does not cease and joy may well follow after woe. That is why Fortune has often been thought a concept essential to Comedy, as Fate is to Tragedy. Fate, too, has its reference in *Troilus and Criseyde*. Troilus from the very beginning of his love for Criseyde feels himself destined to woe. "But, O thow woful Troilus, God wolde,/ Sith thow most loven thorugh thi destine,/ That thow beset were on swich oon that sholde/ Know al thi wo, al lakked hir pitee!" (I, 519-522) he laments, bewildered by the suddenness of his love for a woman he has seen but once and cannot really hope to see again on any intimate terms. And it is the question of the nature of Destiny, of how much man is predestined, that occupies his thoughts in Book IV, as he seeks the solitude of the temple in his grief over the imminent loss of Criseyde. His soliloquy, taken almost word for word from Boethius (Book V, Prosa 3), reveals that in the weighing of the answers to the question he can only resign himself to the conclusion that he is the victim of Fate: "For al that comth, comth by necessitee:/ Thus to ben lorn, it is my destinee" (IV, 958-959).

The joy and sorrow of Troilus are indeed predestined; Fate does have a role in the poem. Both Chaucer and the reader know what is to be the outcome of the story before it begins. Chaucer explicitly states it within the first fifty-five lines, his own awareness of the sadness of the tragedy leading him to make a plea for compassionate understanding, especially from all those who love:

> For so hope I my sowle best avaunce,
> To prey for hem that Loves servauntz be,
> And write hire wo, and lyve in charite,
>
> And for to have of hem compassioun,
> As though I were hire owne brother dere.
> Now herkneth with a good entencioun,
> For now wil I gon streght to my matere,
> In which ye may the double sorwes here
> Of Troilus in lovynge of Criseyde,
> And how that she forsook hym er she deyde.
>
> (I, 47-56)

And from this précis are generated all the ironies, both tragic and comic, that mount in accumulated crescendo to the end. No matter how unhappy Troilus may be at the beginning, we know he is to be unhappy in a more painful way at the end. No matter how secure in bliss the lovers are, we know disaster lies ahead. No matter how extravagant Criseyde's protestations of faithfulness and love, we know of the ultimate betrayal. Troilus is fated by his creator, Chaucer, to suffer, for Chaucer is faithful to his source, Boccaccio.

But this poem, like the early poems of Chaucer, is also a poem of discovery. It is not enough to be in possession of the knowledge of the outcome, any more than it was enough for the poet-dreamer to hear that the Duchess was dead at the beginning of his encounter with "the man in black." The question is, why is Troilus to be unhappy? Why does Criseyde "false him"? What is contained in the concept Fate? The poem thus asks the question Boethius asks, sometimes in the person of Troilus, sometimes in the words of Criseyde, sometimes in the actions of Pandarus, sometimes by means of the shifting course of the war between the Greeks and the Trojans. Thus, in almost every one of its aspects, it dramatizes the question Boethius puts to Philosophy: "Why suffrestow that slydynge Fortune turneth so grete enterchaugngynges of thynges . . .?" (Book I, Prosa 4)

And by its total construct, it suggests the Boethian answers: men get what they deserve, the good are rewarded, the wicked punished, though in ways not clear to the eyes of men who see only in part, or dimly what their mortality condemns them to see. Only God, whose gaze takes in all human action irrespective of time or place, sees this is so: "Ryght so as ye seen some thynges in this temporal present, ryght so seeth God alle thinges by his eterne present" (V, Prosa 6). Only the poet Chaucer, and the reader, can see that Troilus and Criseyde and Pandarus, though acting "for the beste," act out of part knowledge, out of misunderstanding, out of human blindness. "O blynde world, O blynde entencioun!" says Chaucer early in his poem. "How often falleth al the effect contraire/ Of surquidrie and foul presumpcioun" (I, 211-213). Each character gets, alas, "what he deserves," although Troilus cannot see this when toward the end in final despair he cries: "But trewely, Criseyde, swete may,/ Whom I have ay with al my myght yserved,/ That ye thus doon, I have it nat deserved" (V, 1720-1722). For what he deserves he has from the beginning knowingly elected to move toward. Though Chaucer and Boccaccio, history and circumstance, conspire to form the Destiny of the lovers, the characters of Troilus and of Criseyde and of Pandarus freely choose to fulfil that destiny. It is "Simple necessity" that people act like human beings, for "it byhovith by necessite that alle men ben mortal or dedly" (V, Prosa 6); it is "Conditional necessity" that men act in ways their particular circumstances and natures make them act.

Perhaps the most striking characteristic of the condition of being mortal is the limitation of vision. Man in his darkened state may not, in his "derked lookynge . . . knowen the thynne subtile knyttynges of thinges." And things can be known only according to the nature of the knower: "Al that ever is iknowe, it is rather comprehended and knowen, nat aftir his strengthe and his nature, but aftir the faculte *(that is to seyn, the power and the nature)* of hem that knowen" (V, Prosa 4). Troilus can see only in the terms of what he wants and what he thinks Criseyde desires. His love for her while ennobled by the imaginative consideration for her welfare, blinds him to the threat to happiness inherent in her need for the preservation of honor at any cost, and stifles effectively the voice of practical common sense that warns him, in the midst of her confident promises to return, that the danger exists. His pleas with her to run away with him in defiance of the decree of the Trojan parliament come too late to have any effect, and have about them a hopelessness even at the moment of utterance. That he has been blind he is aware at the beginning of Book V. Accompanying Criseyde to the gate of Troy, "so wo-bigon, al wolde he naught hym pleyne,/ That on his hors unnethe he sat for peyne" he has a moment of tragic insight that belies his later complaint that he has not deserved what has happened to him:

> For ire he quook, so gan his herte gnawe,
> Whan Diomede on horse gan hym dresse,
> And seyde to hymself this ilke sawe:
> "Allas!" quod he, "thus foul a wrecchednesse,
> Whi suffre ich it? Whi nyl ich it redresse?
> Were it nat bet atones for to dye
> Than evere more in langour thus to drye?
>
> "Whi nyl I make atones riche and pore
> To have inough to doone, er that she go?
> Why nyl I brynge al Troie upon a roore?
> Whi nyl I slen this Diomede also?
> Why nyl I rather with a man or two
> Stele hire away? Whi wol I this endure?
> Whi nyl I helpen to myn owen cure?"
>   (V, 36-49)

Chaucer, like Philosophy, has the answer, an answer that Troilus cannot have because his vision is one that cannot embrace the whole of the poem, nor comprehend the self:

But why he nolde don so fel a dede,
That shal I seyn, and whi hym liste it spare:
He hadde in herte alweyes a manere drede
Lest that Criseyde, in rumour of this fare,
Sholde han ben slayn; lo, this was al his care.
And ellis, certeyn, as I seyde yore,
He hadde it don, withouten wordes more.

(V, 50-56)

Criseyde, too, is blind, blind to herself, blind to the nature of reality. Ironically, she thinks of herself as wise, as cautious, as practical, and as circumspect; and it is this very combination that gives her a self-assurance so limiting as to deaden her powers of imagination. She is unable to imagine possibility or to predict probability in her concentrated and intense gaze upon the moment, and this she recognizes at the end, though she is still the same Criseyde in spite of the hard-won self-knowledge. Her moment of tragic insight is the most poignant in the poem since it comes to her in terms that reflect the candor she has shown all along.

Ful rewfully she loked upon Troie,
Biheld the toures heigh and ek the halles:
"Allas!" quod she, "the plesance and the joie,
The which that now al torned into galle is,
Have ich had ofte withinne tho yonder walles!
O Troilus, what dostow now?" she seyde.
"Lord! wheyther thow yet thenke upon Criseyde?

"Allas, I ne hadde trowed on youre loore,
And went with yow, as ye me redde er this!
Than hadde I now nat siked half so soore.
Who myghte have seyd that I hadde don amys
To stele awey with swich oon as he ys?
But al to late comth the letuarie,
Whan men the cors unto the grave carie.

"To late is now to speke of that matere.
Prudence, allas, oon of thyne eyen thre
Me lakked alwey, er that I come here!
On tyme ypassed wel remembred me,
And present tyme ek koud ich wel ise,
But future tyme, er I was in the snare,
Koude I nat sen; that causeth now my care."

(V, 729-749)

This resignation so quickly attained makes it inevitable that she will put up little resistance to the approach of Diomede. Uttered before she succcumbs to his wooing, her recognition is itself, ironically, too late.

Pandarus, too, is blind, blind to the true nature of the love he brings to consummation with all his joyous machinations. And his moment of insight comes when, aware, at last, not so much of the falseness of his niece as of the pain felt by Troilus, he is for once unable to utter a word, until "at the laste thus he spak, and seyde:/ 'My brother deer, I may do the namore./ What sholde I seyen? I hate, ywys, Cryseyde;/ And, God woot, I wol hate hire evermore!" (V, 1730-1733). However non-commendable his morality has been he has acted for the best:

> "Havyng unto myn honour ne my reste
> Right no reward, I dide al that the leste.

> "If I dide aught that myghte liken the,
> It is me lief; and of this tresoun now,
> God woot that it a sorwe is unto me!
> And dredeles, for hertes ese of yow,
> Right fayn I wolde amende it, wiste I how.
> And fro this world, almyghty God I preye
> Delivere hire soon! I kan namore seye."
>   (V, 1735-1743)

"Swich is this world, whoso it kan byholde" says Chaucer. "In ech estat is litel hertes reste./ God leve us for to take it for the beste!" (V, 1748-1750).

But the mortal condition that makes the blindness of men inevitable is, *per se,* no more tragic than is the fact of change. Both are subjects for Comedy as well as for Tragedy; in the latter instance the fatal outcome has been effected before insight and wisdom have had time or chance to repair the damage done in blindness. It is not the sad fact of Criseyde's faithlessness nor Troilus' realization of his own blindness, however, that creates the particular emotional quality of the tragedy of *Troilus and Criseyde;* it is the degree of the happiness and joy, of longing and subsequent "blysse," that measures out the quality of the tragic intensity of the poem. With a kind of inexorable justice Chaucer makes it felt that his protagonists shall suffer pain exactly to the degree they have had joy. The "sorwe" is "double" in more ways than one. The tragic emotion created by the poem is great because the joy has been greatly realized. At the risk of reducing to a simplification a complex observation, it is Comedy in the figure of Pandarus that accounts for much of the tragic effect of Chaucer's poem; it is his robust and exuberant presence that transforms so movingly the romance that was Boccaccio's.

The first book of the poetic tragedy begins in a key that is minor. Over and over again Chaucer reminds us that his tale is to be one of sorrow. And for almost five hundred and fifty lines of the ten hundred and ninety-two, the mood remains solemn, the pace sober, the tone one of romantic melancholy. Troilus' woe in the first days of his love for Criseyde dominates this first half of the book. But when Pandarus enters the chamber where Troilus is "bywayling . . . thus allone," the poem is charged with new vitality, and the whole story begins to take on a character markedly different from that of *Il Filostrato*. It is Pandarus, bearing almost no resemblance to his Italian prototype except his name, who transforms the romantic lyricism of the poem into dramatic action, who prods the melancholy Troilus into life, who arranges the meeting with Criseyde, whose vulgar, practical, common sense brings the lovers to their greatest happiness and defines, by ironic contrast, the quality of their love. As the frank sexuality of the common birds in *The Parliament of Fowls* makes believable the romantic attitudes of the royal birds, so Pandarus' conception of love as entirely physical makes Troilus' canonization of it credible.

Pandarus is a comic figure the minute he enters the poem. He is like the narrator in *The Book of the Duchess* as he attempts to lift the spirits of the "langwisshynge" Troilus; he is like the Eagle that took Chaucer "up in a swap" in *The House of Fame*, jovial and paternal and pedantic; he is like the common fowl in *The Parliament* who spoke out for the urgency of mating, impatient with the elaborate delay practiced by the world of courtly nonsense. And at the beginning his excessive activity is comic as he sets about with gleeful relish to bring about something already destined to be. His intrusive busy-ness, his insistent vitality, his well-meant coarseness, his store of maxims, his plotting, all are matters of immediate comic delight; but they are also matters that make him an important part of the tragic effect of the poem. In the last two books his attempts at managing are no longer comic, his busy-ness no longer amusing but futile and pathetic, his coarseness irritating, no matter how well meant. He has played his part in the creation of joy; his efforts to keep the joy going are but gestures, like the helpless flailing of arms. By as much as he ceases to be comic he becomes part of the tragic vision at the end.

Pandarus' genius for machination is set into action by one thing only—his love for love, which means his delight in bringing about the mating of two lovers. The first scene he shares with Troilus reveals that he, like everyone else in the poem except Diomede, does things from the best intentions. His concern for the woeful prince is partly paternal, partly brotherly in its tone. But he is also unable to abide mystery unless he is responsible for its creation, and his sympathy is clearly partly curiosity. The minute Troilus admits that Love is his affliction Pandarus is all business. "How hastow thus unkyndely and longe/ Hid this fro me, thow fol?" he asks and calls forth from Troilus something resembling a spark of life as he offers to help:

> "Paraunter thow myghte after swich oon longe,
> That myn avys anoon may helpen us."
> "This were a wonder thing," quod Troilus
> "Thow koudest nevere in love thiselven wisse:
> How devel maistow brynge me to blisse?"
>   (I, 617-623)

His humorous scorn for Troilus' mooning nonsense awakens our sympathy and our criticism at the same time, making us more attentive to and respectful of the attitude toward love that Troilus has, arousing by its jesting vulgarity even at this early moment a belief in the quality of reality in the kind of love it does not understand. It is clear throughout the poem that Pandarus is never able to comprehend the nature of the love he has played such an active part in bringing to fulfilment, and his blindness is but another way in which Chaucer defines the "blynde world." But for a while his relish is part of the joy that begins to characterize the poem, and his understanding that love and sex are synonymous inspires his genius of manipulation, so that when he finally brings Troilus into the bed of Criseyde he is Fortune's agent in raising Troilus to his greatest "blisse."

Pandarus is indeed the agent of Fortune. He it is who sees her role in human affairs as Philosophy defined it to the suffering Boethius, and his understanding makes of her a goddess of comedy, not of tragedy. His whole attention, once he has discovered the cause of Troilus' woe, is directed toward finding out who the lady is. His tactics reveal that he knows much about human nature, and he shifts from posture to posture in his attempt to make Troilus identify his love. From solemn maxims and old "proverbes" that reprimand Troilus for indulging in fruitless sorrow, to scorn for his romantic languishing—"What womman koude loven swich a wrecche"—to pointing out the stupidity of dying "unknowe, unkist, and lost, that is unsought," he moves to a suggestion that there can be no harm in trying to do something about winning his lady. Troilus' reluctance to be persuaded finds one last defense. He cannot hope to win, for Fortune is his foe: "Ne al the men that riden konne or go/ May of hire cruel whiel the harm withstonde;/ For, as hire list, she pleyeth with free and bonde" (I, 837-840). Pandarus' reply is immediate: Fortune is good as well as bad and she is just as apt to turn woe to joy as not:

> Quod Pandarus, "Than blamestow Fortune
> For thow art wroth; ye, now at erst I see.
> Woost thow nat wel that Fortune is comune
> To everi manere wight in som degree?
> And yet thow hast this comfort, lo, parde,
> That, as hire joies moten overgon,
> So mote hire sorwes passen everechon.
>
> "For if hire whiel stynte any thynge to torne,
> Than cessed she Fortune anon to be.
> Now, sith hire whiel by no way may sojourne,
> What woostow if hire mutabilite
> Right as thyselven list, wol don by the,
> Or that she be naught fer fro thyn helpynge?
> Paraunter thow hast cause for to synge."
>   (I, 841-874)

It is upon this argument that Troilus' resistance breaks. "Allas! of al my wo the welle,/ Thanne is my swete fo called Criseyde!" (1, 873-874).

Like the poet-dreamer in *The Book of the Duchess,* Troilus speaks more than he knows. Fortune is his foe for his fortune is Criseyde "slydynge of corage," as Philosophy had described her who "turneth so grete enterchaungynges of thynges": Criseyde is mutability and mutability is Criseyde. "Allas!" she laments at the end, her yielding to Diomede an accomplished fact,

> ". . . for now is clene ago
> My name of trouthe in love, for everemo!
> For I have falsed oon the gentileste
> That evere was, and oon the worthieste!
>
> "Allas! of me, unto the worldes ende,
> Shal neyther ben ywriten nor ysonge
> No good word, for thise bokes wol me shende.
> O, rolled shal I ben on many a tonge!
> Thorughout the world my belle shal be ronge!
> And wommen moost wol haten me of alle.
> Allas, that swich a cas me sholde falle!"
>   (V, 1054-1064)

"But" she concludes, "al shal passe; and thus take I my leve."

But for Fortune to turn bitter, it must have first been sweet. Criseyde who brings pain to Troilus has also brought him great joy, and she is no mere personification of "Mutabilite." She is a woman of so complex a nature that she has had friends and foes from Chaucer's day to this. It is in the second book that she comes clear as a person and it is through Pandarus that Chaucer touches her into life, and brings into view the complexities of her nature.

The second book of *Troilus and Criseyde* is almost pure comedy. Although we are not allowed to forget that Troy is in a state of siege, the scenes in Criseyde's house, even the glimpses of Troilus, are full of bright gaiety. From the opening lines of the poem with their promise for Troilus of release from despair, to the last stanza that leaves Criseyde on the threshold of Troilus' room and the first meeting, the book is alive with sound and color and movement. Almost all the action takes place among people: Criseyde and Pandarus in the social interchange at her house; Troilus greeted by the admiring crowds; the party at Deiphebus' house, with Helen as the gracious hostess. Solitude is always broken into at moments of significance, and the inner world is swayed by the outer world. Pandarus comes upon Criseyde in the opening scene seated with "two othere ladys . . . withinne a paved parlour." Criseyde's solitary pondering on the news that Pandarus has brought her, her astonishment at the fact that Troilus, the prince of Troy, loves her, is broken into by the noise of the people crying in the street below, "Se, Troilus/ Hath right now put to flighte the Grekes route!" (II, 612-613). Her fear of the Greeks and her withdrawal from public gaze in the first book that have put her in her own state of siege find in the joy of the crowd at Troilus' victory significant comfort:

> Criseÿda gan al his chere aspien,
> And leet it so softe in hire herte synke,
> That to hireself she seyde, "Who yaf me drynke?"
> (II, 649-651)

Her weighing of the dangers and the joys of love is concluded and resolved when, leaving the solitude of her room, she descends into the garden "With hire neces thre, . . . Flexippe, she, Tharbe, and Antigone," for it is Antigone's song with its eloquent praise of Love that calms her fears. Its echo of her own inclination to believe that "no wele is worth, that may no sorwe dryen" brings her conflict to rest for a moment: "And ay gan love hire lasse for t'agaste/ Than it dide erst, and synken in hire herte,/ That she wex somwhat able to converte" (II, 901-903).

Laughter and song fill this book. When Pandarus and Criseyde meet, "thei gonnen laughe." To Criseyde's question about Troilus, "Kan he wel speke of love?", Pandarus "a litel gan to smyle." Her delight in his reply is barely contained in her response, even though she is not pleased by his insinuation that she can only find out if she becomes "his al hool":

> "Nay, therof spak I nought, ha, ha!" quod she;
> "As helpe me God, ye shenden every deel!"
> "O, mercy, dere nece," anon quod he,
> "What so I spak, I mente naught but wel,
> By Mars, the god that helmed is of steel!
> Now beth naught wroth, my blood, my nece dere."
> "Now wel," quod she, "foreven be it here!"
> (II, 589-595)

The laughter she greets Pandarus with when he returns from the first of his bustling journeys to Troilus is gay, but it betrays also a nervousness and an apprehension even as it hints of her joy. "I have a joly wo, a lusty sorwe" says Pandarus, and Criseyde,

> whan that she hire uncle herde,
> With dredful herte, and desirous to here
> The cause of his comynge, thus answerde:
> "Now, by youre fey, myn uncle," quod she, "dere,
> What manere wyndes gydeth yow now here?
> Tel us youre joly wo and youre penaunce.
> How ferforth be ye put in loves daunce?"
>
> "By God," quod he, "I hoppe alwey byhynde!"
> And she to laughe, it thoughte hire herte brest.
> (II, 1100-1108)

That she is reluctant to take the letter Pandarus brings her does not mean she is not pleased. "Refuse it naught" says her uncle, and thrusts it into her bosom. "Now cast it awey anon,/ That folk may seen and gauren on us tweye," he teases, and Criseyde "gan to smyle" as she reminds him she will write no letter in reply. Pandarus' reply "No? than wol I . . . so ye endite" calls forth from her a laugh and an invitation to dine:

> And he gan at hymself to jape faste,
> And seyde, "Nece, I have so gret a pyne
> For love, that everich other day I faste—"

> And gan his beste japes forth to caste,
> And made hire so to laughe at his folye,
> That she for laughter wende for to dye.
>   (II, 1164-1169)

By the time she has been brought to a willingness to meet Troilus she has lost much of her apprehension in the pleasure of knowing herself loved so well, and she laughs to herself as she hears Helen speak seriously of Troilus' "illness." Even Troilus, little given to expressions of gaiety, "gan to smylen" as Pandarus goes out from his chamber to bring Criseyde to him.

The gaiety of this book, the busy comings and goings within the "paved parlour," the long matching of wits between Pandarus and Criseyde, the elaborate plotting to bring the lovers together, are of great significance for the whole tragedy to come. It is not only that in Book II Chaucer thus makes of the rather simply-drawn Criseida of his source a woman of psychological actuality, or that he turns Pandaro into the joyous vulgarian Pandarus; it is, more importantly, that here he prepares for our understanding of the nature of Criseyde's love, which will be the condition for her yielding to Troilus in Book III. By the amount of persuasion Pandarus must exert upon her the full meaningfulness of her words to Troilus, "Ne hadde I er now, my swete herte deere,/ Ben yold, ywis, I were now nought heere!," is realizable.

The social comedy of the second book is the setting for a conflict of wills between uncle and niece. Because we have known from the beginning of the poem that Criseyde will yield to Troilus in the fullest measure, her resistance against doing so is full of comic irony. And at the same time, because we also know that she will yield and then betray, the book is sadly full of preparation for tragedy, the comic ironies at one and the same time premonitorily tragic.

In the immediate scene, Criseyde's contention with herself as she faces the knowledge Pandarus forces upon her has its comic effect. It is a struggle against, and then a struggle for, what Destiny, in the form of Boccaccio and whatever else were Chaucer's sources, has decreed for her. Because we know that she cannot do other than love Troilus, her resistance to the initial attack upon her self-ordained removal from involvement in life by Pandarus, that gives way to a qualified yielding and then to a total acceptance of all that love means, is a progress that crescendos in joy. Her decision to grant Troilus her love, if not her body, reached before the book is ended, is a hard-won decision. All the reasoning that goes into it is clearly rationalization, for the heart "gan enclyne/ To like hym" before the uneasy and cautious mind is quieted. In as far as she can see, in as far as she can understand, she arrives at her willingness to consent to love, freely and willingly, with full and reasonable assent of the mind. Her conflict, so movingly detailed in the scene where, alone in her room, "as stylle as any ston" she weighs the threats against the joys inherent in love, is in miniature an exemplum of Chaucer's understanding of the Boethian definition of the nature of Destiny and Free-Will, for she not only does what Destiny has decreed, but what her nature makes it inevitable for her to do. "Fortune ne schal nevere maken that swiche thynges ben thyne that nature of thynges hath maked foreyne fro the" (Book II, Prosa 5). ". . . Ther is liberte of fre wil. Ne ther ne was nevere no nature of reason that it ne hadde liberte of fre wil," Philosophy points out.

> "For every thing that may naturely usen resoun, it hath doom by which it discernith and demeth every thing; thanne knoweth it by itself thinges that ben to fleen and thinges that ben to desiren. And thilke thing that any wight demeth to ben desiren, that axeth or desireth he; and fleeth thilke thing that he troweth to fleen" (Book V, Prosa 2).

She is not determined by the war, nor by the desertion of Calkas, nor by the lustfulness of her body, nor by the attraction of Troilus to yield to what Destiny has already ordained for her. All these work together in inextricable complexity, so that when the conditions are made right for her, as they are so painstakingly by Pandarus, she can do nothing else but carry out what has been determined for her.

For it is true that without the activity of Pandarus Criseyde would not have yielded. Once more it is important to return to him, the comic figure, as the generator of the tragedy to come. It is by the elaborate cleverness of the persuasion that Pandarus exerts upon her that the degree of her fear and her reluctance is measured. And the degree of her resistance measures the degree of her yielding, so that when, in Book III, she finally opens her arms and gives her body to Troilus with the words "Welcome, my knyght, my pees, my suffisaunce" she is exactly defining her love and describing the measure of her joy. And the measure of her love is the measure of Troilus' "blisse," which in turn, alas, is the measure of his "wrecchidnesse" at the end. Thus the completeness of her yielding is the measure of the tragic pain we feel, and she feels, in the fact of betrayal, made, ironically, after very little persuasion indeed.

It is in Book III that for the moment Fortune holds her turning Wheel still as the lovers and Pandarus arrive at the high point of joy. Book III, like Book II, is predominantly comic. Its comedy, however, is not that of social busy-ness, nor of the brightly sharp exchange of wits; it is the comedy of happiness fulfilled, of love achieved, of agony stilled. Once more it is Pandarus who acts to define the nature of the love that is consummated, his insistent vulgarity and sexuality making the ecstatic lyricism of the love almost unbearably believable by contrast. "O blisful light, of which the bemes clere/ Adorneth al the thridde heven faire!" the book begins; and it ends with "Troilus in lust and in quiet/ . . . with Criseyde, his owen herte swete." And in between, in the room within the room within the house of Pandarus, secure from the world and the "huge rayn," Criseyde has been brought to the arms of Troilus, the desire that is physical has been translated in the act of consummation into the Love that brings full joy to the fearful Criseyde and complete "blysse" to Troilus, ennobling him in all that he is and does:

> In suffisaunce, in blisse, and in singynges,
> This Troilus gan al his lif to lede.
> He spendeth, jousteth, maketh festenynges;
> He yeveth frely ofte, and chaungeth wede,
> And held aboute hym alwey, out of drede,
> A world of folk, as com hym wel of kynde,
> The fresshest and the beste he koude fynde;
>
> That swich a vois was of hym and a stevene
> Thorughout the world, of honour and largesse,
> That it up rong unto the yate of hevene.
> And, as in love, he was in swich gladnesse,
> That in his herte he demed, as I gesse,
> That ther nys lovere in this world at ese
> So wel as he; and thus gan love hym plese.
>
> (III, 1716-1722)
>
> In alle nedes, for the townes werre,
> He was, and ay, the first in armes dyght,
> And certeynly, but if that bokes erre,
> Save Ector most ydred of any wight;
> And this encrees of hardynesse and myght
> Com hym of love, his ladies thank to wynne,
> That altered his spirit to withinne.
>
> In tyme of trewe, on haukyng wolde he ride,
> Or elles honte boor, beer, or lyoun;
> The smale bestes leet he gon biside.
> And whan that he com ridyng into town,
> Ful ofte his lady from hire wyndow down,
> As fressh as faukoun comen out of muwe,
> Ful redy was hym goodly to saluwe.
>
> (III, 1772-1785)

Freed of pride and of arrogance, humble now in the face of the Love he had so mocked in the first book, Troilus is at one and the same time the paragon of the Courtly Lover and the real lover, whose joy is both of the spirit and the flesh.

It is Pandarus who has been intent upon the flesh from the beginning. Although the despair Troilus felt in the first book is clearly as much sexual as "spiritual," his attitude toward the love he has for Criseyde transcends always the purely physical. Love to Pandarus means one thing only, sex. He is open about this to Troilus; to Criseyde he is less so. His whole approach to her barely disguises his enthusiasm for his interest in "the olde daunce" and his words upon meeting her in the opening scene of the second book are full of leering delight: "Do wey youre barbe, and shewe youre face bare," he asks. "Do wey youre book, rys up, and lat us daunce,/ And lat us don to May som observaunce." To which Criseyde, catching the innuendo in the verb "daunce" replies:

> "I? God forbede! . . . be ye mad?
> Is that a widewes lif, so God yow save?
> By God, ye maken me ryght soore adrad!
> Ye ben so wylde, it semeth as ye rave.
> It sate me wel bet ay in a cave
> To bidde and rede on holy seyntes lyves;
> Lat maydens gon to daunce, and yonge wyves."
>
> (II, 113-119)

Book III is full of Pandarus' vast delight in "kenning the olde daunce." From the moment it opens he is busy at getting the lovers into bed. He has no patience whatsoever for Criseyde's initial reserve as she looks upon the sick Troilus: "Pandare wep as he to water wolde,/ And poked evere his nece new and newe,/ And seyde, 'Wo bygon ben hertes trewe!/ For love of God, make of this thing an ende,/ Or sle us both at ones, er ye wende'" (III, 115-119). His tolerance of Troilus' ritualistic and reverential preparation for the physical union with Criseyde is maintained for only a little while, and with great effort. And it is his explosive interruption of Troilus' poeticism that, by its crudeness, makes the preparation really convincing, transforming the words from convention into reality by contrast. "'. . . Blisful Venus, this nyght thow me enspire.'/ Quod Troilus, 'As wys as I the serve,/ And evere bet and bet shal, til I sterve./ . . . O Jove ek, for the love of faire Europe,/ . . . O Mars, . . . For love of Cipris, . . . O Phebus . . . Mercurie . . . Diane, . . . O fatal sustren," Troilus chants until Pandarus can take no more; "Thow wrecched mouses herte,/ Artow agast so that she wol the bite?" (III, 712-737), and into Criseyde's bedroom he brings Troilus "by the lappe."

Pandarus' joy in maneuvering Troilus into Criseyde's arms is restrained by nothing, and if circumstances will not play the game he will create circumstances that do. Fortune, after all, as far as his view of her is concerned, only helps him who helps himself. He is the executor of Fortune, the agent of Destiny, the bringer of joy, and so the irony created by the lie he tells Criseyde—that Troilus is disturbed about a rumor he has heard that she is faithless to him and demands to be seen there and now, in the secret privacy of the bedroom—has overtones that become more and more tragic before the book is over. For a moment the knowledge that she is indeed to "false" Troilus takes the foreground in our minds, and her terror at the thought that Troilus believes her guilty of an act so heinous is deeply and ironically moving, as it breaks forth in the passionate lament—a lament that describes the theme of the whole poem, the mutability of all things, its concept close to that in Boethius, Book II, Prosa 3—

> "O God!" quod she, "so worldly selynesse,
> Which clerkes callen fals felicitee,
> Imedled is with many a bitternesse!
> Ful angwissous than is, God woot," quod she,
> "Condicioun of veyn prosperitee:
> For either joies comen nought yfeere,
> Or elles no wight hath hem alwey here.
>
> "O brotel wele of mannes joie unstable!
> With what wight so thow be, or how thow pleye,
> Either he woot that thow, joie, art muable,
> Or woot it nought; it mot ben oon of tweye.
> Now if he woot it nought, how may he seye
> That he hath verray joie and selynesse,
> That is of ignoraunce ay in derknesse?"
>   (III, 813-826)

There can be no joy then, she sadly concludes, she who is so close to giving Troilus his greatest joy and to finding her own great "blysse." To know that happiness is transitory is to mitigate the happiness, and to realize that one must lose all joy is to make the joy one has "worth ful lite"; "trewely, for aught I kan espie,/ Ther is no verray weele in this world heere" (III, 835-836).

For her resigned melancholy Pandarus has as little tolerance and patience as he had for Troilus' woe, and Criseyde's offer to send her lover a "blewe ring" to assure him of her fidelity, arouses him to scorn:

"A ryng?" quod he, "ye, haselwodes shaken!
Ye, nece myn, that ryng moste han a stoon
That myghte dede men alyve maken;
And swich a ryng trowe I that ye have non.
Discrecioun out of youre hed is gon;
That fele I now," quod he, "and that is routhe.
O tyme ilost, wel mainstow corsen slouthe!"
                                        (III, 890-896)

And he wins from her the willingness to see Troilus at once—"Considered alle thynges as they stoode,/ No wonder is, syn she did al for goode" (III, 923-924).

The scene that follows is one of the most complex in the whole poem. Prefaced by the reminder that joy is brief, that happiness is transitory, it is the most joyous scene of all. Brought into being by the lie of a pander, it is charged into lyric splendor by the most profoundly meaningful love poetry of the whole poem. And its "high seriousness" is constantly accompanied by the comic activity of its vulgar initiator.

The almost ceaseless busy-ness of Pandarus during the first moments of the meeting between the frightened Criseyde and the emotionally tense Troilus betray his eagerness for the success of his scheming, his own barely controlled joy in the joy of the lovers that is so soon to be an accomplished fact, and a real nervousness lest something go awry. He is acutely conscious of the tensions around him: "Pandarus, that so wel koude feele/ In every thyng." To the blushing Criseyde he points out the figure of the kneeling Troilus: "Nece, se how this lord kan knele!/ Now, for youre trouthe, se this gentil man!" And "with that word he for a quysshen ran." On her gentle welcome of Troilus Pandarus comments: "Now wol ye wel bigynne./ Now doth hym sitte, goode nece deere,/ Upon youre beddes syde al ther withinne,/ That ech of yow the bet may other heere." Hopeful that all is well he moves off to the fireplace, "and took a light, and fond his contenaunce,/ As for to looke upon an old romaunce" (III, 960-980).

Surely no meeting of lovers has ever been more comically attended. The figure of Pandarus, discreetly reading an "olde romaunce" by the fire—the presiding spirit and guardian angel—never ceases to arouse laughter, nor to remind us that the world he has taken such pains to forestall from threatening the lovers is really not very far away. It is wise that he has lingered, for his well-made plot almost collapses. Troilus, brave in battle, second only to Hector in reputation for valor, is far from brave in the bedroom, and he swoons just at the crucial moment. Pandarus once more springs into action, and with the cry "O nece pes, or we be lost, . . . Beth naught agast" he picks up the supine lover and "into bed hym caste" voicing his own disgust in no uncertain terms: "O thef, is this a mannes herte?"

For a few moments all is agitation and confusion as Pandarus sets about righting things, and the scene is full of comic business and bustle, a most unlikely prelude to the passionate exchange of romantic love so soon to come. It is Pandarus' scene and the lovers respond helplessly to his managing:

> [He] seyde, "Nece, but ye helpe us now,
> Allas, youre owen Troilus is lorn!"
> "Iwis, so wolde I, and I wiste how,
> Ful fayn," quod she; "Allas, that I was born!"
> "Yee, nece, wol ye pullen out the thorn
> That stiketh in his herte," quod Pandare,
> "Sey 'al foryeve,' and stynt is al this fare!"
>
> "Ye, that to me," quod she, "ful levere were
> Than al the good the sonne aboute gooth."
> And therwithal she swor hym in is ere,
> "Iwys, my deere herte, I am nought wroth,
> Have here my trouthe!" and many an other oth;
> "Now speke to me, for it am I, Criseyde!"
> But al for nought; yit mysht he nought abreyde.
>
> Therwith his pous and paumes of his hondes
> They gan to frote, and wete his temples tweyne;
> And to deliveren hym fro bittre bondes,
> She ofte hym kiste; and shortly for to seyne,
> Hym to revoken she did al hire peyne.
> And at the laste, she gan his breth to drawe,
> And of his swough sone after that adawe.
>
> (III, 1100-1120)

Troilus, now recovered from his swoon and safely in Criseyde's bed, seems finally enough in command to be trusted to do his part in fulfilling Pandarus' plan. Sure that all is now really well, he remarks: "For aught I kan aspien,/ This light, nor I, ne serven here of nought./ Light is nought good for sike folkes yën!" And with a kind of blessing upon the lovers he goes "with a ful goode entente,/ . . . and seyde, 'If ye be wise,/ Swouneth nought now, lest more folk arise!'" (1135-1137; 1188-1190).

The comedy of this scene that makes the lovers almost helpless pawns in the clever hands of Pandarus, that makes of the hero a figure not only quite unheroic, but even somewhat ridiculous, is undeniably intended by Chaucer. Boccaccio's Troilo had not swooned, nor had his coming into the bed of Criseida needed help from anyone. Nor is his faint a part of the "courtly love tradition." Both Pandarus and Criseyde make this clear: "Is this a mannes game?/ What Troilus wol ye do thus for shame?" Why Chaucer does this, why he precedes his most exalted scene with his most farcical, is a question that cannot be answered with satisfaction. But what effects this juxtaposition has can be variously described, though critics will never reach agreement on the judgment of the taste Chaucer seems here to evidence.

It is possible to account for Troilus' faint in something like psychological terms, though for the reader who is at this moment prejudiced against the hero, any explanation sounds like rationalization. One can say, for instance, that Troilus' desire for Criseyde has intensified so greatly that at the moment he is to have her he is unable to bear the emotional force that is released. In a sense, then, his faint measures the degree of his physical need. One can also say that his sense of dignity and honor has been shamed by a knowing and willing participation in the lies and schemes of Pandarus: it is therefore unbearable for him to hear the grief-stricken protests of Criseyde, protests that define her love and fidelity. Nor can he afford to admit that he has been a party to the lie that has so upset her, since he wants what it will bring him more than he wants to maintain his honorableness. The swoon functions also to underscore again Chaucer's insistence that Criseyde, in loving Troilus, "dide al for the beste," and although it almost threatens to make her a victim of the Fate that is hers to fulfill, it moves her into a position of control, of dominance that she freely and frankly exerts.

What the comedy of the scene does to the tragic nature of the whole poem is an even more controversial question. Perhaps the responses to the situation are as many and as varied as there are readers, and any one or two assertions as to the effects can only meet with instantaneous objection. The helplessness of Troilus is funny, but it is also a way in which he contrasts sharply with Diomede, who will make of Criseyde the helpless one in the last book. In nobility of birth the two are well-matched, and in bravery in battle they are equal; but in their attitude to Criseyde they are poles apart. Troilus, like the first royal eagle in *The Parliament of Fowls*, is all courtliness; Diomede, like the third of the eagles, is all open aggressiveness, and no point makes this more clear than the memory of Troilus' swoon. The moment of the faint is surely a moment that symbolizes the only essential difference between the two lovers of Criseyde, and offers some help in understanding the reasons for Criseyde's easy acceptance of the wooing of the "sodeyn Diomede."

The comedy of the situation does not, in my opinion, seriously detract

from the passionate exaltation of the love scene that follows it, any more
than the intrusive figure of Pandarus makes a mockery of what it has
brought to consummation. From the moment the lovers are alone all
comic nonsense is gone, and only joy remains. Their coming together is
full of both sensuous and spiritual "blysse"; framed as it is between the
comic going and the return of Pandarus, following upon the almost
farcical moment of the fainting of Troilus, the love scene, intimate and
glorious, is both of earth and of heaven. The conversation of the lovers
partakes both of the frank sexuality of Pandarus and of the exalted
reverence of Troilus. Relieved by the departure of Pandarus, attention
focuses only upon the lovers, and in particular upon Criseyde, trembling
"as an aspes leef" as she feels Troilus "hire in his armes folde." Troilus,
"al hool of cares colde," is no longer the embarrassed and timid lover;
his joy as he presses Criseyde to him is the joy of one in complete
command and in complete awareness of the nature of the happiness
finally to be his:

> This Troilus in armes gan hire streyne,
> And seyde, "O swete, as evere mot I gon,
> Now be ye kaught, now is ther but we tweyne!
> Now yeldeth yow for other bote is non!"
> (III, 1205-1208)

With free and eager heart Criseyde yields, thinking herself safe from
the threats of the outer and the inner world, her fears quieted, happy in
the illusion that her yielding is, in a way, a measure of her control. And
"al quyt from every drede and tane,/ As she that juste cause hadde hym
to triste," she gave Troilus such gracious love that, says Chaucer, "it
joye was to seene."

This book that had begun with comedy now becomes transformed by
the lyrical ecstasy of the lovers into a book totally infused with joy that
is both earthly and spiritual, physical and "divine." It ends in a moment
of lyric splendor as the two lovers seem almost to sing their farewell in
the *Aubades* that herald their first parting. There is nothing else like
this poetry in all Chaucer and indeed will not be found again in English
poetry until we meet it in the work of Shakespeare and Donne. In context all the lyrical conventions are struck into life.

> But whan the cok, comune astrologer,
> Gan on his brest to bete and after crowe,
> And Lucyfer, the dayes messager,
> Gan for to rise, and out hire bemes throwe,
> And estward roos, to hym that koude it knowe,

Fortuna Major, that anoon Criseyde,
With herte soor, to Troilus thus seyde:

"Myn hertes lif, my trist, and my plesaunce,
That I was born, allas, what me is wo,
That day of us moot make disseveraunce!
For tyme it is to ryse and hennes go,
Or ellis I am lost for evere mo!
O nyght, allas! why nyltow over us hove,
As longe as whan Almena lay by Jove?

"O blake nyght, as folk in bokes rede,
That shapen art by God this world to hide
At certeyn tymes wyth thi derke wede,
That under that men myghte in reste abide,
Wel oughten bestes pleyne, and folk the chide
That there as day wyth labour wolde us breste,
That thow thus fleest, and deynest us nought reste.

"Thow doost, allas, to shortly thyn office,
Thow rakle nyght, ther God, maker of kynde,
The, for thyn haste and thyn unkynde vice,
So faste ay to oure hemysperie bynde,
That nevere more under the ground thow wynde!
For now, for thow so hiest out of Troie,
Have I forgon thus hastili my joie!"
(III, 1415-1442)

Troilus, whose great "gladnesse" is now replaced by "hevynesse," echoes her lament for the passing of the night: "O cruel day, accusour of the joie/ That nyght and love han stole and faste iwryen," "Envyous day," "Dispitous day," "Thou fool," the sun, he cries out. His pledges of love, which intimate her love is not perhaps as great as his, call forth eloquent protests from her that increase his joy, but warn with tragic irony of the end of the poem. "O herte deere" she says, "the game, ywys, so ferforth now is gon,/ That first shal Phebus fallen fro his spere,/ And everich egle ben the dowves feere,/ And everi roche out of his place sterte,/ Er Troilus out of Criseydes herte!" (III, 1493-1498).

The lyrical exaltation that marks the parting of the lovers is barely over when Pandarus bounds in, his joyous curiosity bursting out in vulgar comments of the broadest sort: "Al this nyght so reyned it, allas./ That al my drede is that ye, nece swete,/ Han litel laiser had to slepe and mete./ Al nyght . . . hath reyn so do me wake,/ That som of us, I trowe, hire hedes ake" (III, 1557-1561). Though not in any sense shocked by this sudden intrusion and coarse joviality, Criseyde has her own embarrassment: "She gan hire face for to wrye/ With the shete, and wax for shame al reed" (III, 1569-1570). The scene that had begun with the prodding and poking by Pandarus, his busy figure highly comic as the agent for Fortune and Love, ends with the vision of the prying and peeking Pandarus, curious to know the outcome of his scheming:

> And Pandarus gan under for to prie,
> And seyde, "Nece, if that I shal be ded,
> Have here a swerd and smyteth of myn hed!"
> With that his arm al sodeynly he thriste
> Under hire nekke, and at the laste hire kyste.
> (III, 1571-1575)

Although Book III never again mounts to the rapture of the first meeting, the rest of it is full of the happiness of the lovers. Pandarus, comic realist that he is, sounds a note of warning; he is not "Fortune's" agent for nothing, and he is perfectly well aware that no joy can endure for ever. Ironically it is he who reminds us and Troilus that sorrow is measured in its degree by the happiness that has preceded it. But Troilus, full of his "blisful tyme swete," is not disturbed, and the lovers are "in quyete and in reste." The Wheel of Fortune seems also quietly at rest and the celebration of Love that ends the book for a moment makes us forget the ominous intimations of change in the movement from night to day, in the many partings that foreshadow the last parting:

> But nedes day departe hem moste soone,
> And whan hire speche don was and hire cheere,
> They twynne anon, as they were wont to doone,
> And setten tyme of metyng eft yfeere.
> And many a nyght they wroughte in this manere,
> And thus Fortune a tyme ledde in joie
> Criseyde, and ek this kynges sone of Troie.
> (III, 1709-1715)

When Pandarus next appears in the fourth book there is nothing comic about him. His sorrow at the woe of Troilus is genuine, but it is, like his understanding of the nature of the love between the prince and his niece, limited and limiting. His sympathy leads him to hollow and futile gestures of activity, and his well-meaning efforts to cheer Troilus are grotesquely inadequate. "Syn thi desir al holly hastow had,/ . . . it oughte ynough suffise" (IV, 395-396), he says, with quite uncomic cynicism. Or, "This town is ful of ladys al aboute;/ . . . Forthi be glad, myn owen deere brother!/ If she be lost, we shal recovere an other" (IV, 401; 405-406). New love chases out the old, "syn it is but casuel plesaunce" (IV, 419); "Absence of hire shal dryve hire out of herte" (IV, 427). This is the familiar Pandarus who speaks, the busybody of the first books. But he is no longer funny. His imperception dominates even his kindhearted intentions, and Troilus in fury cries out: "So hold thi pees; thow sleest me with thi speche!" (IV, 455). Pandarus is stilled, and though his familiar figure busies itself in an attempt to right things, to restore happiness, to hold off final disaster, all his efforts are pathetic in the light of the inevitability of events. It is Criseyde who takes upon herself the role of controller of Fortune, who assumes the task of scheming, and becomes, tragically, the personification of the woe into which all will fall.

Books IV and V have, with the exception of the last stanzas of the last book, nothing of joy in them. Unhappiness, the pain of separation, the suffering of loneliness, and the despairing realization that he has been "falsed," fill Troilus, who becomes now the focus of interest. It is in these two books that Chaucer's voice as narrator becomes more distinct. There is real reluctance, even pain, in the moments when, faced with the evidence of his sources, he must accept and relate Criseyde's falseness. And when he reports her final treason in yielding to Diomede he speaks as if he, the poet, had no part in the story at all:

> The morwen com, and gostly for to speke,
> This Diomede is come unto Criseyde;
> And shortly, lest that ye my tale breke,
> So wel he for hymselven spak and seyde,
> That alle hire sikes soore adown he leyde.
> And finaly, the sothe for to seyne,
> He refte hire of the grete of al hire peyne.

> And after this the storie telleth us
> That she hym yaf the faire baye stede
> The which he ones wan of Troilus;
> And ek a broche—and that was litel nede—
> That Troilus was, she yaf this Diomede.
> And ek, the bet from sorwe hym to releve,
> She made hym were a pencel of hire sleve.

> I fynde ek in the stories elleswhere,
> Whan thorugh the body hurt was Diomede
> Of Troilus, tho wepte she many a teere,
> Whan that she saugh his wyde wowndes blede;

> And that she took, to kepen hym, good hede;
> And for to helen hym of his sorwes smerte,
> Men seyn—I not—that she yaf hym hire herte.
>
> But trewely, the storie telleth us,
> Ther made nevere woman moore wo
> Than she, whan that she falsed Troilus.
>   (V, 1030-1053)

Chaucer the narrator, the reteller of "the olde storie," without senti-
mentalizing or condemning accepts the terrible betrayal by Criseyde,
intimating that though in some measure what he has shown her to be—
a person "slydynge of corage," a person of psychologically valid complexity—her action, surrounded as it is by lies to Troilus, by blatant
rationalizations, is ultimately deplorable. As far back as the beginning of
the fourth book, he has expressed sadness at the thought of what it is
he must now write: "Myn herte gynneth blede,/ And now my penne,
allas! with which I write,/ Quaketh for drede of what I moste endite."
Like Philosophy he can do nothing other than view the "wrecchidness"
of men, whose view is so tragically limited that at times it amounts to a
blindness. So, when her betrayal is an accomplished fact, he makes a plea:

> Ne me ne list this sely womman chyde
> Forther than the storye wol devyse.
> Hire name, allas! is punysshed so wide,
> That for hire gilt it oughte ynough suffise.
> And if I myghte excuse hire any wise,
> For she so sory was for hire untrouthe,
> Iwis, I wolde excuse hire yet for routhe.
>   (V, 1093-1099)

Criseyde's mutability, her role as the figure of Change, does not deny
her reality as a person, nor erase the joy that had been, nor ignore the
ugliness of her betrayal. She was "fearful," circumspect, cautious, from
the first; slow to yield, complete in yielding. Like her uncle Pandarus,
she must assert her control, she must believe in the illusion that Fortune
can be made to be kind by sheer force of will. It is "for the beste" that
she will not defy the decree that sends her to her father among the
Greeks; it is "for the beste" that she urges compliance with Fate, becoming even cheerful as she persuades Troilus to believe in her powers of
managing the future. "Er dayes ten" she promises, "I shal ben heere."
"And treweliche, as writen wel I fynde," says Chaucer, "That al this
thyng was seyd of goode entente;/ And that hire herte trewe was and

kynde/ Towardes hym, and spak right as she mente,/ And that she
starf for wo neigh, when she wente,/ And was in purpos evere to be
trewe:/ Thus writen they that of hire werkes knewe" (IV, 1415-1421).
And even when she is frank to admit that she has "lacked the third eye
of Prudence" and that it is "too late" now to undo what has already
been done, she is still the old Criseyde:

> "But natheles, bityde what bityde,
> I shal to-morwe at nyght, by est or west,
> Out of this oost stele on som manere syde,
> And gon with Troilus where as hym lest.
> This purpos wol ich holde, and this is best.
> No fors of wikked tonges janglerie,
> For evere on love han wrecches had envye."
>   (V, 750-756)

With almost exalted resolution to call "felicite" her "suffisaunce," she
concludes "withouten any wordes mo,/ To Troie I wole." "But," says
Chaucer, "God it wot, er fully monthes two,/ She was ful fer fro that
entencioun!" (V, 766-767).

Criseyde is Troilus' woe as much as she is his joy; she is his Fortune,
and Fortune, we recall, is his "fo." And thus she is a significant aspect of
the Human Condition, as Boethius had made clear, and as Chaucer's own
Balade "Fortune," concludes:

> La respounse de Fortune contre le Pleintif
>   Thou pinchest at my mutabilitee,
>   For I thee lente a drope of my richesse,
>   And now me lyketh to withdrawe me.
>   Why sholdestow my realtee oppresse?
>   The see may ebbe and flowen more or lesse;
>   The welkne hath might to shyne, reyne, or hayle;
>   Right so mot I kythen my brotelnesse:
>   In general, this reule may nat fayle.
>
>   Lo, th'execucion of the majestee
>   That al purveyeth of his rightwysnesse,
>   That same thing "Fortune" clepen ye,
>   Ye blinde bestes, ful of lewednesse!
>   The hevene hath propretee of sikernesse,
>   This world hath ever resteles travayle;
>   Thy laste day is ende of myn intresse:
>   In general, this reule may nat fayle.
>   (57-72)

Criseyde, as the embodiment of Troilus' worldly joy, is subject to change and is change itself: she is that which is the necessary condition of the mortal state.

But Chaucer cannot leave Boccaccio's story at this point, nor is he satisfied with the moral his Italian master drew. The poem *Troilus and Criseyde* is not just an exemplum for the assertion that "women are fickle" as *Il Filostrato* had concluded. To the comedy of Pandarus, to the elaboration of the character of Criseyde, to the formal shaping of the theme of mutability, Chaucer added the comedy of the conclusion, and his addition has been as much a matter for controversy among critics as has been the question of Criseyde's betrayal. The vision of Troilus in the "eighthe spere" laughing "at the wo/ Of hem that wepten for his deth so faste," condemning "al oure werk that foloweth so/ The blynde lust, the which that may nat laste," seems to many readers to be an uncomfortable trivializing of the agony that has gone before. Or it seems to destroy in some way the tragic seriousness of the whole poem. It does neither of these things.

What it does do is state finally and explicitly what the poem has been about. Chaucer, the narrator, whose presence has been felt more and more throughout the fifth book, now speaks forth as commentator. In words that remind us of Philosophy's to Boethius he offers his "consolation." "Swich is this world, whoso it kan byholde:/ In ech estat is litel hertes reste," he says. And Troilus' "goost," released from the pain of the tragedy, removed in death from suffering, from the blindness of mortal vision, sees from his perspective the course of his life *sub specie aeternitatis*. This is the perspective Comedy usually gives, and out of context, therefore, this ending seems "comic." But in relation to the whole poem it underscores the intensity of the tragedy, heightening even more the suffering entanglement of the individual characters, whose lives have lacked wisdom and perspective. All the ways in which transitoriness and mutability reveal themselves, in betrayal of trust, in blindness, in assumption and presumption, in the inevitable movement of life from woe to joy, as well as from joy to woe, have been the concern of the poem; to Chaucer, the fact that Eternity and the Infinite are quite other in their unchanging stability does not diminish the particular Reality of the Human Condition. Troilus, we are told, looked down upon "this litel spot of erthe"

> that with the se
> Embraced is, and fully gan despise
> This wrecched world, and held al vanite
> To respect of the pleyn felicite

That is in hevene above; and at the laste,
Ther he was slayn, his lokyng down he caste.
                    (V, 1815-1820)

With the particularizing of his gaze, we too turn our eyes to focus in retrospect upon the story that has just been told. It is no more a story that criticizes the morality of the kind of love it portrays than *Othello* is directed toward condemning marriage between persons of different races; it is a story about a profoundly moving relationship between two lovers in a world where nothing "may laste," neither love, nor honor, nor life itself:

Swich fyn hath, lo, this Troilus for love!
Swich fyn hath al his grete worthynesse!
Swich fyn hath his estat real above,
Swich fyn his lust, swich fyn hath his noblesse!
Swich fyn hath false worldes brotelnesse!
And thus bigan his lovyng of Criseyde,
As I have told, and in this wise he deyde.
                    (V, 1828-1834)

To the readers and the listeners of his poem, in particular to the "yonge lovers" he has been conscious of since the opening stanzas of Book I, Chaucer directs his final words, disparaging not the fact of love, but reminding them of the mutability of it, the sweetest of relationships and thus the best symbol of life's transitory joy: "Thynketh al nys but a faire/ This world, that passeth soone as floures faire." One thing only is unchangeable and that is God's love which in its definition is "eterne and stable":

And loveth hym, the which that right for love
Upon a crois, oure soules for to beye,
First starf, and roos, and sit in hevene above;
For he nyl falsen no wight, dar I seye,
That wol his herte al holly on hym leye.
And syn he best to love is, and most meke,
What nedeth feynede loves for to seke.
                    (V, 1842-1848)

That which Chaucer had attempted, with somewhat unsatisfying results, in *The Parliament of Fowls*—to place the action of the dream within the perspective of Infinity—he here does effectively. A poem about betrayal within betrayal, encompassing the war caused by the theft of Helen, the betrayal of Troy by Calkas, the exchange of Criseyde for the traitor-to-be, Antenor, and the final falsing of Troilus, ends by directing our eyes to God "who nyl falsen no wight," who restores order to all disorder. It ends, in short, by affirming the consolation given by Philosophy, that man "envyrouned and closed withynne the leeste prykke of thilke prykke," the world, suffers in space and in time, but finds in the end that "alle Fortune is good": by it "false joy" is indeed proved false and true joy true; "and God, byholdere and forwytere of alle thingis, duelleth above, and the present eternite of his sighte renneth alwey with the diverse qualite of our dedes, dispensynge and ordeynynge medes to gode men and tormentz to wikkide men" (Book V, Prosa 6).

part two

---

the canterbury tales

chapter 3

MODES OF COMEDY
IN THE FIRST FRAGMENT

"Go, litel bok, go, litel myn tragedye" Chaucer wrote at the end of *Troilus and Criseyde*, "their God thi makere yet, er that he dye,/ So sende myght to make in som comedye." Surely there was never a prayer more graciously answered, never a request more abundantly fulfilled than that which gave to the "Maker" of *The Canterbury Tales* the "myght" of artistry to bring into full view his complex awareness of the comedy of human existence in all its mirth and morality. It matters not that the plan he had in mind as he began the tales was never completed; in outline it was essentially a simple one, structured by means of the journey from London to Canterbury and back again. What matters is the way in which so simple a plan was made dynamically vital by its translation into the complexities of the particular moment. "This world," Boethius had said to Philosophy, "of so manye and diverse and contraryous parties, ne myghte nevere han ben assembled in o forme, but yif ther ne were oon that conjoyned so many diverse thinges; and the same diversitie of here natures, that so discorden the ton fro the other, most departen and unjoynen the thinges that ben conjoynid, yif ther ne were oon that contenyde that he hath conjoynid and ybounden. Ne the certein ordre of nature schulde not brynge forth so ordene moevynges by places, by tymes, by doynges, by spaces, by qualities, yif ther ne were on, that were ay stedfast duellynge, that ordeynide and disponyde thise diversites of moevynges" (Book III, Prosa 12). *The Canterbury Tales* are as finished as they need be, though it will always be a matter of regret that there were not more. The twenty-four tales or beginnings of tales reveal the "diversites of thynges" as completely as one hundred and twenty or one hundred and twenty-eight would have.

73

There is no question about Chaucer's intention to fulfil his plan, for *The Parson's Tale* clearly "knits up" all that has come between the *General Prologue* and its opening lines, though perhaps by the end he had decided to simplify by reducing the numbers of tales; but for us, his readers, there is indeed "God's plenty," and ample evidence that he had arrived at the great expression of his comic genius.

Fragment by fragment, group by group, *The Canterbury Tales* "depart" and "unjoyn" the things "that ben conjoynid." It seems undeniable that the arrangements of groups, their sequences and juxtapositions, were never finally and authoritatively arrived at. Arguments for the Ellesmere order or for any other order suggested by the complicated and confused state of manuscript tradition are, in the long run, subject to contradiction, and are even distractive for this study. But a cursory glance over the tales seems to point to "conjoynings" of some meaningfulness. There is *Fragment I* which contains the *General Prologue, The Knight's Tale, The Miller's Tale, The Reeve's Tale*, the beginning of *The Cook's Tale*, and their dramatic linking in Epilogue and Prologue. There is the so-called Marriage Group, beginning with *The Wife of Bath's Prologue and Tale* and ending with *The Franklin's Tale (Fragments III, IV* and *V* in the Ellesmere order, or D, E and F in the Skeat-Furnivall order), and there is the grouping together in *Fragment VII* (B^2) of six tales, *The Shipman's, The Prioress's*, the two tales told by Chaucer, the pilgrim, and the companion tales of *The Monk* and *The Nun's Priest*. And, finally, there is the moral treatise recited by the Parson that was clearly intended to conclude the pilgrimage. The other tales that interspace these significant groupings are important in their own right, but since they do not seem to work importantly together, they can be thought of as internodes in the larger construct.

In the "Early Poems" and in *Troilus and Criseyde* Chaucer had determinates already worked out for him—the Dream-Vision form, Boccaccio's romantic poem—within which he set into motion those indeterminates of human motivation, of human relationship, of the interaction of circumstance that made the form he had adopted singularly his own. For *The Canterbury Tales* he created his own form, his own determinate, an "ordre, procedinge by an uneschuable byndinge togedre," in which the complex diversity in all its indeterminate ways could be contained. Instead of the fiction of the dream or the fiction of the "olde storie," he makes a fiction of reality in which he as observer and participant is part of his own creation and is subject to its laws along with the rest of the pilgrims. As such, he too can only see what appears, he too must abide by the rules. And he, as writer of the poem, can only "aftir the facultie (that is to seyn, the power and the nature)" of his own observation and knowing, record the diversity of things. As such, he too is viewable in perspective, a willing actor in the carrying out of the general plan.

Chaucer, the pilgrim, has no part in getting the *General Prologue* under way. Before the world of human nature of which he is a part is introduced, the world of Nature is described. The time is April, a time of new and renewed life, of the return of the sap to the plants, of warmth to the world. It is a season of moistness, of stirring into restless movement the vital force of bird and man, of the resumption of the cycle of birth, of fruition, and, in the distant future, of temporary cessation in death. The pattern is one of infinite repetition, yet each particular recurrence has its full measure of joy. The cyclic movement of nature is paralleled by the movement of human beings, both continually reflecting the change that defines both the impermanent and the permanent. "Thanne," as the spring appears, "longen folk to goon on pilgrimages,/ And palmeres for to seken straunge strondes,/ To ferne halwes, kowthe in sondry londes" (12-14).

Chance has its role to play in the world of *The Canterbury Tales*. It is Chance that particularizes the general, that makes of the recurring cycle a unique and special occasion. "Bifil that in that seson on a day" there came together at the Tabard Inn in Southwark "wel nyne and twenty . . ./ Of sondry folk," all meeting "by aventure." "Hap," says Philosophy, is the "unwar betydinge of causes assembled in thingis that ben doon for som oothir thing" (Book V, Prosa I). The most wonderful chance of all is, of course, Chaucer's presence, a pilgrim with the eye of a reporter and an interest in the marvelous diversity possible in human beings. His joy in the occasion is immediate; "and shortly, whan the sonne was to reste/ So hadde I spoken with hem everichon,/ That I was of hir felaweshipe anon."

As observer and reporter, Chaucer places himself exactly in relation to us and to the world of which he is a part. It will be a long time before he is a participator in the plan by telling a tale. Until then he can only tell us what he sees and what he hears, making us co-observers with him, even, at times, an observer of others from a perspective and an understanding more inclusive than his can be. He does not even identify himself at the beginning, for he does not matter. But he does establish quickly our trust in him. With no self-consciousness, no tone of self-importance he states:

> But nathelees, whil I have tyme and space,
> Er that I ferther in this tale pace,
> Me thynketh it acordaunt to resoun
> To telle yow al the condicioun
> Of ech of hem, so as it semed me,

And whiche they weren, and of what degree,
And eek in what array that they were inne.
(35-42)

Gone is the somewhat bemused Dreamer, the saddened teller of Boccaccio's story; in his stead there is the genial pilgrim, possessing like
the other pilgrims "the facultes" of "wit . . . ymaginacioun . . . resoun . . .
and . . . intelligence" (Boethius, Book V, Prosa 4); in short, the power
to see what there is to see—"so as it semed me"—what they were in person and appearance.

Once the observer has defined his position he has also defined the
measure of his detachment. And once he has disarmed us and won
our trust he has created in us an unquestioning readiness to view
what he views, and to arrive at whatever judgments he may arrive at.
With the verb "semed," he says, in effect, that the human beings with
him on the way to Canterbury must be looked at first as they "appear"
to be. At the same time he intimates that appearance may not be the
revealer of the whole truth and our agreement with this makes us ready
to suspect the appearance until proved true, creating in us curiosity and
a willingness to share his ironic vision even before the need arises. What
the degree of detachment is that Chaucer establishes is difficult to
describe. His position as one of the pilgrims, his joy in the "felaweshipe,"
his sense of adventure among human personalities, his response to the
gaiety of the season all intimate a kind of involvement, a kind of com-
mitment. It is thus a detachment that precludes satire or cynicism, that
promises, rather, an attitude that will be more affectionate than critical,
more amused than bitter.

Throughout the rest of the *Prologue* to the point where the Host takes
over, the voice of the observer is heard again and again. He never
assumes a position in the foreground, but the sense of his presence is
never lost, and, at almost the exact moment when we need to be reminded that we are also viewers, we hear the voice that recalls us to
our point of viewing. Of the Squire, following along with his father,
the Knight, the pilgrim-reporter says "of twenty yeer of age he was,
I gesse"; of the Yeoman who accompanies both Knight and Squire he
conjectures "an horn he bar, the bawdryk was of grene;/ An forster
was he soothly, as I gesse." It does not matter whether the phrase "I
gesse" is a filler for the rhyme, or a rhetorical device; what matters is
that it achieves an important effect: It continually disarms us and wins
anew our trust in the observer's honest attempt "to see" clearly the
figures before him. And we are still with him when, after the portraits
are drawn, he speaks to us, redefining once more his position:

> Now have I toold you soothly, in a clause,
> Th'estaat, th'array, the nombre, and eek the cause
> Why that assembled was this compaignye
> In Southwerk at this gentil hostelrye
> That highte the Tabard, faste by the Belle.
>   (715-719)

It is at this point he makes clear what he expects from the "assembled . . . compaignye," and from his expectation we know what Chaucer's intention is. As Philosophy had remarked to Boethius, "thow hast lernyd by the sentence of Plato that nedes the wordis moot be cosynes to the thinges of which thei speken" (Book III, Prosa 12), so the observer-reporter warns us of what might come, reminding us at the same time that he is spectator only, and underscoring our faith in the honesty of his reporting:

> But first I pray yow, of youre curteisye,
> That ye n'arette it nat my vileynye,
> Thogh that I pleynly speke in this mateere,
> To telle yow hir wordes and hir cheere,
> Ne thogh I speke hir wordes proprely.
> For this ye knowen al so wel as I,
> Whoso shal telle a tale after a man,
> He moot reherce as ny as evere he kan
> Everich a word, if it be in his charge,
> Al speke he never so rudeliche and large,
> Or ellis he moot telle his tale untrewe,
> Or feyne thyng, or fynde wordes newe.
> He may nat spare, althogh he were his brother;
> He moot as wel seye o word as another.
> Crist spak hymself ful brode in hooly writ,
> And wel ye woot no vileynye is it.
> Eek Plato seith, whoso that kan hym rede,
> The wordes moote be cosyn to the dede.
> Also I prey yow to foryeve it me,
> Al have I nat set folk in hir degree
> Heere in this tale, as that they sholde stonde.
> My wit is short, ye may wel understonde.
>   (725-746)

There is no doubt that the pilgrims are to speak according "to their natures"; which means, of course, that the tales are to be revelatory as well as entertaining in their own right.

It is in the descriptions of the pilgrims that have preceded these lines that the observer suggests the potential for "wordes" to come. The portraits, which for a time make the *General Prologue* more statically discursive than narrative, are in reality charged with the possibility for dynamic revelation of personality. Furthermore, the observer's apology for not having "set folk in hir degree/ . . . as they sholde stonde," while for a moment quieting the question aroused by the apparent haphazard arrangement of the portraits and intimating that he is proposing no preordained order for the telling of tales, also plants a suspicion that an order other than that of "hir degree" has been behind the sequence of descriptions. And an examination of the portrait section of the *General Prologue* does indeed suggest not only the possibility for dramatic interaction to come but also ways in which the observer is revealing Chaucer's own "moral vision."

For the order of the portraits has meaning, the placing of them does reveal a judgment of the pilgrims that is, in all probability, to be borne out by the tales even as the tellers are to be realized as persons.

Each portrait has within it some degree and some kind of tension. In each instance the tension defines the degree of struggle necessary to maintain equilibrium, to maintain in whatever terms it can the balance between what the pilgrim is and what he senses, or has sensed, he should be. The ironies that convey this "tension in equilibrium" are not ones that hint at a discrepancy between appearance and reality, nor between the false and the true. From the first poem onward, Chaucer's conclusion has been, not that the appearance is the opposite of the reality, but rather that it contains within it the reality if only man had eyes to see and ears to hear. The accidents of things do not contradict their essences. It is the partial vision, the darkened eye, the imperfect "faculte" that makes for misunderstanding, for miscomprehension. The order of the portraits reveals a grouping principle that suggests a kind of spectrum of human nature in its struggle to maintain equilibrium. And that the struggle is in some way or other continually successful, though at great cost, is the reason the irony of the portraits is comic and not something else. The spectacle of the "warring soul" is not comic, *per se;* but it is full of potential for comedy if its efforts to avoid disaster either from the self or the outer world at the same time affirm the right of human beings to stay upright, to contain the tension, and thus simply to continue "to live." That the struggle to maintain balance is comic and thus pleasurable to see, that it does not preclude moral or ethical judgment on the part of the viewer, goes without saying. And indeed the observer of the pilgrims gathered at the Tabard Inn on that April day sees more morally than he knows he sees, since the "condicioun . . . the degre . . . and the array," as the appearances of the reality, indicate that reality itself.

The descriptive section of the *Prologue* begins and ends with the portraits of the Knight and the Pardoner. Both pilgrims are exactly what they appear to be, and what they are as human beings puts them poles apart. Because Chaucer the pilgrim-observer has won our trust in his honesty, we have no reason to suspect the meaning of the terms he uses to describe the Knight. That the portrait is created in somewhat clear and simple outline by the delineation of his appearance, by the factual cataloguing of battles that can be dated historically, and by the repetition of the word "worthy" at all significant points does not make of this, the first and the highest in social rank of the pilgrims, an oversimplified portrayal. Not once but five times the Knight is called "worthy." Each repetition qualifies in some admirable way the meaning of the word and points out the actual nature of the man. By the time the portrait is finished the exact limits of the connotations of the word are unquestionably and unironically clear; the Knight is truly and unromantically "worthy" in all the ways it is possible for him to be: in fulfilling the ideals of chivalry, in battle, in society. He is exactly what he should be, no more, no less, literally "a verray, parfit gentil knyght." But, as the reiteration suggests, he is limited, uncomplex, single in vision. The observer's insistence upon defining the one apparent quality of his nature hints at the comic possibilities in the tensions that may arise between the limited human being and the complex reality of the world.

The Pardoner, like the Knight, is also what he appears to be. He too is "gentil"; he too has recently come from afar—"streight . . . fro the court of Rome." He too is to be commended for the way he becomes his profession: "He was in chirche a noble ecclesiaste." Like the Knight he makes no pretense at being other than he is. Yet he is clearly wicked as the Knight is clearly good. And this is so not simply because Chaucer counted upon his readers to respond to him as to the stereotype of pardoners whose activities were so openly condemned in the period. It is true because what he is, unlike what the Knight is, is conscious pretense. In all frankness he rejoices in his hypocrisy. With unabashed glee he is consciously and intentionally unscrupulous, proud of his ingenuity in preying upon the foolish:

> And thus, with feyned flaterye and japes
> He made the person and the peple his apes.
>
> .   .   .   .
>
> Wel koude he rede a lessoun or a storie,
> But alderbest he song an offertorie;
> For wel he wiste, whan that the song was songe,
> He moste preche and wel affile his tonge

> To wynne silver, as he ful wel koude;
> Therefore he song the murierly and loude.
>
> (705-714)

This pilgrim, with his false relics, his "pigges bones" and holy pillow cases, amuses not so much because he is so clearly a faker as because he is so proud of what he is. He obviously relishes his own somewhat repulsive physical appearance: his hair "as yellow as wex" that hung smoothly "as dooth a strike of flex"—

> . . . thynne it lay, by colpons oon and oon
> But hood, for jolitee, wered he noon,
> For it was trussed up in his walet.
> Hym thoughte he rood al of the newe jet;
> Dischevelee, save his cappe, he rood al bare.
>
> (679-683)

The observer, Chaucer, indicates little of his own response, but the particular details he records convey something like wonder at the blatant vainglory of the Pardoner's figure. His voice "as smal as hath a goot," his eyes "glarynge as an hare," his sexlessness, "I trowe he were a geldyng or a mare," might well be details to disgust us, but they do not because they are the very aspects of his appearance he glories in. His obliquity is clearly manifested to everyone, most of all to himself. Since he is so patently malicious, he is no threat to the pilgrims, nor to the observer, nor to us. He can only be threatened by his own limitations, even as the Knight. His self-assurance, like that of the Knight, is destructible if subjected to the greater complexity of the outside world. What wickedness the figure of the Pardoner embodies is not yet clear, of course, any more than what the "good" is that is imaged in the Knight. This will, we are led to expect, emerge in the telling of their tales, and in their participation in the social interaction of the pilgrimage. But it is clear that these, the first and the last of the pilgrims in the order of the portraits, define some opposites of a moral sort.

The variety of ways in which the pilgrims reveal to the observer the tension in equilibrium and all its possibility for the comedy to come almost defies analysis. So seldom does Chaucer repeat himself that the temptation is strong to subject each portrait to a line by line examination. To do so in this literal and schematic way would be, of course, to labor the point far beyond its usefulness. What follows may seem, in the light of this observation, to be unnecessarily detailed. Since the *General Prologue* is full of its own kind of comedy in its own right, it is important to see something of the minutiae that go into the "diversite of thingis." And although it is true that it is the tales and the pilgrimage that bring to realization the potentials latent in the portraits, it is possible to add significantly to a definition of Chaucer's comedy by pausing a little longer over the *General Prologue*.

Between the portraits of the Knight and the Pardoner are the portraits of twenty-four pilgrims. They can rightly be called "portraits," it seems to me, for, even though the literature of the Middle Ages abounds with characters clearly delineated in appearance, Chaucer's characters, however closely they seem to resemble those in *The Romaunt of the Rose* or in *Piers Plowman* do not really do so upon more careful reading. In his hands the allegorical figure that serves to concretize the abstraction becomes a character the details of whose external appearance convey complex psychological reality. Thus, they are portraits in a special sense of the word.

The portraits can be generally grouped into three social classes that resemble the "Three Estates" of medieval society. There are those who fight, those who work, and those who pray. But Chaucer's awareness of the "diversite of thingis" extends beyond this simple arrangement. From a study of the juxtaposition of descriptive details that differs from pilgrim to pilgrim, it can be seen that each pilgrim within his group has a position within a moral spectrum. And the sequence of the portraits reveals in various ways the moral stance of the observer as, with deceptive detachment, he presents them one after the other.

Following upon the portrait of the Knight are those of the Squire and the Yeoman, painted in much the same way. This small group representing "those who fight" is also what its members appear to be. Each, in his own way, is also limited. The Squire is "fresshe," a lover in the romantic and courtly sense of the word and a knight in training in the best tradition of the day. The Yeoman is efficient: "Wel koude he dresse his takel yemanly"; his arrows "drouped noght with fetheres lowe." These three are no more comic in their own right than are the royal eagles in *The Parliament of Fowls*—even less so. But what they are will be contrasted almost immediately with those in whose company they travel, and the first portrait that follows, that of the Prioress, begins to provide that contrast.

The observer, disarmed by the clear reality of the appearances met in the Knight, the Squire, and the Yeoman, looks at the highest rank among the group of religious, the lady Eglentine, prioress. So disarmed are we by the literal truth of the words "worthy," "fressh," "yemanly" in the portraits just described that we hardly notice at first the difference in the kind of key word that serves as the pointer to the essential characteristic of this lady of the church. The word is "semely"; and it is played upon in all its connotations until it defines precisely what kind of religious she is.

The portrait of the Prioress is the first one that is obviously "comic." What she is as a lady and what she should be as a religious are immediately contrasted in our minds. She seems to be entirely contained in a harmony of self, a lady before she is anything else, elegant of manners, properly pious, efficient as the head of a convent of nuns. But the terms of the observer's description point to something more significant. The apparent harmony is made up of a tension within her nature between the secular and the sacred. The tension offers no threat to her unquestionable serenity, but it makes of her a figure of irony and of comic amusement.

The details that outline the portrait are placed in a sequence that defines the tension; they may be described as "sacred, secular, sacred, secular" in almost exact alternation. The beginning and the end of the portrait, both "sacred" in nature, contain the discordancies that are inherent in the whole. And so exact has been the "secular-sacred" alternation that it is impossible to determine which element in her nature predominates. Is she more spiritual than she is secular? Or is she more worldly than she is religious? She sings elegantly, but it is the divine office she sings. Her manners, her social graces are those of a lady, but they also befit a prioress:

> At mete wel ytaught was she with alle:
> She leet no morsel from hir lippes falle,
> Ne wette hir fyngres in hir sauce depe;
> Wel koude she carie a morsel and wel kepe
> That no drope ne fille upon hire brest.
> In curteisie was set ful muchel hir lest.
>
> (127-132)

She is "plesant," "amyable of port," conscious of her position as lady and as religious administrator: "and peyned hire to countrefete cheere/ Of court, and to been estatlich of manere." Her heart is tender, her charitableness evident, though directed toward "smale" animals. Her beauty is undeniable and her awareness of it almost amounts to an indulgence in vanity. But the care she takes with her clothes, the ways in which she shows forth her beauty are, though perhaps not for "the greater glory of God," certainly not without reverence for her position in the Church:

> Ful semyly hir wympul pynched was;
> Hir nose tretys, hir eyen greye as glas,
> Hir mouth ful smal, and thereto softe and reed;
> But sikerly she hadde a fair forheed;

It was almoost a spanne brood, I trowe;
For, hardily, she was nat undergrowe.
Ful fetys was hir cloke, as I was war.
(151-157)

All this wordly vanity becomes directed into the spiritual in the last lines that once more conjoin the two worlds, the secular and the spiritual, into harmony:

Of smal coral aboute hire arm she bar
A peire of bedes, gauded al with grene,
And theron heng a brooch of gold ful sheene,
On which ther was first write a crowned A,
And after *Amor vincit omnia.*
(158-162)

What Chaucer means by the ambiguous ending of the portrait has been defined by all the details that lead up to it: love of elegance, love of manners, love of small "houndes," compassion for helpless mice, fondness for position, love of the reverence due her as a lady in the service of the Church. The coexistence within her nature of worldly and spiritual elements and her unawareness of them make her the first of the complex portraits, and the first figure for amused contemplation of all the Canterbury pilgrims. She too is clearly limited, but she is not simplified.

Toward the Monk and the Friar, the next portraits in the group of "those who pray," the observer looks with less affection than he looks at the Prioress. It is clear that he sees the contrast between the ideal that these two religious should be and the real that they are and his tone is implicitly condemnatory. Once again, however, the source of the comedy is not in just this contrast, but in the vision of human nature sustaining in constant balance the tensions that threaten. Both men are what they are because they have successfully rationalized the conflict between the religious and the worldly life. Both men live within their rationalizations with joy and vitality.

The Monk, obviously to the eye "a manly man, to been an abbot able," has arrived consciously at an "opinion" that has settled for him whatever conflict there has been between the spirit and the flesh, and, remarks Chaucer, the pilgrim-observer, "I seyde his opinioun was good." Robust and vigorous, this Monk who loved hunting, whose boots were "souple," whose horse was "in greet estaat," whose approach was heralded by the jingling of his bridle—"gynglen in a whistlynge wynd als cleere/ And eek as loude as dooth the chapel belle," scorned all rule that threatened this life as old-fashioned:

> What sholde he studie and maken hymselven wood,
> Upon a book in cloystre alwey to poure,
> Or swynken with his handes, and laboure,
> As Austyn bit? How shal the world be served?
> Lat Austyn have his swynk to hym reserved!
> (184-188)

In similar ways, whatever war has gone into the making of the equilibrium of the Friar "cleped Huberd" has been won long before he joined the pilgrims at the Tabard. That there had once been some kind of contention within him between the secular and the spiritual is clear in the rationalization that exalts the secular in the service of the sacred. Women and money, good food, good company, and "daliaunce" are proper objects for his attention and for his religious zeal, for women need absolving and the Church and his order need the "profit." The life he has led, the values he has openly cultivated, all have been to the greater glory of the order. "Wantowne and . . . merye,/ A lymytour, a ful solempne man," he was the best gossip in all the four orders. His sexual and social activities have indeed made him into a "noble post" in the Church: the young girls he has married off "at his owene cost"; the rich franklins of the countryside have been graced with his visits, the "worthy women" have had the sweetness of his absolution:

> For he hadde power of confessioun,
> As seyde hymself, moore than a curat,
> For of ordre he was licenciat.
> Ful swetely herde he confessioun,
> And plesaunt was his absolucioun:
> He was an esy man to yeve penaunce,
> Ther as he wiste to have a good pitaunce.
> For unto a povre ordre for to yive
> Is signe that a man is wel yshryve;
> For if he yaf, he dorste make avaunt,
> He wiste that a man was repentaunt;
> For many a man so hard is of his herte,
> He may nat wepe, althogh hym soore smerte.
> Therfore in stede of wepynge and preyeres
> Men moote yeve silver to the povre freres.
> (218-232)

It is evident that the gullible and the wise have corroborated his rationalization, and his success has justified the cultivation of his whole temperament. The result is a genial, jovial, thoroughly pleasant companion.

There is no secret that he is a hypocrite, but because we "see" the rationale of his hypocrisy, and because the world he "fools" is no better than himself, the "evil" that is his is contained and is realizable as comedy. Though more threatening to society than either the Prioresse or the Monk, he is far less dangerous to the human soul than the Pardoner. And there is no doubt that he contributes to social joy, something the Pardoner, singing his drunken duet with the Summoner does not do:

> And certeinly he hadde a murye note:
> Wel koude he synge and pleyen on a rote;
> Of yeddynges he baar outrely the pris.
> (235-237)

And the relish he has in his physical appearance is somehow a proper relish: white of neck, "as the flour-de-lys," mighty of muscle, courteous of manner, he was not at all like a "cloysterer":

> But he was lyk a maister or a pope.
> Of double worstede was his semycope,
> That rounded as a belle out of the presse.
> Somwhat he lipsed, for his wantownesse,
> To make his Englissh sweete upon his tonge;
> And in his harpyng, whan that he hadde songe,
> His eyen twynkled in his heed aryght,
> As doon the sterres in the frosty nyght.
> (261-268)

The four portraits that follow upon those of the religious represent the first grouping of the Third Estate, those "who work." The members of this Estate far outnumber those of the other two among the pilgrims, as indeed was inevitable in view of the nature of English society in Chaucer's day. The men in this group, the Merchant, the Clerk, the Sergeant of Law, and the Franklin, are fourteenth-century professionals. How much their appearance intimates what they really are, or contrasts with what they should be, the observer-pilgrim is not quite sure. He sees and he hears, and he suggests that he suspects he sees and hears dimly. Each of the four pilgrims, though socially and professionally alike in rank, exists as an isolate. True, the Franklin and the Lawyer are together, but it seems more a companionship by accident than by design. And of the four two seem secretive, two seem open, two somewhat sinister, two really innocent.

The Merchant "with a forked berd," clad elegantly in motley, reserved even in the posture he maintains upon his horse—"and hye on

horse he sat"—is known to the observer only by what he says. From his
concern with money and with the threat of piracy at sea there seem
to be hints of dishonesty and double-dealing. The observer, perhaps at
loss for a word, uses once more the adjective "worthy," though, obviously
he does not mean it literally as he had for the Knight; and though he is
ironic, he seems ambiguously so. The whole portrait, though drawn in
what seems to be exact and precise detail, leaves curiously no vital impression at all. This man, "so estatly was he of his governaunce," remains a figure apart from the others, and the observer dismisses him
almost with relief:

> For sothe he was a worthy man with alle,
> But, sooth to seyn, I noot how men hym calle.
> (283-284)

The portrait of the Clerk is of a man quite different in nature. He,
too, is a man apart; but about him there is no hint of the sinister. Re-
ticent and reserved—"Noght o word spak he moore than was neede,/
And that was seyd in forme and reverence,/ And short and quyk and ful
of hy sentence"—he is preoccupied with himself in a totally inner way.
His lean and threadbare appearance, his lean horse, contrast sharply
with the elegantly dressed Merchant, even as his reticence speaks
of the inner world concerned with Aristotle and "his philosophie" in
contrast to the reticence of the Merchant that hints only of dishonesty.

The Lawyer and his companion, the Franklin, are in similar opposition.
What characterizes them both is their extreme busyness; what differ-
entiates them both is what this busyness reveals. The Sergeant at Law,
"war and wys," takes great pains to impress the world with his knowledge, with his adroitness in things legal, with his importance in his
profession. And it all, says the observer, is a "seeming." His discretion,
his dignity, are conscious impositions upon the world—"He semed
swich, his wordes weren so wise," says the observer. "Nowher so bisy a
man as he ther nas,/ And yet he semed bisier than he was." In markedly
clear contrast to him rides the Franklin, sanguine and open in temperament—"whit was his berd as is the dayesye." This owner of manor and
field lives with delight and sumptuous joy, "for he was Epicurus owene
sone." About him there is no hint of the sinister, of the secretive, of the
dishonest. The observer's summation of the Franklin's appearance has
a note of happy relief that there is among them a pilgrim so obviously
genial:

> At sessiouns ther was he lord and sire;
> Ful ofte tyme he was knyght of the shire.

An anlaas and a gipser al of silk
Heeng at his girdel, whit as morne milk.
A shirreve hadde he been, and a contour.
Was nowher swich a worthy vavasour.
(355-360)

What I have called the Three-Estate pattern of the *General Prologue,*
that pattern of social order that is the skeletal structure of the
introduction of the pilgrims, is at this point made its most complex.
"Those who work," the Third Estate, as might be expected, provide the
greatest number of pilgrims. They, too, can be seen to form subgroups
of social import. The group portrait of the five guildsmen, described as
members of a species rather than as individuals, amusing in their solemn
pretense to position and elegance, introduces the portraits of the members of the working class: those who have their own businesses, as the
Cook, the Shipman, the Physician (not, in the Middle Ages, a professional
as was the Lawyer), and the Wife of Bath; and certain ones of those who
work for others or make their livelihood living off society in ways more
dishonorable than honorable—the Miller, the Manciple, the Reeve, the
Summoner, and the Pardoner. Separating these two subgroups are the
portraits of the Parson and the Plowman, the most clearly idealized
figures on the pilgrimage, the priest and the worker, dedicated to service
rather than to self, significantly the "ideal" at the heart of the "real."

The observer looks at these companions of his as he has looked at
those of higher rank, noting "array," at times aware of inner complexity,
at times suspicious of what reticence may imply, though withholding
anything suggesting moral judgment unless the appearance of the
pilgrim clearly calls for it. So it is that the questionable moral natures
of the last five pilgrims, because so openly recognized, become more
obviously comic as they are more clearly fearsome. What these people
are the whole world can see. "The "gold thumb" of the Miller advertises
his thievery, and the observer has no difficulty in reading the dishonesty
of the Manciple, regardless of his skill in cheating the law students he
takes care of. The whole world of the manor served by the Reeve, that
"sclendre colerik man," was "adrad" of him "as of the deeth"; and of
the Summoner, diseased and filthy, children were "aferd." The Pardoner,
revealing with relish the total perversity of his nature, the last of the
portraits and the most obviously reprehensible of the pilgrims, is clearly
wicked. But because he so unquestionably is what he appears to be
he offers no more threat to society at large than the Knight does.

Of the pilgrims seen before the Parson and the Plowman, three—the
Cook, the Shipman, and the Physician—hint by their appearance at
something sinister, at something dishonest in the practice of their

businesses. It is as if the observer can interpret from how they look no more certainly than he can the natures of the professional pilgrims. But about the Wife of Bath there is no puzzle, no suggestion of the secretive or the sinister.

It is still a while before the Wife of Bath is heard in all her robust lustiness, but even in the few lines of her portrait she has implications for broad comedy. The largeness of her body and the huge vitality of her soul are unembarrassedly evident in the open vowels of the words that describe her: "a good Wif . . . of biside Bathe" who was "somdel deef, and that was scathe./ . . . Gat-tothed was she, soothly for to seye,/ Upon an amblere esily she sat,/ Ywympled wel, and on hir heed an hat/ As brood as is a bokeler or a targe;/ A foot-mantel aboute hir hippes large" (468-472). In many ways the observer sees her in terms similar to those he was aware of when he looked at the Prioress. But her nature is a complex one, full of tensions that are barely kept in balance.

The initiation of laughter, deep and affectionate, comes in the first sentence of the portrait, in the apparent *non sequitur* that is created by the conjunction "but," which qualifies in a way deliberately ambiguous, the adjective "good":

> A good Wif was ther of biside Bathe,
> But she was somdel deef, and that was scathe.
> (445-446)

The rest of the description, apparently artlessly haphazard in organization, qualifies more and more exactly the ironic ambiguity of the dominant adjective, "good." She is "good" as a business woman, expert in the making of cloth. She is "good" in her sense of superiority, and aggressively proud:

> In al the parisshe wif ne was ther noon
> That to the offrynge bifore hire sholde goon;
> And if ther dide, certeyn so wrooth was she,
> That she was out of alle charitee.
> (449-452)

She was "good" in size, ample and florid and exuberantly padded:

> Hir coverchiefs ful fyne weren of ground;
> I dorste swere they weyeden ten pound
> That on a Sonday weren upon hir heed.
> (453-455)

And "good" means prosperous:

> Hir hosen weren of fyn scarlet reed,
> Ful streite yteyd, and shoes ful moyste and newe,
> (456-457)

as it also means "large of spirit," and boundless in vigor.

She also, says the observer, is "worthy" and he makes clear what he means. Two things chiefly make up her "worthiness," connected significantly by the conjunction "and":

> She was a worthy womman al hir lyve:
> Housbondes at chirche dore she hadde fyve,
>
> .   .   .   .
> And thries hadde she been at Jerusalem.
> (459-463)

The adjectives "good" and "worthy" with all their qualifications suggest excellence that is physical and sexual and also spiritual. And with the evidence of her great restlessness—thrice at Jerusalem, once at least "at Rome," "at Boloigne," "In Galice at Seint-Jame, and at Coloigne," and now with the pilgrimage to Canterbury—they convey the sense of enormous energy created by the tensions that are the complex of her nature:

> In felaweshipe wel koude she laughe and carpe,
> Of remedies of love she knew per chaunce,
> For she koude of that art the olde daunce.
> (474-476)

Here the war between the spirit and the flesh has been, and is being waged. And it is by no means certain that the flesh has been granted victory of any lasting sort.

*   *   *

"Now have I toold you soothly, in a clause,/ Th'estaat, th'array, the nombre, and eek the cause/ Why that assembled was this compaignye/ In Southwerk at this gentil hostelrye/ That highte the Tabard," says the observer-pilgrim as the last of his descriptions is ended. Without explicit acknowledgement he has created an order of moral values, though in no specifics, and has established within the portraits probability for dynamic action, though of an indeterminate nature.

It is not to be the fate of any one of the pilgrims to energize the pilgrimage into dramatic life. Chance has not only gathered them together at the Tabard Inn but has, more importantly, provided that Inn with a Host who by his very nature seems to sense in his guests great possibilities for "mirth." For above all, the observer sees, "Oure Hooste" is a man in love with mirth. "A semely man . . . a large man . . . boold of his speche, and wys, and wel ytaught, . . . a myrie man" whose joy in the collection of pilgrims inspires him to formulate the plan for the journey that will bring about the telling of the Canterbury Tales. " 'Now lordynges' " he says,

> "Ye been to me right welcome, hertely;
> For by my trouthe, if that I shal nat lye,
> I saugh nat this yeer so myrie a compaignye
> Atones in this herberwe as is now.
> Fayn wolde I doon yow myrthe, wiste I how."
> (761-765)

What motivates the Host to suggest the telling of tales and to offer to go along on the pilgrimage as guide has been variously conjectured. Perhaps he wants to get away from a shrewish wife, perhaps he has some desire to escape from some responsibility or other. It seems motive enough to the observer, however, that he is a man by temperament full of the relish for "pleye," a large-spirited human cousin to the small "whelp" of *The Book of the Duchess,* to the genial Eagle of *The House of Fame,* to the insistent Scipio of *The Parliament,* to Pandarus in his love of managing the "diversite of thinges." "And of a myrthe I am right now bythoght,/ To doon yow ese, and it shal coste noght," he promises. His plan is a simple one at first: each pilgrim shall tell two tales on the way to Canterbury and two on the way back to London; and for the tale of the "best sentence and moost solas" there will be a reward—"a soper at oure aller cost/ Heere in this place, sittynge by this post." One rule must be followed—"whoso wole my juggement withseye/ Shal paye al that we spenden by the weye." Agreement is immediate and enthusiastic:

> This thyng was graunted, and oure othes swore
> With ful glad herte, and preyden hym also
> That he wolde vouche sauf for to do so,
> And that he wolde been oure governour,
> And of our tales juge and reportour,
> And sette a soper at a certeyn pris,
> And we wol reuled been at his devys
> In heigh and lough; and thus by oon assent
> We been acorded to his juggement.

And therupon the wyn was fet anon;
We dronken, and to reste went echon.
(810-820)

The Host's proposal is the first clear hint at some plan for the sequence of the narratives to follow. Chaucer, it is true, seems to suggest in the order of the portraits a possible order for the telling of tales. But that suggestion is no longer tenable the moment the Host takes over the leadership and dominates the pilgrims. He certainly has every intention of managing, not only the nomination of the teller but also the preservation of order and good spirits: "Now, by my fader soule that is deed,/ But ye be myrie, I wol yeve yow myn heed!" How he meant to choose the tellers of the tales that were to follow, or in what order will, of course, never be known. Chance, "cas," provides him with the first speaker, the Knight. That Chance, by giving the "cut" to the Knight, is showing almost human wisdom, is true. But to the Knight the lot does fall—"Syn I shal bigynne the game,/ What, welcome be the cut, a Goddes name!"—and his position as the first of the portraits, as well as his "worthiness," are reaffirmed. The first tale is, however, the only one told "by lot." Once the plan is under way, once some suggestion as to a possible order is given, the Host steps in as he had intended. The next teller is to be the Monk, says the Host. And it is possible to conjecture that he planned to choose the rest of the tellers in an order that might correspond to his sense of hierarchy, or of some protocol or other known only to himself. But neither the Host nor Chance is to rule the pilgrims; neither will determine the sequence of tales. From the moment the drunken Miller bursts out with his demand to be allowed to tell the tale "to quite with the Knyghtes tale," the Host becomes an umpire, a keeper of peace and of good temper, his energies spent more or less successfully in maintaining "myrthe" and harmony, and in re-establishing the threatened balance and equilibrium of the whole pilgrimage. In the process he emerges as a figure of comedy in his own right. But it is as the Keeper of Mirth rather than as the Figure of Mirth that he is the most important single character in the dramatic and dynamic organization of *The Canterbury Tales.*

By the time *The Knight's Tale* is ended and *The Miller's Tale* is begun, what is to be the informing principle of *The Canterbury Tales* begins to come clear. It is to be the principle of *agon* made to function dynamically in a variety of ways, first as "game," then as "quiting," then as contention. And each manifestation is richly comic, is, indeed, the source of the complex comedy of the whole.

The "Game-Concept" that is explicit in the plan worked out by the Host is rich in comic potential. It is entered into with great gusto by all the pilgrims. The Knight, solemn as he has seemed to be, says "Syn I shal bigynne the game,/ What, welcome be the cut, a Goddes name!" (853-854). And the joy of the Host after the Knight has told his tale is the joy of anyone who has planned well: "Lat se now who shal telle another tale;/ For trewely the game is wel bigonne" (I, 3116-3117). If the project for insuring "confort [and] myrthe" is to be thought of as a game then what is not game-like in spirit can be taken in the same way as that which is; at least whatever is perhaps offensive or solemn or romantic should not ultimately be taken in "earnest." Chaucer the pilgrim reminds us of this when he introduces the first of the fabliaux, *The Miller's Tale*:

> And therfore every gentil wight I preye,
> For Goddes love, demeth nat that I seye
> Of yvel entente. . . .
>
> .   .   .   .
>
> The Millere is a cherl, ye knowe wel this;
> So was the Reve eek and othere mo,
> And harlotrie they tolden bothe two.
> Avyseth yow, and put me out of blame;
> And eek men shal nat maken ernest of game.
>
> (I, 3171-3186)

The pilgrimage is not long upon the road before the Host has to make a similar reminder. Evidently irritated by the Cook's inordinate glee at the end of *The Reeve's Tale*, he hesitates not at all to sketch in vivid detail the loathsome filth of the Cook's shop, though he at the same time attempts to avert any real protest at the attack:

> "Now telle on, Roger, looke that it be good;
> For many a pastee hastow laten blood,
> And many a Jakke of Dovere hastow soold
> That hath been twies hot and twies coold.
> Of many a pilgrim hastow Cristes curs,
> For of thy percely yet they fare the worse,
> That they han eten with thy stubbel goos;
> For in thy shoppe is many a flye loos.
> Now telle on, gentil Roger by thy name.
> But yet I pray thee, be nat wroth for game;
> A man may seye ful sooth in game and pley."
>
> (I, 4345-4355)

Roger gets the point. He understands the paradox fully and goes the Host one better:

"Thou seist ful sooth," quod Roger, "by my fey!
But 'sooth pley, quaad pley,' as the Fleming seith."
(I, 4356-4357)

If there is truth in "pley," then there is unpleasantness in "pley"; but since both are play and the spirit of mirth prevails, then both can be mutually suffered.

The concept of "game" includes in its connotative cluster more than an attitude of a special kind, more than a spirit of jest and play; it includes also the understanding that there are participants whose relationships are determined or created by rules of some sort. A game, whatever kind it is, is a determinate, and its participants, as long as they are consciously part of it, must remain within its disciplines no matter how, as individuals, they carry out the rules. A game is an ordered world in which the erratic can be contained, in which the agonistic impluses can be profitably used to fulfil its aims. And a game, though unique in one sense, is never really over in one trial. There is always another day. The "tragedy," the "injustice," the "disappointment" of one day's loss or defeat are intensely felt for the moment, but the woeful moment is temporal: there is another day, or another year. The world of the game, of the great organized sports, of tournaments, of horse-racing, of the World Series, is the world of Comedy, its figure also that of Fortune and her turning wheel—for what goes up to victory will inevitably go down to defeat but go on to rise again. Chaucer's own experience as builder and overseer of grandstands and arenas hints at his understanding of the world of organized sports. But it is, of course, his essential vision of life, that sees life as unique and yet continual, subject to rules and disciplines and yet exhibiting a variety of possible plays; it is only incidental that such vision corresponds to some of his professional activities.

A game, although entered into in a spirit of mirth and play, once begun becomes a matter of serious concern on the part of the participants. When the concern becomes too "ernest" and the order of the game is threatened, there must be someone to right things, someone to separate the contestants, someone to judge the winner. This is, of course, the role the Host consciously assumed at the beginning. It was he who formed the plan and stated the rules of the game and it was he who got the whole pilgrimage on its way: "Amorwe, whan that day bigan to sprynge,/ Up roos oure Hoost, and was oure aller cok,/ And gadrede us togidre alle in a flok" (822-824). And it is he, who throughout the whole journey acts the part of umpire and master of ceremonies, always intent upon keeping the rule of mirth.

As master of the game, one of the Host's more obvious duties is to invite the pilgrims to participate. When he does so, more often than not, his manner of speaking reveals his admirable qualities as a Host. Conscious of the personality, or profession, or rank of most of the pilgrims, he carefully adapts his address to the particular person. To the Man of Law he speaks in legal terms: "So have ye blis,/ Telle us a tale anon, as forward is,/ Ye been submytted, thurgh youre free assent,/ To stonden in this cas at my juggement./ Acquiteth yow now of youre biheeste;/ Thanne have ye do youre devoir atte leeste" (II, 33-38). As "wel ytaught" in the respect due a lady religious as he is in the jargon of the law, he bows, verbally, to the Prioress in a filigree of subjunctives (VII, 446-450). So often is he correct in his appraisal of the pilgrims that when he is mistaken he, too, becomes a figure of laughter, a reminder that though appearances suggest reality they can be misread even by the most practiced observer.

In addition to his task as the one to begin and the one to end the "game" of the telling of tales, he has the responsibility to keep the peace among the members of the pilgrimage. It is no easy task, given the aggressive individualities of his companions. As he functions dramatically throughout the journey, he proves himself to be almost always alert to the tensions that threaten to explode into a disruption of the "mirth." The first tale is barely over before his skill as keeper of the peace is taxed by the drunken Miller, roaring out his insistence on being the next to speak after the Knight, an insistence he wisely submits to. During the altercation between the Friar and the Summoner, when the antipathy that is both personal and professional between the two threatens to flare up into a fist fight, his shouts of "pees" just barely keep the situation under control. He is obeyed, and his reiterated requests for "pees" make it possible for the near venomous hatred between the two apparently irreconcilable pilgrims to work itself out verbally in their tales. And peace at almost any cost seems to motivate his last act to maintain some sort of harmony among the pilgrims. Though himself once threatened by the Cook, he comes to that one's defense against the sardonic humor of the Manciple even as he comes to the defense of the mirth and the "confort" of the whole company. Stepping in between the thoroughly drunken Cook and the sarcastically accusatory Manciple, he wards off whatever action might arise by reminding the Manciple that he should be careful, on "another day . . . peraventure" this same Cook might well retaliate. And his approval of the Manciple's response both defies any possible threat from the Cook and insures his continued oblivion. As more wine is poured down the Cook's throat, the Host laughs "wonder loude" and says:

"I se wel it is necessarie,
Where that we goon, good drynke with us carie;
For that wol turne rancour and disese
T'accord and love, and many a wrong apese.
   O thou Bacus, yblessed by thy name,
That so kanst turnen ernest into game!
Worshipe and thank be to thy deitee!"
                    (IX, 94-101)

But the Host is also a member of the pilgrimage, a participator as well as a guide and an umpire. As he emerges in his own person from the epilogues and prologues that join many of the tales together and make them organically vital to the whole design of the pilgrimage, he is a comic figure in his own right. His joy is seldom ruffled. Frank to relish whatever is lusty and bawdy, coarsely articulate in his anti-feminism and anticlericalism, on guard against whatever he fears may be boring, sentimentally moved by tales of simple holiness, he wins, by his robust openness, our willing attention, sometimes our respect, sometimes our amused disapproval.

Thus the "game" has its creator, its umpire, and its participant in "Herry Bailly," the Host. And as long as its important rule, that mirth prevail, is kept, whatever way its aim of entertaining the pilgrims along the way is fulfilled is up to the tellers themselves. It is they who in the process of interacting invent the dynamics of the first fragment, for the tales that are told come into being agonistically. From the moment the Miller announces he will tell "a noble tale . . . with which" he will "quite the Knyghtes tale," he generates the vital principle that brings the tales of the Reeve and the Cook to life, and, retrospectively he makes the *Knight's Tale* part of the group. Not only is each tale a "quiting" of another tale, but each is about some form of quiting and each makes a statement about the nature of justice and affirms the existence of order in social and ethical and moral spheres.

THE KNIGHT'S TALE

The first of the tales, *The Knight's Tale*, is a romance and at first reading seems hardly comic at all. Certainly in its genre it is not conventionally supposed to be, and it is not comic because it is in any sense parodic or satiric. Nor is it comic merely because the Miller's tale that follows points up its somewhat solemn absurdities. Its comedy is far less obvious than this, and far more meaningful.

That the pilgrims expect the Knight to comply with the Host's request for entertainment that is merry, is clear; they greet with joy his election by "Cas" and the "cut" as the first to tell a tale: "ful blithe and glad was every wyght." And that they were not disappointed is also clear, for their approval is explicit:

> In al the route nas ther yong ne oold
> That he ne seyde it was a noble storie,
> And worthy for to drawen to memorie;
> And namely the gentils everichon.
> Oure Hooste lough and swoor, "So moot I gon,
> This gooth aright; unbokeled is the male.
> Lat se now who shal telle another tale;
> For trewely the game is wel bigonne."
>   (I, 3110-3117)

So in spite of its gentle solemnity and its quiet seriousness, in spite of its "tragic" moments, *The Knight's Tale* has not threatened to violate the Host's cardinal rule.

The approval of the pilgrims and particularly of the Host indicates also an assent to, even a ratification of, the Knight's thesis about life, a thesis that is in simplified ways Boethian in essence. It is the thesis that is undoubtedly Chaucer's, and though its simplification in the tale points up humorously the Knight's character, its tenets are in no way subject to question. The tale is about order more importantly than it is about anything else. The Knight, worthy in so many ways, "verray" and "parfit gentil" in identifying himself with his hero, Duc Theseus, voices what are medieval commonplaces that are nonetheless meaningful as an accounting for the mysteries of human existence. All of nature, animate and inanimate, is in ordered arrangement; each thing, each human being, has a place and a relationship to every other human being, and all are but parts derived from the great Whole:

> Wel may men knowe, but it be a fool,
> That every part dirryveth from his hool;
> For nature hath nat taken his bigynnyng
> Of no partie or cantel of a thyng,
> But of a thyng that parfit is and stable,
> Descendynge so til it be corrumpable.
>   (I, 3005-3010)

It is wise, therefore, in the face of God's great plan, says Theseus, to make "vertu of necessitee," confident that if all is not for the best in the best of all possible worlds, it is for the best in the best of all possible universes. It is, indeed, even the duty of man to be "merye" in the

face of life; to "grucchen" is to be wilful and contrary, to complain is
to waste energy and time and hence is fruitless:

> "Why grucchen we, why have we hevynesse,
> That goode Arcite, of chivalrie the flour,
> Departed is with duetee and honour
> Out of this foule prisoun of this lyf?
> Why grucchen heere his cosyn and his wyf
> Of his welfare, that loved him so weel?
> Kan he hem thank? Nay, God woot, never a deel,
> That both his soule and eek himself offende,
> And yet they mowe hir lustes nat amende.
>   What may I conclude of this longe serye,
> But after wo I rede us to be merye,
> And thanken Juppiter of al his grace?
> And er that we departen from this place
> I rede that we make of sorwes two
> O parfit joye, lastynge everemo."
>   (I, 3058-3072)

To hold that from two sorrows can come "one perfect joy" is not to
minimize the pain of the sorrows. As a matter of fact, it is to accept the
fact that the sorrows of this world usually outnumber the joys. But one
does not, for that reason, deliberately set about cultivating and multiply-
ing the conditions of woe. Thus when the Knight, indignant at the
Monk's endless recitation of "tragedies," interrupts him later in the
journey with "hoo, . . . good sire, namoore of this!" he does so "in
character." And at the same time, in his defense of his rudeness he gives
a definition of comedy to counter the Monk's definition of tragedy:

> "Hoo!" quod the Knyght, "good sire, namoore of this!
> That ye han seyd is right ynough, ywis,
> And muchel moore; for litel hevynesse
> Is right ynough to much folk, I gesse.
> I seye for me, it is a greet disese,
> Whereas men han been in greet welthe and ese,
> To heeren of hire sodeyn fal, allas!
> And the contrarie is joye and greet solas,
> As whan a man hath been in povre estaat,
> And clymbeth up and wexeth fortunat,
> And there abideth in prosperitee.
> Swych thyng is gladsom, as it thynketh me."
>   (VII, 2767-2778)

So he restores "mirth" to the company of pilgrims, even as his intervention between the Host and the Pardoner has earlier restored peace
and order:

> "Now," quod oure Hoost, "I wol no lenger pleye
> With thee, ne with noon oother angry man."
> But right anon the worthy Knyght bigan,
> Whan that he saugh that al the peple lough,
> "Namoore of this, for it is right ynough!
> Sire Pardoner, be glad and myrie of cheere;
> And ye, sire Hoost, that been to me so deere,
> I prey yow that ye kisse the Pardoner.
> And Pardoner, I prey thee, drawe thee neer,
> And, as we diden, lat us laughe and pleye."
> Anon they kiste, and ryden forth hir weye.
>   (VI, 958-968)

The Knight becomes almost a symbol of Order, even as the Host is the
symbol of Mirth, and though he acts only twice as such, his tale, as the
first to be told, proclaims the existence of Order before the "diversite of
thynges" in the rest of the Canterbury Tales takes over.

The ordered world of the Knight is revealed in almost every narrative
and thematic detail of his tale. He chose for his source Boccaccio's
Teseida, a lyrical, somewhat sentimental account of the winning of
Hippolita by Theseus, and of the love of Palamon and Arcite for the
lady Emilia, a romance in no way comic. Although the world of the
Italian poem is stylized and therefore "ordered," the Knight in his retelling of it sharpens and reshapes the suggestions for order in every
possible way. His narrative, unlike that of his source in its division into
twelve books, is related in four parts, almost precisely equal in numbers
of lines. Each of the parts in turn has its own pattern, repeating in
miniature the pattern of the whole: a pattern of twos, of "tweye and
tweye," a pattern that embodies the concept of ordered balance. The
narrative style almost exactly reflects the same balance and equalization.
The numbers of pairings of verbs, of adjectives, of descriptive and narrative detail, are remarkable. They give to the tale much of its stately
dignity, but more importantly they reveal the mind of the narrator and
its view of life, a view that is essentially comic, "gladsom . . . and of
greet solas."

Part One of the tale presents the *dramatis personae*: Duc Theseus,
Palamon and Arcite, and the "fresshe Emelye the shene." The narrative
moves with unhurried and deliberate pace to the central issue: the love
of Palamon annd Arcite for Emelye. Because this is to be the concern of

his story, the Knight is willing to omit many details from his source that, one expects, he might have liked to include were it not for his sense of proportion and fitness:

> And certes, if it nere to long to heere,
> I wolde have toold yow fully the manere
> How wonnen was the regne of Femenye
> By Theseus and by his chivalrye;
> And of the grete bataille for the nones
> Bitwixen Atthenes and Amazones;
> And how asseged was Ypolita,
> The faire, hardy queene of Scithia;
> And of the feste that was at hir weddynge,
> And of the tempest at hir hoom-comynge;
> But al that thyng I moot as now forbere.
> I have, Got woot, a large feeld to ere,
> And wayke been the oxen in my plough.
> The remenant of the tale is long ynough.
> (I, 875-888)

And by "two and two" he unfolds the important "remenant of the tale." In the field of battle Theseus' men find "two yonge knyghtes liggynge by and by"; "nat fully quyke, ne fully ded they were." Back to Athens the "yonge two" are taken

> And in a tour, in angwissh and in wo,
> This Palamon and his felawe Arcite
> For everemoore, ther may no gold hem quite.
> (I, 1030-1032)

There they remain, "yeer by yeer and day by day" until, on a May morning, one after the other they catch sight of the lovely Emelye, "that fairer was to sene/ Than is the lylie upon his stalke grene,/ And fressher than the May with floures newe" (I, 1035-1037). "Bright was the sonne and cleer that morwenynge" when Palamon from the "tour heigh" looked down upon her in the garden and was smitten with love. Arcite, attracted to the window by Palamon's cry of woe also "gan espye" Emelye below, and is also instantly smitten with love:

> . . . if that Palamon was wounded sore,
> Arcite is hurt as muche as he, or moore.
> And with a sigh he seyde pitously:
> "The fresshe beautee sleeth me sodeynly
> Of hire that rometh in the yonder place,

> And but I have hir mercy and hir grace,
> That I may seen hire atte leeste weye,
> I nam but deed; ther nis namoore to seye."
> (I, 1115-1122)

Whereupon Palamon, more in sadness than in anger, calls Arcite a traitor, and reminds him of their sworn brotherhood with its simple, but binding pledge:

> This Palamon gan knytte his browes tweye.
> "It nere," quod he, "to thee no greet honour
> For to be fals, ne for to be traitour
> To me, that am thy cosyn and thy brother
> Ysworn ful depe, and ech of us til oother,
> That nevere, for to dyen in the peyne,
> Til that the deeth departe shal us tweyne,
> Neither of us in love to hyndre oother,
> Ne in noon oother cas, my leeve brother;
> But that thou sholdest trewely forthren me
> In every cas, as I shal forthren thee,--
> This was thyn ooth, and myn also, certeyn;
> I woot right wel, thou darst it nat withseyn."
> (I, 1128-1140)

Thus, that which had bound the "two" into "o joye" of brotherhood is now "unjoyned" into conflict; two equal forces are now brought to tension.

Before the first part of the tale is over, Fate, in the person of Duc Perotheus, has arranged the release of Arcite from the tower. His unhappiness at being set free from the prison where at least he could see Emelye is equaled by the unhappiness of Palamon, who envies his "freedom" and his chance to pursue his "felicitee" even though he is supposed to go from the country. In their operatic solemnity, the two laments are Boethian in content, one reflecting the protests of the imprisoned Boethius, the other, the consolations of Philosophy, both together summarizing the Boethian concept of Fortune. "How greet a sorwe suffreth now Arcite" says the Knight. But so "upon that oother syde" does Palamon, and both weep "salte teeres wete." The lament of the freed Arcite sets the pattern:

> . . . "Allas that day that I was born!
> Now is my prisoun worse than biforn;
> Now is me shape eternally to dwelle,

Noght in purgatorie, but in helle.

.   .   .   .

"O deere cosyn Palamon," quod he,
"Thyn is the victorie of this aventure.
Ful blisfully in prison maistow dure,—
In prison? certes nay, but in paradys!
$\qquad$ (I, 1223-1226, 1234-1237

And it is echoed by the imprisoned lover:

"Allas . . . Arcita, cosyn myn,
Of al oure strif, God woot, the fruyt is thyn.
Thow walkest now in Thebes at thy large,
And of my wo thow yevest litel charge.
Thou mayst, syn thou has wisdom and manhede,
Assemblen alle the folk of oure kynrede,
And make a werre so sharp on this citee,
That by som aventure or som tretee
Thou mayst have hire to lady and to wyf
For whom that I moste nedes lese my lyf."
$\qquad$ (I, 1281-1290)

For Arcite Fortune is indeed whimsical, life ironic. Clearly it would have been better to have had the fortune to have been kept in prison than to have had the fortune to be set free:

"Allas, why pleynen folk so in commune
On purveiaunce of God, or of Fortune,
That yeveth hem ful ofte in many a gyse
Wel bettre than they kan hemself devyse?

.   .   .   .

We witen nat what thing we preyen heere:
We faren as he that dronke is as a mous.
A dronke man woot wel he hath an hous,
But he noot which the righte wey is thider,
And to a dronke man the wey is slider.
And certes, in this world so faren we;
We seken faste after felicitee,
But we goon wrong ful often, trewely."
$\qquad$ (I, 1251-1254, 1260-1267)

Palamon in prison is also occupied with the sense of the irony of life, though he puts his meditation on the enigma of existence in the form

of questions, as had Boethius. Why must the innocent suffer, he asks.
Why is there injustice? Why must some be victims? He can only conclude
that "it may stonden so."

> "The answere of this lete I to dyvynys,
> But wel I woot that in this world greet pyne ys.
> Allas, I se a serpent or a theef,
> That many a trewe man hath doon mescheef,
> Goon at his large, and where hym list may turne."
>
> (I, 1323-1327)

Part One closes upon another question: which of the two, Palamon
or Arcite, "hath the worste." The answer is, of course, that neither has
"the worse" since both have equal woe. And another question is intimated: which of the two will eventually have "the best," which will
win the hand of Emelye, and what principle will determine the award.
It is once more the question debated by the *Parliament of Fowls*: which
of the tercel eagles will have the formel. That debate was never resolved;
this one is.

In Part Two it is clear that the lady is not to be awarded as a prize of
simple contest; bravery will have little to do with determining who
deserves the fair. For both lovers are equally brave and equally matched
in battle. The meeting between Palamon, now escaped from prison, and
the disguised Arcite is wonderfully funny, though the Knight relates it
with unwavering solemnity. The pledge of brotherhood, the obligations
of chivalry are maintained in the most literal way even as the two who
were once one are engaged in "mortal struggle. "I wol be deed, or elles
thou shalt dye;/ Thou shalt not love my lady Emelye" cries Palamon, as
he bursts out of the bushes upon the unsuspecting Arcite.

> This Arcite, with ful despitous herte,
> Whan he hym knew, and hadde his tale herd,
> As fiers as leon pulled out his swerd,
> And seyde thus: "By God that sit above,
> Nere it that thou art sik and wood for love,
> And eek that thow no wepne hast in this place,
> Thou sholdest nevere out of this grove pace,
> That thou ne sholdest dyen of myn hond.
>
> .   .   .   .
>
> But for as muche thou art a worthy knyght;
> And wilnest to darreyne hire by bataille,
> Have heer my trouthe, tomorwe I wol nat faille,
> Withoute wityng of any oother wight,

That heere I wol be founden as a knyght,
And bryngen harneys right ynough for thee;
And ches the beste, and leef the worste for me.
And mete and drynke this nyght wol I brynge
Ynough for thee, and clothes for thy beddynge."
(I, 1596-1600, 1608-1616)

Arcite is indeed an honorable man. Disguised as he is as a servant in
the court of Theseus, he is able to see to it that the escaped Palamon
is well armed for the battle. Back he returns carrying on his horse "al
the harneys hym biforn." And then

Ther nas no good day, ne no saluyng,
But streight, withouten word or rehersyng,
Everich of hem heelp for to armen oother
As freendly as he were his owene brother;
And after that, with sharpe speres stronge
They foynen ech at oother wonder longe.
(I, 1649-1654)

Upon this scene of bloody woe, for "up to the ancle foghte they in hir
blood," comes Duc Theseus "with hunte and horn and houndes hym
bisyde." And though he is willing to agree with Palamon that they "bothe
two" are deserving of death, this prince yields to the pleas of "alle the
ladyes in the compaignye," especially those of the queen and Emelye,
and proposes battle by tournament: ". . . aslaked was his mood/ For
pitee renneth soone in gentil herte" (I, 1760-1761). If there is to be a contest for a prize it will be a contest governed by rule and subject to
judgment and order. Theseus decrees

That ech of yow shal have his destynee
As hym is shape.
(I, 1842-1843)

Each knight is to go "frely, withouten raunson or daunger," far and wide
in search of a hundred knights apiece; in "fifty wykes" each is to return
"armed for lystes . . ./ Al redy to darreyne hire by bataille." Whichever of
the two slays "his contrarie" or drives him out of the "lystes"—"Thanne
shal I yeve Emelya to wyve." And the Second Part that had begun in woe
and lament ends in joy:

Who looketh lightly now but Palamoun?
Who spryngeth up for joye but Arcite?

> Who kouthe telle, or who kouthe it endite,
> The joye that is maked in the place
> Whan Theseus hath doon so fair a grace?
> But doun on knees wente every maner wight,
> And thonked hym with al hir herte and myght,
> And namely the Thebans often sithe.
> And thus with good hope and with herte blithe
> They taken hir leve, and homward gonne they ride
> To Thebes, with his olde walles wyde.
>
> (I, 1870-1880)

The Knight, the symbol of Order, rejoices in the restoration of order, in the establishment of rule for the controlling of chaos.

The first suggestion that the simple principle of victory in battle is not to be the principle by which Emelye is won comes in Part III. To the temples erected in "noble theatre" that Theseus has built for the tournament, come the three, Palamon, Arcite, and Emelye, one by one. Each prays to a different god and in so doing raises another question: whose prayer will be answered and by what principle? There is to be, clearly, something other than "might is right" to be brought to bear upon the outcome. From the Knight's recital of the prayers it is apparent that though his heart is probably with the "warrior" Arcite in his prayer to Mars, his sense of the way things should be in a tale of Courtly Love tells him that the reward must go to Palamon, the supplicant to Venus. Love, in short, is to win out. But basic to this principle is one even more vital and essential, the principle of Distributive Justice: as each prays so each receives, as each asks so each is given. Or to put it in another way, each character gets exactly what he or she deserves.

Palamon, the first to love Emelye, proves his worthiness to have been the first the minute he goes into the temple of Venus to prepare himself for the coming battle with Arcite:

> The Sonday nyght, er day bigan to sprynge,
> Whan Palamon the larke herde synge
> (Although it nere nat day by houres two
> Yet song the larke) and Palamon right tho
> With hooly herte and with an heigh corage,
> He roos to wenden on his pilgrymage
> Unto the blisful Citherea benigne,—
> I mene Venus, honourable and digne.
>
> (I, 2209-2216)

In words of gentle humility and reverence he makes his request, revealing the exact degree to which he is the very model of a courtly lover:

> "Faireste fo faire, O lady myn, Venus,
> Doughter to Jove, and spouse of Vulcanus,
> Thow gladere of the mount of Citheron,
> For thilke love thow haddest to Adoon,
> Have pitee of my bittre teeris smerte,
> And taak myn humble preyere at thyn herte.
> (I, 2221-2226)

Promising always to be her "trewe servant/ And holden werre alwey with chastitee," he asks not for victory in the battle, nor fame, nor "veyne glorie/ Of pris of armes blowen up and doun":

> "But I wolde have fully possessioun
> Of Emelye, and dye in thy servyse."
> (I, 2242-2243)

Of her power over Mars he has no doubt, and if she grants him his love,

> "Thy temple wol I worshipe everemo,
> And on thyn auter, where I ride or go,
> I wol doon sacrifice and fires beete."
> (I, 2251-2253)

But if it is not to be, then he asks for death: "This is th'effect and ende of my preyere:/ Yif me my love, thow blisful lady deere" (I, 2259-2260).

Arcite, alas, can have little chance in a contest of love, for he prays to Mars: "I moot with strengthe wynne hire in the place/ . . . Thanne help me, lord, tomorwe in my bataille . . . and do that I . . . have victorie" (I, 2399-2405). By the time his prayer is over it sounds suspiciously as if he wants the victory even more than he wants Emily. And she, Emelye "the shene," whose prayer has been to Diana, has no wish except to be allowed to live in chastity, though aware that it cannot be:

> . . . if my destynee be shapen so
> That I shal nedes have oon of hem two,
> As sende me hym that moost desireth me.
> (I, 2323-2325)

And although each god manifests a favorable answer to each prayer, "destynee" seems more and more clearly to be pointing in the direction of Palamon.

In Part Four the Knight answers all the questions he has raised in his tale. Under the rule of Order the battle is fought; the two "worthy knights" are tested. To each contestant comes the answer to his prayer: Palamon loses the battle that Arcite wins; but Arcite loses his life and his lady; and Emelye is awarded to the one who loves "her moost." It is not merely that Love wins even among the gods, but that Justice does. As Arcite laments in his farewell speech that gives to Palamon the lady they have fought over:

> "What is this world? What asketh men to have?
> Now with his love, now in his colde grave
> Allone, withouten any compaignye."
>
> (I, 2777-2779)

But no woe is permanent, and all misfortune is ultimately good fortune; though both worthy knights have suffered both are made "blisful" at the end: Arcite is released from "this foule prisoun . . . lyf" and

> . . . with alle blisse and melodye
> Hath Palamon ywedded Emelye.
> And God, that al this wyde world hath wroght,
> Sende hym his love that hath it deere aboght;
> For now is Palamon in alle wele,
> Lyvynge in blisse, in richesse, and in heele,
> And Emelye hym loveth so tendrely
> And he hire serveth al so gentilly,
> That nevere was ther no word hem bitwene
> Of jalousie or any oother teene.
>
> (I, 3097-3106)

Thus Chaucer in setting *The Knight's Tale* before all the other tales of the Canterbury pilgrims makes a clear statement about the nature of human existence that is to be taken seriously, as the Knight is taken seriously by all the pilgrims. It is without any doubt a statement that is thoroughly optimistic, completely cheerful in essence. That it is made in what is really an oversimplified way, and in a way that is comic, in no way detracts from the seriousness at its heart.

For this tale of the two "gentil knyghtes," the "faire Emelye," and the magnanimous "Duc," is at every moment, even its most woeful, wonderfully provocative of laughter. If it was not explicitly clear that the Knight is to be taken in the way the observer, Chaucer, has described him in the *General Prologue*, it would be tempting to see in the course of his tale something close to a "spoof" on the courtly romances so popular in the middle ages. But the Knight is no satirist, no literary critic, or if he is, Chaucer is playing an unfair joke on pilgrims and readers.

Nor is he a figure of ridicule. He is a certain kind of person who invites respect from his fellow pilgrims and at the same time, amused affection from Chaucer's readers. He is a pilgrim among the pilgrims, and although a "worthy man," he is in no sense idealized; and he tells a tale in a way that clearly indicates his limitations, revealing simplifications about Human Nature and Reality that Chaucer, even in his earliest poems, never conceded to. What is funny about *The Knight's Tale* depends not on its absurdities, but rather upon what those absurdities tell us about the teller, who thus assumes in clearer detail the distinct personality outlined in his portrait. His tale, by its simplifications, does not so much make literal use of the Boethian philosophy as it skeletalizes it. It states thematically in an uncomplex way what is to be the essential vision of life in all its diversity revealed in the rest of *The Canterbury Tales*, until at the end the Parson once more outlines it in his own simple way.

The limitations in the Knight's view of actuality are obvious. He is a sentimentalist through and through, old-fashioned in his ideals of chivalry, uninterested in, certainly uncurious about the complex motives or the conflicts of human beings. As Order characterizes his universe, rule governs its inhabitants. There are rules for everything: rules for brotherhood, rules for battle, rules for the game of love, and even rules for sorrow. Reality is made up of prescribed attitudes, of formulas that his characters follow with a literalness that is simple and exact. So Theseus, who can kill and pillage with the rest of his warriors, is gentle and mild to the "ladyes"; so Arcite sees to it that Palamon has the best armor for their combat; so Emelye, so reluctant to wed in the first place, wails aloud at the death of Arcite, along with all the rest of the city of Thebes:

> Shrighte Emelye, and howleth Palamon,
> And Theseus his suster took anon
> Swownynge, and baar hire fro the corps away.
> What helpeth it to tarien forth the day
> To tellen how she weep bothe eve and morwe?
> For in swich cas wommen have swich sorwe.
>
> .   .   .   .
>
> Infinite been the sorwes and the teeres
> Of olde folk, and folk of tendre yeeres,
> In al the toun for deeth of this Theban,
> For hym ther wepeth bothe child and man.
>
> (I, 2817-2822, 2827-2830)

And Arcite, dead, "as was that tyme the gyse," is burned to "asshen colde," his funeral held in all the proper pomp, his Emelye, making "vertu of necessitee," as willing to take Palamon as she had been to take him.

Nor has he any more skill in handling the complex problems of narration than he has in creating the complexities of his characters. Except for the moment when experience gives him suddenly notable articulateness in his account of the feast and the preparation before the tournament, he is awkward and graceless in style, given to statements about what he will relate next, apt to leave characters in suspended motion, totally unaware of the logic of time. And his characters, though clearly enough distinguished one from the other, speak all alike, and all of them seem, with the exception of Emelye, but projections of himself: worthy, wise, and prudent. Humorless and kind, motivated by the best of values—"trouthe, honour, knyghthede,/ Wysdom, humblesse, estaat, and heigh kynrede,/ Fredom, and al that longeth to that art"—the Knight voices the simple conclusion that for all its cliché quality is fundamentally the conclusion of *The Canterbury Tales,* a conclusion that is elaborated upon in more detail by the Parson at the end—a conclusion that is a cheerful one in spite of its reference to "wo":

> This world nys but a thurghfare ful of wo,
> And we been pilgrymes, passynge to and fro.
> (I, 2847-2848)

THE MILLER'S TALE

The Miller's Tale is also about love and it is also about justice exactly distributed; it does indeed "quite the Knyghtes tale." What the Host has wanted from the Monk when he turns to him as the next narrator after the Knight is a happy tale to match a happy tale, for his joy in the "game" well begun and his vision of the "bagful" of tales still to be told fills him with confidence and assurance. What he gets from the Miller, instead, is a tale that more than realizes his request. The story of the carpenter and his wife, of "hende Nicholas" and Absolon, her lovers, is richly comic in its own right. It is also comic in its relation to *The Knight's Tale,* not simply because in many ways it parodies the romance, but more importantly, because its vulgar and lusty view of "love" and "justice" makes the Knight's views in retrospect less incredibly idealized, less impossibly sentimentalized. Together, in exact juxtaposition, *The Miller's Tale* and *The Knight's Tale* present a more probable "whole" of Reality than either alone suggests, much as the disparate views of love revealed by the royal and the common birds in *The Parliament of Fowls* worked together. And, finally, because it is a tale that infuriates the Reeve, a carpenter in his spare time, it arouses the first dramatic contention among the pilgrims, thus making dynamic the "game" the Host had so genially proposed.

From the moment the Host utters the word "quite," he generates a potential for narration that he is not yet aware of. The whole first fragment, from the tale told by the Knight to the last word of the unfinished *Cook's Tale*, is dominated by the quiting concept that makes the pilgrimage tense with hostilities barely held in check. "Stynt thy clappe!/ Lat be thy lewed dronken harlotrye," cries the Reeve. But he holds in abeyance the full blast of his rage until the tale of the Miller is done, his malice ripening all the time. Permitted to retaliate with his own tale, he, too, announces the intention of "quiting"—meaning, obviously, not "matching," but "out-matching":

> "Now, sires," quod this Osewold the Reve,
> "I pray yow alle that ye nat yow greve,
> Thogh I answere, and somdeel sette his howve;
> For leveful is with force force of-showve.
>   This dronken Millere hath ytoold us heer
> How that bigyled was a carpenteer,
> Peraventure in scorn, for I am oon.
> And, by youre leve, I shal hym quite anoon;
> Right in his cherles termes wol I speke.
> I pray to God his nekke mote to-breke."
>   (I, 3909-3918)

And the Cook, at the end of *The Reeve's Tale*, picks up the word when, peeved by the Host's explicit attack on the filth in his shop, he bristles:

> "And therfore, Herry Bailly, by thy feith,
> Be thou nat wrooth, er we departen heer,
> Though that my tale be of an hostileer.
> But nathelees I wol nat telle it yit;
> But er we parte, ywis, thou shalt be quit."
>   (I, 4358-4362)

Thus, in all its possible meanings, the word "quite" is the keyword for the tales of the first fragment, uniting them dramatically, qualifying the nature of "the game" they are a part of, and joining them together as explorations of a common subject: justice, distributive and retributive.

The Miller's Tale depends for its comedy upon the exactness of the distribution of justice. The laughter that openly greets this tale is aroused, of course, by its wonderful high jinks. But the comic joy that is too deep for laughter, that generates more and more relish the more it is contemplated, comes because our wishful thinking that we live in a world of justice and order is hilariously encouraged.

To define "justice" in *The Miller's Table* is to define its comedy. In unambiguous and unequivocal terms this tale reveals that as you reap so shall you sow, as you do so shall you be done unto, as you pretend so shall you be fooled, as you deserve so shall you get. In short, the Miller's world is in essence the same world as the Knight's; its differences are accidents only. If the obvious parody of the courtly love situation of the "noble tale" points up anything, it points up this. Love in the one instance may be something of the spirit, and in the other something of the flesh, but in both instances it is contained in an ordered and just universe that punishes and rewards in ways that are not determined by human law but in ways that are, in a manner of speaking, supra-ethical, supra-societal, supra-legal.

There are four important characters in *The Miller's Tale* as there had been in the Knight's, and, in exact ways, each is clearly the opposite: the carpenter is foolish as Theseus had been wise; Nicholas and Absolon are full of treachery and open malice as Palamon and Arcite had been full of brotherly loyalty and chivalric rivalry; and Alisoun is all animal as Emelye had been all gentlewoman. The Miller, whose experience in life has been with people like those in his tale, is a far more skillful narrator than is the Knight, whose art of relating is as rusty as his armor. A natural raconteur, his "cherles tale" tells of people whose motivations are recognizable, and whose characters produce their own destiny and bring about their own punishment.

The carpenter is a "riche gnof" who has married an eighteen-year-old wife. And though he loved her "more than life," his jealousy was so great he "heeld hire narwe in cage,/ For she was wylde and yong, and he was old,/ And demed hymself been like a cokewold" (I, 3224-3226). Had he been a man of learning, says the Miller, he would have known his "Catoun," who had long ago pointed out that youth and age are "at debaat" and that marriage between those so disparate in age is bound to be disastrous. The tale that follows proves how right both predictions are.

In addition to being old and jealous, the carpenter is also "sely"—a significant word in Chaucer. It means "innocent" and "foolish"; it also means "hapless" and "gullible," and at times, "happy" and "fortunate." This carpenter is a perfect prey for the shrewd wit of his boarder, the clerk "hende Nicholas," for like most men of little learning he has unquestioning reverence for what is in Nicholas' head. Fool that he is, he accepts Nicholas' assertion that he is to be singled out by God as a second Noah, and he sets to work to follow out Nicholas' instructions, that are, after all, "divinely inspired":

> "But whan thou hast, for hire and thee and me,
> Ygeten us thise knedyng tubbes thre,

> Thanne shaltow hange hem in the roof ful hye,
> That no man of oure purveiaunce spye.
> And whan thou thus hast doon, as I have seyd,
> And hast oure vitaille faire in hem yleyd,
> And eek an ax, to smyte the cord atwo,
> Whan that the water comth, that we may go,
> And breke an hole an heigh, upon the gable,
> Unto the gardyn-ward, over the stable,
> That we may frely passen forth oure way,
> Whan that the grete shour is goon away,
> Thanne shaltou swymme as myrie, I undertake,
> As dooth the white doke after hire drake."
>   (I, 3563-3576)

Because he is naïve and presumptuous, jealous and old, he carries out the instructions to the last letter and to his own total exhaustion. And because he is so literal in the carrying out of the instructions, he brings about his own punishment, an ignominious collapse of the whole fantastic contraption and the consequent public delight at his stupidity. At the agonized outcry of Nicholas, whose own punishment is being painfully administered, the old "sely" man

> . . . out of his slomber sterte,
> And herde oon crien "water" as he were wood,
> And thoughte, "Allas, now comth Nowelis flood!"
> He sit hym up withouten wordes mo,
> And with his ax he smoot the corde atwo,
> And doun gooth al.
>   (I, 3816-3821)

His cuckolding has been accomplished and his foolishness has brought its own punishment.

The nature of the carpenter makes possible the conditions for his downfall and circumstances of the action of the comedy. Nicholas, his wily boarder, gentle, courteous, lecherous, sly, initiates the action and suffers, appropriately, the most painful physical punishment in consequence. His intentions toward Alisoun, the young wife, are frankly and openly lecherous; his first approach to her is physical, his plan for the fooling of the old husband is motivated by lust, and his punishment is, fittingly, given him in the exact spot on his body where his "lust" is most in evidence: "The hoote kultour brende so his toute,/ And for the smert he wende for to dye./ As he were wood, for wo he gan to crye,/ 'Help! water! water! help, for Goddes herte!' " (I, 3812-3815).

Absolon, who has been the one to administer the punishment to Nicholas, the one who has applied "the hoote kultour" and who is thus his own avenger, has also been made to pay for his own foolishness, has likewise come in for a share of "poetic justice." His crime has been not lechery, but pretension and vanity. Of all the characters in the tale, Absolon is the most clearly drawn. And rightly so, for in his appearance lurks his downfall. Gay, self-consciously elegant, somewhat effeminate, pretentiously delicate in array and manners, he presumed to be a "lady's man":

> Crul was his heer, and as the gold it shoon,
> And strouted as a fanne large and brode;
> Ful streight and evene lay his joly shode.
> His rode was reed, his eyen greye as goos.
> With Poules wyndow corven on his shoos,
> In hoses rede he wente fetisly.
> Yclad he was ful smal and proprely
> Al in a kirtel of a lyght waget;
> Ful faire and thikke been the poyntes set.
> And therupon he hadde a gay surplys
> As whit as is the blosme upon the rys.
> A myrie child he was, so God me save.
> (I, 3314-3325)

This "myrie child," with his self-image of elegant bourgeoiserie, considers himself in every way far above the villagers and their two most evident crudities, farting and swearing, for, says the Miller with what must have been anticipatory glee:

> . . . sooth to seyn, he was somdeel squaymous
> Of fartyng, and of speche daungerous.
> (I, 3337-3338)

This parish clerk sets out to woo Alisoun with all the manners of a courtly lover, village style, and prepares for himself his own downfall. The parodies of the convention are obvious: he serenades her at her window, he sends her messages, he gives her gifts of spiced wine, of mead, of ale, and of "wafres, pipyng hoot out of the gleede." But all is in vain; the "faire Emelye" may have no favorite, but Alisoun has:

> She loveth so this hende Nicholas
> That Absolon may blowe the bukkes horn;
> He ne hadde for his labour but a scorn.
> (I, 3386-3388)

There is no discouraging Absolon, however; his pretensions as a courtly lover are inherent in his vanity. The relish with which the Miller describes Absolon's elaborate preparations for winning a kiss from Alisoun regardless of her scorn warns us that some climax is near, that some punishment of the proper sort lies in store, for such aspirations to gentility must not be allowed to go unmocked. "This Absolon, ful joly . . . and light," aware that the carpenter is not around (though not aware, of course, of the exhausting occupation of the old man in his endeavor to erect the tubs and carry out Nicholas' plans), promises himself at least one kiss as reward for his faithfulness as a lover. "Up rist" Absolon, says the Miller

> And hym arraieth gay, at poynt-devys.
> But first he cheweth greyn and lycorys,
> To smellen sweete, er he hadde kembd his heer.
> Under his tonge a trewe-love he beer,
> For therby wende he to ben gracious.
> (I, 3688-3693)

And in echoes of the Song of Songs, this delicate and "somdeel squaymous" village lover serenades his "sweete Alisoun":

> "My faire bryd, my sweete cynamome
> Awaketh, lemman myn, and speketh to me!
> Wel litel thynken ye upon my wo,
> That for youre love I swete ther I go.
> No wonder is thogh that I swelte and swete;
> I moorne as dooth a lamb after the tete.
> Ywis, lemman, I have swich love-longynge,
> That lik a turtel trewe is my moornynge.
> I may nat ete na moore than a mayde."
> (I, 3699-3707)

What happens to Absolon happens to him fittingly: his mouth, the index to his vanity, is subject to punishment most vulgarly for its absurd pretensions. And fittingly, his enraged delicacy precipitates its own vulgar revenge, and starts the chain of punishments that reach a climax in the hullabaloo attending the collapse of the carpenter and his tubs.

The character of Alisoun, though sketched with vitality, is not more than a sketch. Though "sikerly she hadde a likerous ye," she is, in a manner of speaking, more sinned against than sinning. Justice is meted out to her, but in so slight a measure that she can be said to have hardly suffered punishment at all. The Miller makes clear his own attitude toward her in the terms he uses to describe her, terms that are both delicate and sensuous.

> Fair was this yonge wyf, and therwithal
> As any wezele hir body gent and smal.
> A ceynt she werede, barred al of silk,
> A barmclooth eek as whit as morne milk
> Upon hir lendes, ful of many a goore.
>
> .   .   .   .
>
> She was ful moore blisful on to see
> Than is the newe pere-jonette tree.
> And softer than the wolle is of a wether.
>
> .   .   .   .
>
> Ful brighter was the shynyng of hir hewe
> Than in the Tour the noble yforged newe.
> But of hir song, it was as loude and yerne
> As any swalwe sittynge on a berne.
> Therto she koude skippe and make game,
> As any kyde or calf folwynge his dame.
> Her mouth was sweete as bragot or the meeth,
> Or hoord of apples leyd in hey or heeth.
> Wynsynge she was, as is a joly colt,
> Long as a mast, and upright as a bolt.
>
> .   .   .   .
>
> She was a prymerole, a piggesnye,
> For any lord to leggen in his bedde,
> Or yet for any good yeman to wedde.
>
>   (I, 3233-3237; 3247-3249; 3255-3264; 3268-3270)

This "yonge wyf" is no more subject to moral judgment or social criticism than is the weasel, or the early pear tree, or the new-born lamb, or the swallow, or the calf, or the apples, or the trillium. Free of pretensions of any sort, Alisoun lives simply according to her nature. Caught in the midst of the chain of disasters that befall her husband and her two lovers, she maintains her position by simply letting circumstances run their course. Her "tee-hee" as she "clapped the window to" and set Absolon on his way to revenge is her only important comment on all that happens. Jealousy has been punished, pretensions have been uncovered, the trickster has been caught in his own trick, punishment has been made precisely to fit the crime, and the joyous cavorting of the village at the end of the tale signifies the restoration of disorder to order, the exposure of the private defiance of public good to the eyes of all:

The folk gan laughen at his fantasye;
Into the roof they kiken and they cape,
And turned al his harm unto a jape.
For what so that this carpenter answerde,
It was for noght, no man his reson herde.

(I, 3840-3844)

THE REEVE'S TALE

The comedy in the *Reeve's Prologue and Tale,* because it follows upon *The Miller's Tale* and is created by the Reeve's enraged and paranoic response, is the most complex of the first fragment of *The Canterbury Tales.* There is comedy in the portrayal of the Reeve, for he is the first of the pilgrims to emerge in any degree of dimensionality before he tells a tale. There is riotous farce in the tale itself. And there is the suggestion of a "quiting" that is more than successful in the portrait the Reeve gives of Robin, the Miller—for the miller of the tale does indeed suffer for his own foolish pride.

In his conception of the Reeve, Chaucer for the first time elaborates upon a portrait in the *General Prologue,* making full use of all the suggestions there for the comedy of the stereotype. A "sclendre colerik man," sharp in the governing of his lord's manor, taciturn, asocial, hated by those he has to oversee, he is fated by Medieval Physiology to dyspeptic malice and to paranoia; and by the Medieval Theory of Contraries, he is fated to hate the vigorous and sanguine Miller. In their imbalance his bodily humors have made his temperament; his temperament makes it certain that he will feel a personal as well as a professional slight in the Miller's portrayal of the old carpenter and his "yonge, wilde wyf." And as a bailiff, well aware of the professional slyness of millers in general, he is ready to retaliate as soon as he can. As carpenter and bailiff, as one choleric by nature, "Osewold" the Reeve, even before he tells his tale, has great potential for comedy.

The Reeve is also old and thus belongs to an ancient tradition of comedy. As an old man he is not, however, made the butt of the joke, nor is he made a fool of, nor is his anger against the Miller merely the vitriol of age. Although he makes somewhat of a spectacle of himself, he contains his rage in a tale of brilliant comedy that quits the Miller without awakening anyone's displeasure or resentment. And as a character he is richly comic in the way he reveals himself to be always asserting and maintaining his balance, his equilibrium in the face of all of life's threats. The Reeve is the first of the portraits to come alive to the exact degree he shows himself to be "at war" with himself and with the world.

Old age and its deprivations are not something new for the Reeve. He has never really been young, for even from his cradle he has lacked vitality. Indeed his petulance and his irascibility have been his surest ways to assert life. Self-pity and whining peevishness are in everything he says in the prologue to his tale, but the relish with which he whines affirms a kind of denial of despair. The images he sees himself in are images of life and of living things whose very condition for life and maturity lies in their imminent decay, even in their rottenness:

> "So theek," quod he, "ful wel koude I thee quite
> With bleryng of a proud milleres ye,
> If that me liste speke of ribaudye.
> But ik am oold, me list not pley for age;
> Gras tyme is doon, my fodder is now forage;
> This white top writeth myne olde yeris;
> Myn herte is also mowled as myne heris,
> But if I fare as dooth an open-ers,—
> That ilke fruyt is ever the lenger the wers,
> Til it be roten in mullok or in stree.
> We olde men, I drede, so fare we:
> Til we be roten, kan we nat be rype;
> We hoppen alwey whil the world wol pype.
> For in our wyl ther stiketh evere a nayl,
> To have an hoor heed and a grene tayl,
> As hath a leek; for though oure myghte be goon
> Oure wyl desireth folie evere in oon.
> For whan we may nat doon, than wol we speke;
> Yet in oure asshen olde is fyr yreke."
>   (I, 3864-3882)

In his ill-tempered way he is obsessed with life and with the sexual power that he never seems to have had much of:

> "Foure gleedes han we, which I shal devyse,—
> Avauntyng, liyng, anger, coveitise;
> Thise foure sparkles longen unto eelde.
> Oure olde lemes mowe wel been unweelde,
> But wyl ne shal nat faillen, that is sooth.
> And yet ik have alwey a coltes tooth,
> As many a yeer as it is passed henne
> Syn that my tappe of lif bigan to renne.
> For sikerly, whan I was bore, anon
> Deeth drough the tappe of lyf and leet it gon;
> And ever sithe hath so the tappe yronne
> Til that almoost al empty is the tonne.

The streem of lyf now droppeth on the chymbe.
The sely tonge may wel rynge and chymbe
Of wrecchednesse that passed is ful yoore;
With olde folk, save dotage, is namoore!"
(I, 3883-3898)

And yet, the tale this old and impotent man tells burst with vitality. It is a fabliau depending for its action upon sexual trickery, full of noise and bustle and nervous energy, its narrator revealing an ear for dialogue and a sense of narrative pace that makes it more vigorously comic than the fabliau told by the far more virile Miller.

The Reeve's Tale is also about "justice," but about "retributive" rather than "distributive" justice. As the clerk Allen says, "ther is a lawe that says thus,/ That gif a man in a point be agreved,/ That in another he sal be releved" (I, 4180-4181). And the clerk, like his creator, the Reeve, also "will have esement,/ By Goddes sale, it sal neen other bee!" (I, 4186-4187).

With elaborate care the Reeve draws his portrait of the miller who is to be the object of the joke of the tale. We cannot know how closely Symkyn resembles Robin, the pilgrim, but it is clear that he is the Reeve's idea of the Miller who has so enraged him. Of the whole tale of some four hundred lines, almost seventy-five are descriptive of Symkyn and his pride:

As any pecok he was proud and gay,
Pipen he koude and fisshe, and nettes beete,
And turne coppes, and wel wrastle and sheete;
Ay by his belt he baar a long panade,
And of a swerd ful trenchant was the blade.
(I, 3926-3930)

Three things make him vain: his strength—"Ther was no man, for peril, dorste hym touche"; his skill at cheating his customers—"A theef he was for soothe of corn and mele,/ And that a sly, and usuant for to stele"; and pride in his wife's birth, for she was the illegitimate daughter of the village priest, and thus indeed nobly connected and properly educated:

A wyf he hadde, ycomen of noble kyn;
The person of the toun hir fader was,
With hire he yaf ful many a panne of bras,
For that Symkyn sholde in his blood allye.
She was yfostred in a nonnerye;
For Symkyn wolde no wyf, as he sayde,

> For she were wel ynorissed and a mayde,
> To saven his estaat of yomanrye.
> And she was proud, and peert as is a pye.
> (I, 3943-3950)

These two haughty and vainglorious people have two children, a daughter "of twenty yeer," and a son "in cradel . . . a propre page." The daughter, however, is the heir of all Symkyn's pride: "thikke and wel ygrowen . . ./ With kamus nose, and eyen greye as glas,/ With buttokes brode, and brestes rounde and hye;/ But right faire was hire heer; I wol nat lye" says the Reeve, and in his shrill and nasal voice recounts with joy how Symkyn's pride in his slyness brings his pride in his brawn, in his wife's fine birth, and in his daughter's inheritance to woeful disaster. Symkyn, the "deynous," gets exactly what he deserves with compound interest.

From the moment he turns his thieving sharpness to tricking the ill manciple of the "Soler Halle at Cantebregge" by stealing from the two clerks, Aleyn and John, who have come to represent the manciple, he is in for trouble. Absolutely confident in his own superior ingenuity, he gets rid of the watchful and suspicious clerks by untying their horse, steals enough grain to hide in baking a loaf of bread, and in turn has his wife and daughter "swyved," his loaf taken, his body and head battered and beaten, and sees the clerks go off scot-free. The Reeve's relish in recounting his swiftly moving tale is wonderful to hear. He knows exactly how to convey the confusion, the chaotic hubbub, the sharp interchange of noise and action of crucial scenes. His nasal twang rings out shrilly as he tells of the pursuit of the horse; his Norfolk accents are brittle and sharp as they convey the glee he feels as he nears the climax of his tale that will so thoroughly "quite" the Miller from the south.

> This John goth out and fynt his hors away,
> And gan to crie, "Harrow!" and "Weylaway!
> Oure hors is lorn, Alayn, for Goddes banes,
> Step on thy feet! Com of, man, al atanes!
> Allas, our wardeyn has his palfrey lorn."
> This Aleyn al forgat, bothe mele and corn;
> Al was out of his mynde his housbondrie.
> "What, whilk way is he geen?" he gan to crie.
> The wyf cam lepynge inward with a ren.
> She seyde, "Allas! youre hors goth to the fen
> With wilde mares, as faste as he may go."
>
> .   .   .   .
>
> Thise sely clerkes rennen up and doun

With "Keep! keep! stand! stand! jossa, warderere,
Ga whistle thou, and I shal kepe hym heere!"
But shortly, til that it was verray nyght,
They koude nat, though they dide al hir myght,
Hir capul cacche, he ran alwey so faste,
Til in a dych they caughte hym atte laste.
                (I, 4071-4081; 4100- 4106)

His tale and its complications find resolution in a riotous scene in the best tradition of farce, in a wild and furious interchange of blows. The nervous clarity with which the Reeve describes the scene conveys, even acts out, the full vigor of his own rage at the Miller on the pilgrimage:

. . . By the throte-bolle he caughte Alayn,
And he hente hym despitously agayn,
And on the nose he smoot hym with his fest.
Doun ran the blody streem upon his brest;
And in the floor, with nose and mouth tobroke,
They walwe as doon two pigges in a poke;
And up they goon, and doun agayn anon,
Til that the millere sporned at a stoon,
And doun he fil bakward upon his wyf.

        .   .   .   .

    This John stirte up as faste as ever he myghte,
And graspeth by the walles to and fro,
To fynde a staf; and she stirte up also,
And knew the estres bet than dide this John,
And by the wal a staf she foond anon,
And saugh a litel shymeryng of a light,
For at an hole in shoon the moone bright;
And by that light she saugh hem bothe two,
But sikerly she nyste who was who,
But as she saugh a whit thyng in her ye.
And whan she gan this white thyng espye,
She wende the clerk hadde wered a volupeer,
And with the staf she drow ay neer and neer,
And wende han hit this Aleyn at the fulle,
And smoot the millere on the pyled skulle,
That doun he gooth, and cride, "Harrow! I dye!"
                (I, 4273-4281; 4292-4307)

The Reeve's satisfaction in his "moral" and in the way his tale has illustrated his concept of justice gives his final lines something of a tone

of fatigue as if the personal venom had been exhausted in the telling
of the tale, and his spleen had suddenly subsided:

> Lo, swich it is a millere to be fals!
> And therfore this proverbe is seyd ful sooth,
> "Hym thar nat wene wel that yvele dooth;
> A gylour shal hymself bigyled be."
> And God, that sitteth heighe in magestee,
> Save al this compaignye, grete and smale!
> Thus have I quyt the Millere in my tale.
> (I, 4318-4324)

Though he has made the miller suffer for his blindness, a blindness
inevitable in all egocentric and proud people, though he has directed
all his irony to the miller's blindness, it is really his excitement in the
"brainy opportunism" of the two clerks, amoral though they may be,
that makes of this tale a gay and brilliant comedy. For what might have
been a bitter and even a cynical attack becomes, before it is over, a tale
exuberant in its celebration of the triumph of right over might, even
though that "right" is simply the cause of those who have been wronged.
"Ha! ha! . . . for Cristes passion," says the Cook in his glee at the end
of the tale: "This millere hadde a sharp conclusion/ Upon his argument
of herbergage!" And within the tale itself, the words of John that echo
the words of Theseus at the end of *The Knight's Tale* point up the
"moral" of this tale:

> "Now, Symond," seyde John, "by seint Cutberd,
> Ay is thou myrie, and this is faire answerd.
> I have herd seyd, 'man sal taa of twa thynges
> Slyk as he fyndes, or taa slyk as he brynges,'"
> (I, 4127-4130)

To make a "vertu of necessitee' and make "of sorwes two/ O parfit joye,
lastynge everemo" begins to seem to be a philosophy of life, a guide to
the conduct of existence in the midst of the hostilities of self and the
world, that is common to the pilgrims. At least, it is one rule by which
one can "play the game" and hope for a win; it is a conclusion that
helps to give the strength to hang on to the turning wheel of Fortune.
And always encompassing the turns of the wheel—the interrelations of
people and of things—there is a concept of Justice that will be brought
into materialization by the actors themselves.

chapteR 4

COMEDY IN THE TALES
LARGELY RELIGIOUS AND MORAL

The Man of Law's Tale that follows upon the tales of the first fragment, is told in compliance with the Host's invitation and is generated by no contention with any pilgrim. Nor does Chaucer indicate that it arouses any response from anyone. It is, in a sense, isolated from the vital give-and-take, from the attack and counterattack that surround it. Three other tales, *The Physician's, The Second Nun's,* and *The Prioress',* are similarly isolated, narrated simply as part of fulfilling the rules of the Host's game. Therefore, it seems possible to remove them from their respective fragments and to examine them together. All four are important for the general definition of Chaucer's comedy, and each in its own way is significant for the understanding of how diverse its particulars are.

In the simplest of ways the four tales are comic: they have to do with the rewarding of suffering or of endurance; they are, in other words, concerned with justice that is divine, with happiness that is won, whether in heaven or on earth, after trial. If "this world nys but a thurghfare ful of wo" and the turning of Fortune's Wheel will cast us into suffering as often as it gives us joy, there is, at least, happiness in the promise that "Deeth is the ende of every worldly soore," or in the hope that he who hangs on long enough to the turning Wheel will ultimately arrive at some enduring moments of "blysse."

Of the four tales, that of the Second Nun is the most obvious and the plainest in intent, though what kind of person its teller was is not clear. Indeed, there is even some doubt about whether Chaucer intended to assign the tale to the Prioress' companion, since the teller speaks of herself, or himself, as "unworthy sone of Eve." Both the prologue and the tale do, however, sketch out a character with enough suggestion of inner conflict to make her sufficiently vital to be included among the more boldly and fully drawn pilgrims. She is a simple woman, somewhat preoccupied with the "sin of ydelnesse," though the thematic connection with the Saint's Legend she relates is not at all intimate. True, she has "doon [her] feithful bisynesse" to make a translation of the Legend "Right of thy glorious lif and passioun,/ Thou with thy gerland wroght with rose and lylie,—/ Thee meene I, mayde and martyr, Seint Cecile," and has thus put from her "ydelnesse,/ That cause is of so greet confusioun" (VIII, 22-28). But the theme of idleness, a variant on the subject of Accidia, has no place in the recounting almost word for word of the details pious tradition had attached to the person of Saint Cecilia. And so we are no closer to knowing the kind of figure Chaucer really intended his "Second Nun" to be than we were. In the simplest way, the tale illustrates that perseverance in faith and the enduring of pain upon earth will be rewarded with happiness in heaven. In what ways more complex than this Chaucer might have planned to make this teller and her tale more intimately a part of his comedy, we shall never know.

The Physician's Tale offers more of interest. Although its theme, the preservation of "holy chastity" at the cost of life, makes it akin to hundreds of similar tales so popular in the Middle Ages, its emphasis on punishment, on retributive justice, makes it more significantly a revelation of Chaucer's comic thesis. The whole tale illustrates not so much that virtue is its own reward, but that vice will be punished. The retribution that descends upon the wicked judge, Apius, and upon the "fals cherl," Claudius, is sudden and terrible. The people, horrified at the arrest of Virginius who has killed his daughter, Virginia, to preserve her holy purity, thrust the two wicked men into prison:

> Ther as [Apius] slow hymself; and Claudius,
> That servant was unto this Apius,
> Was demed for to hange upon a tree,
> But that Virginius, of his pitee,
> So preyde for hym that he was exiled;
> And elles, certes, he had been bigyled.
> The remenant were anhanged, moore and lesse,
> That were consentant of this cursednesse.
>   (VI, 268-276)

The tale ends upon a note of warning: "Heere may men seen how synne hath his merite./ Beth war, for no man woot whom God wol smyte" (VI, 277-278), for the justice of God is sure and inevitable, at times violently retributive. The Host sees the point clearly:

> Oure Hooste gan to swere as he were wood;
> "Harrow!" quod he, "by nayles and by blood!
> This was a fals cherl and a fals justise.
> As shameful deeth as herte may devyse
> Come to thise juges and hire advocatz!
> Algate this sely mayde is slayn, allas!"
>   (VI, 287-292)

There has been some questioning about the attribution of this tale of
Virginia and Virginius. The Physician is as likely a narrator as not, and
for the purpose of this study any argument for or any argument against
his "fitness" as the teller is not relevant. It is clear that Chaucer meant
to characterize someone, for the tale, unlike that given to the Second
Nun, is no translation of a legend. Chaucer's teller attributes the tale to
"Titus Livius" and critics have pointed out the indebtedness to a section
in *The Roman de la Rose*. But the tale is apparently Chaucer's own
concoction, worked out to suggest certain qualities of a pilgrim, qualities
that are not hard to arrive at but that do not really hint at how they
were to function comically in the whole plan. The Physician of the
General Prologue has been seen by the observer, Chaucer, as a certain
kind of person; the narrator of this pious tale is also, clearly, a kind of
person. And what he is neither corroborates nor contradicts the portrait, though, it is safe to guess, Chaucer might have made the two
"one" if he had had time (or inclination) to revise.

The teller of the tale of Virginius is not unlike the Knight in his
somewhat simplified view of Reality. But unlike the Knight, he is given
to flatly dogmatic statements about the values he is concerned with in
his tale. And unlike the Knight, he has neither zest nor joy in the world
he sees with humorless and impoverished eyes. There is something of
the puritan and of the preacher in this man, and he reduces the complexities of life to the simple contest between alternate abstractions.
Virginia, the "mayde" of "excellent beautee," is beautiful because Nature, not Art, has made her so, and is therefore "a thousand foold moore
vertuous." She has kept her "vertu" and "her maydens shamefastness"
by running away from evil company, by fleeing "festes, revels, . . . and
daunces." "Swich thynges maken children for to be/ To soone rype
and boold" (VI, 67-68), says the Physician, and lectures the pilgrims
about the raising of children:

> Ye fadres and ye moodres eek also,
> Though ye han children, be it oon or mo,
> Youre is the charge of al hir surveiaunce,
> Whil that they been under youre governaunce.

> Beth war, that by ensample of youre lyvynge,
> Or by youre necligence in chastisynge,
> That they ne perisse; for I dar wel seye,
> If that they doon, ye shul it deere abeye.
> Under a shepherde softe and necligent
> The wolf hath many a sheep and lamb torent.
>   (VI, 93-102)

And the *vita* of the beautiful maiden Virginia, subject to the lustful desires of Apius, and decreed to die by her father, Virginius, a "shepherde" neither "softe" nor "necligent," is his *exemplum* for the text. His characters are simple illustrations of his thesis; even the moment when Virginia seems to have some emotional response is only a gesture to her human nature. It is more important as it functions to point up the pathos of the choice she must make between "death or shame." "O mercy, deere fader!" she cries,

> And with that word she bothe hir armes layde
> Aboute his nekke, as she was wont to do.
> The teeris bruste out of hir eyen two,
> And seyde, "Goode fader, shal I dye?
> Is ther no grace, is ther no remedye?"
>   "No, certes, deere doghter myn," quod he.
>   "Thanne yif me leyser, fader myn," quod she,
> "My deeth for to compleyne a litel space;
> For, pardee, Jepte yaf his doghter grace
> For to compleyne, er he hir slow, allas!
> And, God it woot, no thyng was hir trespas,
> But for she ran hir fader first to see,
> To welcome hym with greet solempnitee."
> And with that word she fil aswowne anon,
> And, after, whan hir swownyng is agon,
> She riseth up, and to hir fader sayde,
> "Blissed be God, that I shal dye a mayde!
> Yif me my deeth, er that I have a shame;
> Dooth with youre child youre wyl, a Goddes name!"
>   And with that word she preyed hym ful ofte
> That with his swerd he sholde smyte softe;
> And with that word aswowne doun she fil.
> Hir fader, with ful sorweful herte and wil,
> Hir heed of smoot, and by the top it hente,
> And to the juge he gan it to presente,
> As he sat yet in doom in consistorie.
>   (VI, 231-257)

The Host can hardly stand the pitifulness of the tale: "But wel I woot thou doost myn herte to erme,/ That I almoost have caught a cardynacle" (VI, 312-313), he cries and, though he does not know it yet, suggests to the Pardoner, the next to tell a tale, the degree to which he might be susceptible to an emotional appeal, particularly one having to do with sin, since *The Physician's Tale* had ended significantly:

> Heere may men seen how synne hath his merite.
> Beth war, for no man woot whom God wol smyte
> In no degree, ne in which manere wyse
> The worm of conscience may agryse
> Of wikked lyf, though it so pryvee be
> That no man woot therof but God and he.
> For be he lewed man, or ellis lered,
> He noot how soone that he shal been afered.
> Therfore I rede yow this conseil take:
> Forsaketh synne, er synne yow forsake.
> (VI, 277-286)

Thus, although neither the Physician nor his tale have much that is particularly noteworthy about them as comedy except as they hold out reward for suffering, they both function in the dramatic structure of the whole plan. The Host's response will lay him open to the invitation of the Pardoner to step up for a pardon as the "moost envoluped in synne," and will move the pilgrimage to one of its most important climaxes.

The tale told by the Prioress also has a function in the linking of the tales, for, as will be seen when the group in *Fragment VII* is examined, it serves as an important transition to some of Chaucer's most complex comedy. But thematically, it belongs to the stories told by the Second Nun, by the Physician, and by the Man of Law; it too, tells of reward and punishment, of joy in heaven won by suffering on earth, and of the terrible justice meted out to those responsible for the suffering. Here, however, the comedy is of character as much as it is of theme.

Except for the reference to what she thinks monks ought to be, a reference that might indicate she has heard *The Shipman's Tale* with some distress—"This abbot, which that was an hooly man,/ As monkes been, or elles oghte be" (VII, 642-643)—the Prioress seems unaffected by the lusty pilgrims around her. The Host's excess of respect removes and isolates her from the more vital and earthy pilgrims. That Chaucer intended to insulate her in this way seems clear. She is included in the dramatic plan of the pilgrimage, but not included in the dramatic give-and-take that vitalizes the friction between the others into comic action. And the uncritical solemnity that marks the pilgrims' reception of her tale seems to reaffirm her isolation and her insulation from the world she moves in. "Whan seyd was al this miracle, every man/ As sobre was that wonder was to se" characterizes the response of her hearers, a response that the Host, as keeper of the mirth, must break in upon in order to return the travelers to "the game."

The observer-pilgrim, Chaucer, has been exactly correct in his reading of her appearance. Though what she is may not be what, as Prioress, she ought to be, she is, without pretense or pretension, what she seems. The paucity of language, its poverty in the absence of metaphor, of synonym, of variety, in her prologue and in her tale—all underscore her simplicity and her innocence. That she thinks of herself as specially affined to the child of her tale is clear from the last stanza of her Prologue:

> "My konnyng is so wayk, o blisful Queene,
> For to declare thy grete worthynesse
> That I ne may the weighte nat susteene;
> But as a child of twelf month oold, or lesse,
> That kan unnethes any word expresse,
> Right so fare I, and therfore I yow preye,
> Gydeth my song that I shal of yow seye."
> (VII, 481-487)

And her whole tale, devoted to the celebration of the instinctual piety of the "litel clergeon" in the "litel scole of Cristen folk," reveals the limited imagination of a "holy innocent." The child's murder at the commànd of the Jews holds no more horror for her than does the sight of a "mous,/ Kaught in a trappe, if it were deed or bledde." For both she can weep in charity and pity as for tiny, defenseless, and holy things. She has little perception of the agony of human suffering; the search made by the child's mother she describes briefly and in general terms:

> This poure wydwe awaiteth al that nyght
> After hir litel child, but he cam noght;
> For which, as soone as it was dayes lyght,
> With face pale of drede and bisy thoght,
> She hath at scole and elleswhere hym soght,
> Til finally she gan so fer espie
> That he last seyn was in the Juerie.
> (VII, 586-592)

And the gentle way in which she relates the mercilessly wholesale punishment given "thise Jewes" reveals not so much her anti-Semitism- as a

child-like sense of justice that would find wholesale slaughter quite the
proper and fitting retribution for the death of one small boy. Apparently
it does not occur to her that the vengeance is grimly ruthless, as she says:

> With torment and with shameful deeth echon.
> This provost dooth thise Jewes for to sterve
> That of this mordre wiste, and that anon.
> He nolde no swich cursednesse observe.
> "Yvele shal have that yvele wol deserve";
> Therfore with wylde hors he dide hem drawe,
> And after that he heng hem by the lawe.
> (VII, 628-634)

Her tale of innocence and murder is, however, a happy one, and her
piety, limited and sentimental as it is, reaches what degree of lyricism
it can as she narrates the last moments of the child:

> "My throte is kut unto my nekke boon,"
> Seyde this child, "and, as by wey of kynde,
> I sholde have dyed, ye, longe tyme agon.
> But Jesu Crist, as ye in bookes fynde,
> Wil that his glorie laste and be in mynde,
> And for the worship of his Mooder deere
> Yet may I synge *O Alma* loude and cleere.

> "This welle of mercy, Cristes mooder sweete,
> I loved alwey, as after my konnynge;
> And whan that I my lyf sholde forlete,
> To me she cam, and bad me for to synge
> This anthem verraily in my deyynge,
> As ye han herd, and whan that I hadde songe,
> Me thoughte she leyde a greyn upon my tonge.

> "Wherefore I synge, and synge moot certeyn,
> In honour of that blisful Mayden free,
> Til fro my tonge of taken is the greyn;
> And after that thus seyde she to me:
> 'My litel child, now wol I fecche thee,
> Whan that the greyn is fro thy tonge ytake.
> Be nat agast, I wol thee nat forsake.'"

> This hooly monk, this abbot, hym meene I,
> His tonge out caughte, and took away the greyn,

And he yaf up the goost ful softely.
And whan this abbot hadde this wonder seyn,
His salte teeris trikled doun as reyn,
And gruf he fil al plat upon the grounde,
And stille he lay as he had ben ybounde.
(VII, 649-676)

What is in a very real way a portrait of naïvete, a portrait of imperception and of childlike piety, is saved from satire and contained within the comic world of the pilgrimage by the way in which Chaucer isolates her completely from the world of complex reality, and by the ways he insures the retention of her innocence. The portrait in the *General Prologue* that is made up of the combination of the spiritual and the worldly is resolved in her tale, and her childlike innocence, which is neither spiritual nor worldly, places her among the blessed, if not very intelligent, worshippers of God. "O yonge Hugh of Lyncoln, slayn also" she prays at the end, "Preye eek for us, we synful folk unstable,/ That, of his mercy, God so merciable/ On us his grete mercy multiplie,/ For reverence of his mooder Marie. Amen" (VII, 684-690).

The Prioress, too, is part of the "diversity of thyngis," and as long as her oversimplification of Reality is contained within her own world, it threatens neither her equilibrium nor that of those around her, and she can, like the Knight, continue to exist in the company of those quite different. And grimly ironic (at least to our ears) as her final prayer for "mercy" may seem to be in the light of the revenge taken on the Jews that she has so blandly related, the moral of the tale—that the innocent suffering of mother and child will be rewarded in heaven, and that "Yvele shal have that yvele wol deserve"—makes of this tale yet another statement of "the comic vision" of *The Canterbury Tales*.

Although *The Man of Law's Tale* precedes those just discussed in the order of tales, I have reserved an examination of it as the last of the religious and moral tales that are not interrelated to other tales within the large plan. It is by far the most complex of the four, and in many ways, Chaucer's finest single religious tale.

On the most obvious level, the story of Dame Custance and her trials is comic in the divine sense of the word. Like the heroines of the other religious tales, she is subject to much suffering, but unlike them, she is rewarded in life, her husband restored to her, her son welcomed as the grandson of the Emperor of Rome, her last years full of honor and happiness. Her persecutors too are punished. Whether the Man of Law was really intended to be the narrator is another question that once more is not relevant for this study. But every element of the tale, even the insistence upon reward and punishment here upon earth, point to him as the more than probable choice, and it seems justifiable to read the tale, not as it makes him a figure of comedy, but as his legalistic and formalistic mind fashions a comic explanation for suffering and happiness. His view is not a complex one, but his presentation of it is.

The whole tale, which moves with slow and somewhat majestic pace, is patterned upon the simple definition of Comedy that was Boethian in inspiration: comedy, the literal opposite of tragedy, exists when "a man hath been in povre estaat,/ And clymbeth up and wexeth fortunat,/ And there abideth in prosperitee." "Swich thyng is gladsom" for the Man of Law even as it was for the Knight. Like *Troilus and Criseyde*, this story also moves in accordance with the concept of the turning Wheel, from woe to joy, then to woe and further joy, followed by woe and final joy. So transparently inevitable is the movement that this tale, having to do with separation, with apparent injustice as well as real injustice, with terrible death, mounts in its turning to greater joy and happiness. As the Man of Law approaches the two scenes of recognition and the last part of his narrative, he uses the word "joy" over and over again, contrapuntally reminding us that the unhappiness of the scenes he is immediately describing are but temporarily so. "Long was the sobbyng and the bitter peyne" of Constance when she found herself face to face with Alla, her husband. "I pray yow alle my labour to relesse;/ I may nat telle hir wo until tomorwe,/ I am so wery for to speke of sorwe," says the Man of Law (II, 1065-1071). But "wo" and "sorwe" are not lasting; joy will follow and, though reluctant to be explicit about the degree of woe, the Man of Law has no such reticence about the degree of joy.

> . . . finally, whan that the sothe is wist
> That Alla giltelees was of hir wo,
> I trowe an hundred tymes been they kist,
> And swich a blisse is ther bitwix hem two
> That, save the joye that lasteth everemo,
> Ther is noon lyk that any creature
> Hath seyn or shal, whil that the world may dure.
> (II, 1072-1078)

Husband and wife, Alla and Constance together go to meet the Emperor, her father. The circle of her wanderings is about to return to its starting point, the exile and the outcast is about to be reunited with her people and her world. The first recognition scene was merely a prelude to the joyousness of the second.

> The morwe cam, and Alla gan hym dresse,
> And eek his wyf, this Emperour to meete;
> And forth they ryde in joye and in gladnesse.
> And whan she saugh hir fader in the strete,
> She lighte doun, and falleth hym to feete.
> "Fader," quod she, "youre yonge child Custance
> Is now ful clene out of youre remembrance.
>
> I am youre doghter Custance," quod she,
> "That whilom ye han sent into Surrye.
> It am I, fader, that in the salte see
> Was put allone and dampned for to dye.
> Now, goode fader, mercy I yow crye!
> Sende me namoore unto noon hethenesse,
> But thonketh my lord heere of his kyndenesse."
>
> Who kan the pitous joye tellen al
> Bitwixe hem thre, syn they been thus ymette?
> But of my tale make an ende I shal;
> The day goth faste, I wol no lenger lette.
> This glade folk to dyner they hem sette;
> In joye and blisse at mete I lete hem dwelle
> A thousand foold wel moore than I kan telle.
>   (II, 1100-1120)

Lest his hearers be left, however, with the thought that earthly joy, wonderful as it is, is lasting, the Man of Law reminds them that "joye of this world, for tyme wol nat abyde;/ Fro day to nyght it changeth as the tyde" (II, 1133-1134).

Constance has surely earned her happiness, for her trials have been many. The Man of Law has narrated the tale of her persecution and her wanderings with faithful respect for his source, Nicholas Trivet's account in his Anglo-Norman Chronicle. But he has been disturbed somewhat by the strain put upon his sense of the credible and the probable, and he pauses at moments to face certain questions with all the philosophy at his command, philosophy he seems to have got from reading Pope Innocent's *De Contemptu Mundi*. "Men myghten asken why she was nat sleyn/ Eek at the feste" he comments, forced to account for the fact that she alone of all the guests at her own wedding feast survived the dreadful slaughter instigated by the "wicked sultaness," her mother-in-law to be. His answer, in its cheerful rhetoric, begs the question but it acknowledges that God's plan, mysterious as it is, is good, and human suffering is but a passing thing:

Who saved Danyel in the horrible cave
Ther every wight save he, maister and knave,
Was with the leon frete er he asterte?
No wight but God, that he bar in his herte.

God liste to shewe his wonderful myracle
In hire, for we sholde seen his myghty werkis;
Crist, which that is to every harm triacle,
By certeine meenes ofte, as knowen clerkis,
Dooth thyng for certein ende that ful derk is
To mannes wit, that for oure ignorance
No konne noght knowe his prudent purveiance.
                    (II, 473-483)

To God also is to be attributed her survival at sea, without "oar or pole" for three years, and then for five:

Now sith she was nat at the feeste yslawe,
Who kepte hire fro the drenchyng in the see?
Who kepte Jonas in the fisshes mawe
Til he was spouted up at Nynyvee?
Wel may men knowe it was no wight but he
That kepte peple Ebrayk from hir drenchynge,
With drye feet thurghout the see passynge.

Who bad the foure spirites of tempest
That power han t'anoyen lond and see,
Both north and south, and also west and est,
"Anoyeth, neither see, ne land, ne tree"?
Soothly, the comandour of that was he
That fro the tempest ay this womman kepte
As wel whan she wook as whan she slepte.

Where myghte this womman mete and drynke have
Thre yeer and moore? how lasteth hire vitaille?
Who fedde the Egipcien Marie in the cave,
Or in desert? No wight but Crist, sanz faille.
Fyve thousand folk it was as greet mervaille
With loves fyve and fisshes two to feede.
God sente his foyson at hir grete neede.
                    (II, 484-504)

Trivet's matter-of-fact explanation of his heroine's strength at the moment when she is sexually assaulted by the "lordes styward" does not entirely satisfy Chaucer's narrator. It may be, as Trivet suggested, that she was more clever than strong as she crept up behind the lustful servant and pushed him into the sea; but for the Man of Law some other force was at work:

> How may this wayke womman han this strengthe
> Hire to defende agayn this renegat?
> O Golias, unmesurable of lengthe,
> Hou myghte David make thee so maat,
> So yong and of armure so desolaat?
> Hou dorste he looke upon thy dredful face?
> Wel may men seen, it nas but Goddes grace.
>
> Who yaf Judith corage or hardynesse
> To sleen hym Olofernus in his tente,
> And to deliveren out of wrecchednesse
> The peple of God? I seye, for this entente,
> That right as God spirit of vigour sente
> To hem, and saved hem out of meschance,
> So sente he myght and vigour to Custance.
> (II, 932-945)

It seems clear that what is bothering the Man of Law is that he cannot quite accept Constance merely as an allegorical figure, a personification of the constancy of the good and holy soul in the face of persecution; she seems to him, apparently, at times to be more of a human being than this, and at such times he feels the need to account for the wonder and the mystery that surrounds her. At moments, therefore, he gives her some emotional responses to her unhappiness. There is sadness in her farewell to her father, and fear as she kneels before Alla, the "kyng of al Northhumbrelond":

> Have ye nat seyn somtyme a pale face,
> Among a prees, of hym that hath be lad
> Toward his deeth, wher as hym gat no grace,
> And swich a colour in his face hath had,
> Men myghte knowe his face that was bistad,
> Amonges alle the faces in that route?
> So stant Custance, and looketh hire aboute.
> (II, 645-651)

And the prayer she utters as, with her baby in her arms, she is forced once more out of happiness and away from the love of her husband, the

King, once more persecuted by a wicked mother-in-law, is full of lyrical grief:

> Hir litel child lay wepyng in hir arm,
> And knelynge, pitously to hym she seyde,
> "Pees, litel sone, I wol do thee noon harm."
> With that hir coverchief of hir heed she breyde,
> And over his litel eyen she it leyde,
> And in hir arm she lulleth it ful faste,
> And into hevene hire eyen up she caste.
>
> "Mooder," quod she, "and mayde bright, Marie,
> Sooth is that thurgh wommannes eggement
> Mankynde was lorn, and damned ay to dye,
> For which thy child was on a croys yrent.
> Thy blisful eyen sawe al his torment;
> Thanne is ther no comparison bitwene
> Thy wo and any wo man may sustene.
>
> "Thow sawe thy child yslayn bifore thyne yen,
> And yet now lyveth my litel child, parfay!
> Now, lady bright, to whom alle woful cryen,
> Thow glorie of wommanhede, thow faire may,
> Thow haven of refut, brighte sterre of day,
> Rewe on my child, that of thy gentillesse,
> Rewest on every reweful in distresse.
>
> (II, 834-854)

The question she asks is the Boethian one and, although it is not the thematic question of the tale, it is an important one:

> "O litel child, allas! what is thy gilt,
> That nevere wroghtest synne as yet, pardee?
> Why wil thyn harde fader han thee spilt?
> O mercy, deere constable," quod she,
> "As lat my litel child dwelle heer with thee;
> And if thou darst nat saven hym, for blame,
> So kys hym ones in his fadres name!"
>
> (II, 855-861)

But, of course, there is never any doubt that Constance will survive her many trials. Sad though at times she may be, she is simple perseverance and fortitude personified and in due time all will be well. It is also not surprising that in course of time each one of her persecutors will be punished; the Man of Law makes that quite clear. In fact, his belief in the inevitable administering of Justice provides him with a way to bring the theme of Justice full circle even as he is bringing the wandering Constance back to Rome and to the final rest of the turning Wheel in happiness. For this he had no suggestion in his source. Nor does the large coincidence bother him. For after many years the Roman army has fought with the pagans under the command of the evil sultaness, she who was the first to send Constance into exile and suffering. Triumphant, they are returning to Rome when they happen upon the floating boat holding the heroine and her child, and pick her up for her return home. Nine years or more have intervened, but at the last moment the first crime is punished as surely as all the others have been. There is hardly an incident in this tale that does not affirm its narrator's optimistic view of human life, even though that view is more deterministic than humanistic.

There is, of course, no question about Chaucer's genuine seriousness in selecting these pious tales for his pilgrims. That they are simple proclamations of a simple faith has nothing to do with their comic value, except in so far as they hold out the promise of final joy, of the happy ending either here on earth or in heaven. Chaucer is holding up for critical laughter neither the simplicity of the tales nor of their tellers. Indeed, it is stories such as these that he speaks of in his "Retraction" at the end of *The Canterbury Tales*, hoping that they will serve to win him forgiveness for others he has written, less clearly moral and religious in theme. These tales are comic because they are joyful in the holy sense of the word; and they are necessary complements to the more earthy and complex tales that outnumber them.

One of the other tales is like those just examined—that of The Clerk. Out of dramatic context, the story of the persecution and testing of the Patient Griselda reads like *The Man of Law's Tale* of the persevering Constance. But its context makes it an organic and integral part of the comedy of the pilgrimage, and gives it far greater complexity. It cannot be removed from its position in the "Marriage group" no matter how serious its professed allegorical intention may be.

All these tales, illustrating as they do, reward after suffering, are simple affirmations of the workings of Justice in a Divine sense rather than in an earthly sense, though punishment immediate and exact may be also in evidence. And presenting, as they do, examples of contention, of agon, of contest, they are as much a part of Chaucer's "comic vision" as are the more obvious comic tales of the pilgrimage.

chapteR 5

THE COMEDY OF
THE MARRIAGE GROUP

Contention and conflict, argument and counterargument, strife that is verbal and once, almost physical, "conjoyn" into one dramatic whole the seven tales from *The Wife of Bath's* to *The Franklin's*. It seems evident that Chaucer intended the sequence, and no matter what important manuscript tradition is followed, they are always grouped together, whatever group-position they have within *The Canterbury Tales*. And although three of the tales, *The Friar's, The Summoner's,* and *The Squire's,* may not fit the description exactly, there is no reason to quarrel with Kittredge's suggestion that the tales in *Fragments III, IV,* and *V* (as designated in the Robinson-Ellesmere text) form "The Marriage Group." Marriage, the relation between the sexes, love, and lust are the subjects dynamically realized in the tales told by the Wife of Bath, the Clerk, the Merchant, and the Franklin. *The Squire's Tale* is in too unfinished a state to justify any conclusions about the nature of its subject or its theme, except that it is about "romantic love" as well as about adventure. But unfinished as it is, it has within it many of the important concerns that have occupied the Wife of Bath and that will occupy the Franklin. The altercation between the Friar and the Summoner leading to the two stories that "quit" each other has nothing to do with marriage or love. But it has to do with the situational comedy of the contention between the pilgrims and the efforts of the Host to keep "pees," so that it does not really violate the unity of the group. Since, however, *The Friar's Tale* and *The Summoner's Tale* and the comic activity that accompanies them deserve attention in their own right, I have removed them from fragment-context and will discuss them separately in the next chapter.

The subject of marriage is introduced by the Wife of Bath. It was a subject particularly rich in potential for comedy, for in it come together all the motifs that have interested Chaucer since *The Book of the Duchess;* in it are brought to focus all the important ways in which human beings show that life is a matter of struggle and contention, of inner and outer conflict; in it is the possibility of defining the nature of the equilibrium that must coexist with the tension caused by strife. And because it was a subject sure to arouse opinion charged with emotion, it was certain to create dramatic response of one sort or another. An opinion about marriage uttered by so robust and vital a woman as the Wife of Bath must inevitably generate response that is contentious; indeed, any opinion about anything she might put before the pilgrims was bound to stir feelings in some way.

She has not moved far into the monologue that prefaces her tale before she is interrupted. Her relish in the power she has had over her husbands, a power to which even the Bible entitles her—"I have the power durynge al my lyf/ Upon his propre body, and noght he;/ Right thus the Apostel tolde it unto me"—is, apparently, more than the Pardoner can bear:

> Up stirte the Pardoner, and that anon:
> "Now, dame," quod he, "by God and by Seint John!
> Ye been a noble prechour in this cas.
> I was aboute to wedde a wyf; allas!
> What sholde I bye it on my flessh so deere?
> Yet hadde I levere wedde no wyf to-yeere!"
>   (III, 163-168)

Her reply is genial, almost benign, and calls forth from the Pardoner a remark that betrays his resentment of her open and frankly sexual rich nature. To her promise that she will reveal much more than he can guess "of tribulacion in mariage,/ Of which I am expert in al myn age," his sneering words seem charged with all the hatred the impotent have for that which is vitally alive:

> "Dame, I wolde praye yow, if youre wyl it were,"
> Seyde this Pardoner, "as ye bigan,
> Telle forth youre tale, spareth for no man,
> And teche us yonge men of youre praktike."
>   (III, 184-187)

"Gladly," she says, "sith it may you like," and the brief moment of interchange is over, leaving us aware that the illusion of the pilgrimage is still dramatically a part of the telling of tales, reminding us that the Wife is being listened to by those around her, and suggesting that Chaucer intends to contrast the Pardoner to her in some essential way.

At the end of her prologue and before she can begin her tale, she is once more a part of the dramatic action of the pilgrimage. The Friar intimates some boredom with her monologue— somehow she must have been like many of the "worthy wommen of the toun" among whom he moved with such profit and joy, and he may have heard all this before. To Alisoun's announcement that she will now "seye" her tale, he laughs. "Now dame," he says, "so have I joye or blis,/ This is a long preamble of a tale!" The brief contention between the Summoner and the Friar that delays the beginning of her tale seems not to perturb her. She merely waits for the Host to quiet the altercation, though she takes cognizance of the Friar's presence and evident reputation. "Al redy, sire," she replies to the Host's request that she begin, "If I have license of this worthy Frere." And before she is very far into her tale she makes sure that she has a moment of retaliation. It is, she says, to be a tale about other days and other ways, about the England of King Arthur and of elves and fairies—all, alas, long departed—departed by force of the Church:

> . . . now kan no man se none elves mo,
> For now the grete charitee and prayeres
> Of lymytours and othere hooly freres,
> That serchen every lond and every streem,
> As thikke as motes in the sonne-beem,
> Blessynge halles, chambres, kichenes, boures,
> Citees, burghes, castels, hye toures,
> Thropes, bernes, shipnes, dayeryes—
> This maketh that ther been no fayeres.
> (III, 864-872)

And good-naturedly she directs a barb straight to the Friar, the innuendo clear in its meaning of anyone who has the ears to hear:

> For ther as wont to walken was an elf,
> Ther walketh now the lymytour hymself
> In undermeles and in morwenynges,
> And seyth his matyns and his hooly thynges
> As he gooth in his lymytacioun.
> Wommen may go now saufly up and doun.
> In every bussh or under every tree
> Ther is noon oother incubus but he,
> And he ne wol doon hem but dishonour.
> (III, 873-881)

The irony in the multiple negatives needs time to untangle, and the Wife of Bath does not wait for the Friar or for anyone else to do so. She moves immediately into her tale and the only comment the Friar has to make at the end is about the "learning" she has revealed, though he finds the display of it not in keeping with the occasion: "But, dame, heere as we ryde by the weye,/ Us nedeth nat to speken but of game,/ And lete auctoritees, on Goddes name,/ To prechyng and to scole eek of clergye" (III, 1274-1277). His own desire is to get on with the revenge he has promised the Summoner, and for awhile, the attention of the pilgrims, and the focus of the comedy is turned to the altercation between the two men. But the Wife of Bath, though she does not speak again, is never from this moment out of mind; her presence is felt in many ways and she becomes, simply by the aura of her being, a symbol of Life, of Endurance, of the Triumph of Joy—in short, of Comedy itself.

The observer is proved accurate in his portrayal of the Wife of Bath. What he has seen has been the restless movement from place to place, the bold and colorful vitality of a personality that must dominate or cease to exist, the zest in "felaweshipe"; what her monologue in all its candor reveals is the complex war within the self that generates all the vital forces the observer has noted. To put it simply, the comedy of the Wife of Bath is the comedy of tensions and conflicts kept in balance, the comedy of the warring self, whose very life depends upon the continual battle. Though the content of her prologue is "the battle of the sexes" and is thus by tradition and convention "comic," battle within the self is what makes her far more richly and significantly comic.

From the opening lines of her prologue, the threats, the hostile forces, the warring elements come clear. And her joy in sustaining them, her relish in living in the face of them, resounds in every word. It seems almost impossible for her to say the word "woe" without following it with the word "joy." Indeed, "woe" in marriage is her first concern and the intended subject of her autobiographical monologue. But the gusto, the vigor, the triumph with which she describes and accepts the woe makes of it a subject that is anything but doleful. The first sentence is not ended before her joy in survival is clear:

> "Experience, though noon auctoritee
> Were in this world, is right ynogh for me
> To speke of wo that is in mariage;
> For, lordynges, sith I twelve yeer was of age,
> Thonked be God that is eterne on lyve,
> Housbondes at chirche dore I have had fyve,—

If I so ofte myghte have ywedded bee,—
And alle were worthy men in hir degree."
(III, 1-8)

That her experience with marriage has been a hard one, she is most willing to admit; but that she should not have had that experience, that she should have been limited to one husband and one only, she cannot believe. Misuse, controversy, indignities there have been, but "Yblessed be God that I have wedded fyve!/ Welcome the sixte, whan that evere he shal./ For sothe, I wol nat kepe me chaast in al" (III, 44-46).

The lusty exuberance of her nature has not allowed the solemn voice of ecclesiastical authority to upset her. But it is clear she has some respect for what the Church has to say about chastity and the needs of the flesh. Her concern for the judgments and pronouncements of authority and her rationalizations because of them suggest that she has felt a constant threat and has warred insistently to keep at arm's length the full force of the Church's censure. The battle has been almost life-long, and it is now made more threateningly fatal by "age." The Reeve may have been old before he was ever young; Alisoun has known all the full vitality of youth and it causes her a pang to accept its loss. Fearsome as growing old may be, she will not deny its reality, nor be for more than a moment frightened of its limitations upon the flesh. For a second she sounds like the Reeve as she almost yields to self-pity:

'But, Lord Christ; whan that it remembreth me
Upon my yowthe, and on my jolitee,
It tikleth me aboute myn herte roote.
Unto this day it dooth myn herte boote
That I have had my world as in my tyme.
But age, allas! that al wole envenyme,
Hath me biraft my beautee and my pith."
(III, 469-475)

But the moment is over almost as soon as it has begun. With a resurgence of joy she finishes the thought, her vigorous healthiness affirming life "as it is":

"Lat go, farewel! the devel go therwith!
The flour is goon, ther is namoore to telle;
The bren, as I best kan, now moste I selle;
But yet to be right myrie wol I fonde."
(III, 476-479)

That she has learned to accept "what is" since her early years has not freed her of struggle. Although she has arrived at some measure of self-understanding, she has won no final victory over the tensions she feels between herself and the world, which by now are for her specifically focused in the Church. Her return again and again in the course of her autobiographical self-defense to a reference to or an examination of the position of the Church or the attitude of society toward what she so openly is betrays her respect for the forces she feels oppose her, and make of her struggle to keep her hard-won equilibrium something wonderfully heroic. Though sustained by rationalizations, she is never complacent, nor indifferent, nor self-satisfied, nor morally irresponsible.

In the most clear-sighted way she has seen that the source of her endurance in the "wo that is mariage" has been her joy in sex. Sex and the sexual act have been, what is more, the source of her control over the hostile forces that have always threatened her: society, as it has forced her to marry; men, as they have used her body; the Church, as it has frowned upon the flesh; the self, as it has sought through lust something more closely resembling love. Sex and her recognition of her sexual richness have been the basis of her self-knowledge, the clear center of her self-identity: "Jhesu Crist us sende," she concludes her tale, "Housbondes meeke, yonge, and fressh abedde," for, in spite of her advancing age and all the decrees of the Church, some people cannot be chaste, anymore than all vessels can be made of gold:

> "I graunte it wel, I have noon envie,
> Thogh maydenhede preferre bigamye.
> It liketh hem to be clene, body and goost;
> Of myn estaat I nyl nat make no boost.
> For wel ye knowe, a lord in his houshold,
> He nath nat every vessel al of gold;
> Somme been of tree, and doon hir lord servyse.
> God clepeth folk to hym in sondry wyse,
> And everich hath of God a propre yifte,
> Som this, som that, as hym liketh shifte."
>   (III, 95-104)

Never has the doctrine of the Charismata been more willfully employed! Without any grudge or malice she is frank to admit that "virginitee is greet perfeccioun," but she reminds her listeners:

> ". . . Crist, that of perfeccion is welle,
> Bad nat every wight he sholde go selle
> Al that he hadde, and gyve it to the poore

And in swich wise folwe hym and his foore.
He spak to hem that wolde lyve parfitly;
And lordynges, by youre leve, that am nat I.
I wol bistowe the flour of al myn age
In the actes and in fruyt of mariage."
                                        (III, 107-114)

Her ceaseless search to explain the lustful and sexual nature she knows is hers has led her to draw upon all the resources at her command. Like her restless moves from shrine to shrine, her search through the Old Testament for examples of multiple marriages, through the New Testament and the Church Fathers for any admonitions about chastity to argue with or against, through astrology and the theories of medieval physiology—this search says clearly that though undaunted in her sexuality, she is not entirely content with it. The vigor and the energy of her mind are not much less than those of her body. Rationalist that she is, she seems to have sought out bravely the most censorious admonishments in order to turn them to her own advantage. That such ingenious, often witty, use of the Scriptures for her own ends sounds at times like blasphemy is indisputable; at moments she seems to enjoy her cleverness at the cost of reverence. "I nyl envye no virginitee" she says—

> "Lat hem be breed of pured whete-seed,
> And lat us wyves hoten barly-breed;"

and with a gleam of sheer joy in the sexual implications of the pun she concludes:

> "And yet with barly-breed, Mark telle kan,
> Our Lord Jhesu refresshed many a man."
>   (III, 143-146)

Authority indeed can tell her nothing of the "wo that is in mariage" that experience has not told her first. The forces of the Church and Society that condemn her behavior have created in her a continuing vitality of defense; the forces that have confronted her in her experiences with her husbands have created in her a continuing vitality of offense. Married at the age of twelve, she learned early how to maintain the upper hand over elderly husbands, for both age and lust put them in her power and their money won her willingness to call them "good." She still relishes her triumph over them:

> "As help me God, I laughe whan I thynke
> How pitously a-nyght I made hem swynke!
> And, by my fey, I tolde of it no stoor.
> They had me yeven hir lond and hir tresoor;
> Me nedeth nat do lenger diligence
> To wynne hir love, or doon hem reverence.
> They loved me so wel, by God above,
> That I ne tolde no deyntee of hir love!
> A wys womman wol bisye hire evere in oon
> To gete hire love, ye, ther as she hath noon.
> But sith I hadde hem hooly in myn hond,
> And sith they hadde me yeven al hir lond,
> What sholde I taken keep hem for to plese,
> But it were for my profit and myn ese?
> I sette hem so awerke, by my fey,
> That many a nyght they songen 'weilaway!' "

> (III, 201-216)

Her sense of justice is as simple and as primitive as the Miller's or the Reeve's. Her "olde lecchour" husbands got exactly what they deserved, and were "quit" even before they had offended. She more than hints that God, justly, comes in for His own desert:

> "For al swich wit is yeven us in oure byrthe;
> Deceite, wepyng, spynnyng God hath yive
> To wommen kyndely, whil that they may lyve.
> And thus of o thyng I avaunte me,
> Atte ende I hadde the bettre in ech degree,
> By sleighte, or force, or by som maner thyng.

> .   .   .   .

> I wolde nat spare hem at hir owene bord;
> For, by my trouthe, I quitte hem word for word,
> As helpe me verray God omnipotent,
> Though I right now sholde make my testament,
> I ne owe hem nat a word that it nys quit.
> I broghte it so aboute by my wit
> That they moste yeve it up, as for the beste,
> Or elles hadde we nevere been in reste."

> (III, 400-405; 421-428)

Fate, or Fortune, of Life, what you will—the Wife does not label it— has kept its greatest irony for her age. After the thoroughly grim fourth marriage with a husband as promiscuous as she, a marriage that left her embittered—for after all she gave as good as she received: "By God! in erthe I was his purgatorie,/ For which I hope his soule be in glorie" (III, 489-490)—she has fallen in love as she had never fallen before. "Now of my fifthe housbonde wol I telle," she says. "God lete his soule nevere come in helle," for although he was the "mooste shrewe" he was "in oure bed . . . so fressh and gay,/ And therwithal so wel koude he me glose,/ Whan that he wolde han my *bele chose*,/ That thogh he hadde me bete on every bon,/ He koude wynne agayn my love anon" (III, 504-512). The paradox seems for her to be in the course of things: "I trowe I loved hym best, for that he/ Was of his love daungerous to me" (III, 513-514).

The courtship had been clandestine and lovely. Her heart had been given finally into his keeping when at the funeral of her fourth husband she had caught sight of his delicately formed legs:

> "As help me God! whan that I saugh hym go
> After the beere, me thoughte he hadde a paire
> Of legges and of feet so clene and faire
> That al myn herte I yaf unto his hoold."
> (III, 596-599)

It is this last and most unhappy love that brings to her the realization of her age and of her failing vitality and calls forth from her the great defiance of decay that is the final affirmation of her joy in life as it is:

> "He was, I trowe, a twenty wynter oold,
> And I was fourty, if I shal seye sooth;
> But yet I hadde alwey a coltes tooth.
> Gat-tothed I was, and that bicam me weel;
> I hadde the prente of seinte Venus seel.
> As help me God! I was a lusty oon,
> And faire, and riche, and yong, and wel begon."
> (III, 600-606)

What matter that this fifth husband she loved so well caused her mental woe and physical pain, what matter that in his sadistic glee he badgered her with nightly readings about the evil caused by women or brought on her deafness by a blow to her head. She had outwitted him in the long run and had achieved a certain time of happiness:

> "And whan that I hadde geten unto me,
> By maistrie, al the soveraynetee,
> And that he seyde, 'Myn owene trewe wyf,
> Do as thee lust the terme of al thy lyf;

> Keep thyn honour, and keep eek myn estaat'—
> After that day we hadden never debaat.
> God helpe me so, I was to hym as kynde
> As any wyf from Denmark unto Ynde,
> And also trewe, and so was he to me."
>   (III, 817-825)

It is quite possible to accept the hypothesis that the tale attributed to the Shipman and placed in another sequence was the one that Chaucer originally planned for the Wife of Bath. It is also possible to argue that it may have been intended for her second tale. As a fabliau that tells how a woman tricked her husband as well as her lover, it underscores her conviction that woman are from birth, and from hard experience, full of "wit, . . . deceite, wepyng, spynnyng" so that "atte ende" they may have "the bettre in ech degree,/ By sleighte, or force, or by som maner thyng." The tale has her vigor and her rationale, and its amorality confirms part of her view of life. There is zest and earthiness and economy in its narration that make it sound like her far more than it does the somewhat sinister Shipman of the *General Prologue*. But the tale Chaucer gave her instead is much more richly revealing than this, for its almost childlike romanticism hints at aspects of her nature that even her clear-sighted view of herself has not recognized. Deep beneath the acknowledged tensions that in sustained balance have given her a kind of joyous equilibrium, there is still a simple belief in romance, in the ideals of natural gentility, in the saving and transforming power of submission to love. The "foul wyf" who possesses the knowledge about women that saves the life of the young knight is Alisoun, and the magical transformation into a lovely and youthful maiden which she undergoes is wishful thinking of the most poignant sort:

> And whan the knyght saugh verraily al this,
> That she so fair was, and so yong therto,
> For joye he hente hire in his armes two,
> His herte bathed in a bath of blisse.
> A thousand tyme a-rewe he gan hire kisse,
> And she obeyed hym in every thyng
> That myghte doon hym plesance or likyng.
>   (III, 1250-1256)

The narrative power she reveals in her tale is as marked as are her powers of argumentation and rationalization. Sensitive to timing, to economy of detail, to ways of creating suspense and the sure rise to the climactic moment, she tells a small gem of a short story. Whatever her source has been she has markedly changed it, for from the many analogues of the Loathly Lady story it is clear that she has feminized it. The young knight is no more chivalric than most young men are, and the court of King Arthur, "of which that Britons speken greet honour," is in reality under the controlling hand of the queen, to whose jurisdiction the King hands over the young knight, the "lusty bachelor" who has been imprisoned for having raped a young girl. For his crime he is given the task of discovering the answer to the queen's question, "What thyng is it that wommen moost desiren." The many answers he gets in the course of his twelve-month travels bear the amused corroboration of Alisoun's experience and rationale:

> Somme seyde wommen loven best richesse,
> Somme seyde honour, somme seyde jolynesse,
> Somme riche array, somme seyden lust abedde.
> And oftetyme to be wydwe and wedde.
> Somme seyde that oure hertes been moost esed
> Whan that we been yflatered and yplesed.
> He gooth ful ny the sothe, I wol nat lye.
> A man shal wynne us best with flaterye;
> And with attendance, and with bisynesse,
> Been we ylymed, bothe moore and lesse.
>   And somme seyen that we loven best
> For to be free, and do right as us lest,
> And that no man repreve us of oure vice,
> But seye that we be wise, and no thyng nyce.
> For trewely ther is noon of us alle,
> If any wight wol clawe us on the galle,
> That we nel kike, for he seith us sooth.
> Assay, and he shal fynde it that so dooth;
> For, be we never so vicious withinne,
> We wol been holden wise and clene of synne.
>   (III, 925-944)

One answer the knight picks up arouses her honest objection and leads her to a brief retelling of the legend of King Midas. That women like to be thought "stable and eek secree" is to her a sheer absurdity, because her own self-candor proves it not at all so. And to illustrate her point— for after all she was given to talk freely to her godmother and her niece and to a friend "bet than oure parisshe preest"—she draws upon her reading of "Ovyde" and his tale of Midas, his asses' ears, and the ultimate betrayal of his disfigurement by his wife, who ran to the marsh in her utter inability to contain the secret, "And as a bitore bombleth

in the myre,/ . . . leyde hir mouth unto the water doun" and revealed
that her husband "hath longe asses erys two" (III, 972-976). By now it is
clear, so ambiguous are her pronouns, that she is making an identification in the story she is telling that she is not aware of.

As she moves to the first climactic moment of the tale, she reveals
how sensitive she is to the effects of suspense. What the answer to the
queen's question is that is given to him by the foul hag the knight
finally meets in his wanderings, is, in the sources, given immediately. But Alisoun, after making clear that he must promise to wed her
in return for the answer that will save him, saves the revelation for her
audience until the knight faces the court of the queen in a moment of
brief but dramatic tension. Except for the presence of the young man,
the court seems teeming with women:

> Whan they be comen to the court, this knyght
> Seyde he had holde his day, as he hadde hight,
> And redy was his answere, as he sayde.
> Ful many a noble wyf, and many a mayde,
> And many a wydwe, for that they been wise,
> The queene hirself sittynge as a justise,
> Assembled been, his answere for to heere;
> And afterward this knyght was bode appeere.
> (III, 1023-1030)

Alisoun's joy in the moment is evident, for the answer the knight will
give is her hard-won conviction about marriage even as, ironically, it
is about to commit him to an enslavement far more complete than he
knows:

> To every wight comanded was silence,
> And that the knyght sholde telle in audience
> What thyng that worldly wommen loven best.
> This knyght ne stood nat stille as doth a best,
> But to his questioun anon answerde
> With manly voys, that al the court is herde:
>   "My lige lady, generally," quod he,
> "Wommen desiren to have sovereynetee
> As wel over hir housbond as hir love,
> And for to been in maistrie hym above.
> This is youre mooste desir, thogh ye me kille.
> Dooth as yow list; I am heer at youre wille."
> In al the court ne was ther wyf, ne mayde,

> Ne wydwe, that contraried that he sayde,
> But seyden he was worthy han his lyf.
> (III, 1031-1045)

Worthy to have his life he is, but a bargain is a bargain in the world of the queen, and of Alisoun; in spite of his despair at the realization, he must marry the "foul and aged hag."

"Greet was the wo the knyght hadde in his thoght,/ Whan he was with his wyf abedde ybroght," says Alisoun (III, 1083-1084). And although the "olde wyf" has another trick in store for him in her imminent transformation into all that he wants, she will not play it until she has lectured him about each of his objections to her:

> "Thou art so loothly, and so oold also,
> And thereto comen of so lough a kynde,
> That litel wonder is thogh I walwe and wynde.
> So wolde God myn herte wolde breste!"
> (III, 1100-1103)

Her "prechyng," as the Friar calls it, wins his submission, but that is only incidental to what is really revealed in it about the Wife of Bath, the narrator. Of the three accusations he makes, those of poverty and age bother her little: "For filthe and eelde, also moot I thee,/ Been grete wardeyns upon chastitee." It is the phrase "Thou art . . . therto comen of so lough a kynde" that concerns her most. It is not that she must prove herself of high birth, for this she cannot do, indeed would not do, since history has shown that the gentle-born often do un-gentle deeds. Both Christ and Dante have made clear that true "gentillesse" belongs not to the nobility, nor to the poor, but to him "that dooth gentil dedis." That such idealism, spoken as it is with all the ring of true conviction, can come from the robustly vulgar and openly coarse Wife of Bath confirms the existence of a dimension in her that is hinted at all through her prologue. But it is the close association she (as the "olde wyf") makes between "gentilesse" and sinlessness that is the most deeply moving revelation of her whole nature. The intensity of her concern is disclosed as with more and more frequency the word "sin" enters into her "prechyng," and the concluding lines say more about the moving force behind her restlessness than all her conscious rationalizations:

> "He nys nat gentil, be he duc or erl;
> For vileyns synful dedes make a cherl.
> For gentillesse nys but renomee
> Of thyn auncestres, for hire heigh bountee,

Which is a strange thyng to thy persone.
Thy gentillesse cometh fro God allone.
Thanne comth oure verray gentillesse of grace;
It was no thyng biquethe us with oure place.

.   .   .   .

And therfore, leeve housebonde, I thus conclude:
Al were it that myn auncestres were rude,
Yet may the hye God, and so hope I,
Grante me grace to lyven vertuously.
Thanne am I gentil, whan that I bigynne
To lyven vertuously, and weyve synne."
(III, 1157-1176)

That the Wife of Bath has made no really conscious identification with her heroine seems clear; she does not use her, as the Merchant will use his protagonist, to stir sympathy or pity for herself. Her ceaseless search for ways to keep her "synful" vitality coexistent with the world that condemns her depends for its success upon not taking to heart "thanne am I gentil, whan that I bigynne/ To lyven vertuously, and weyve synne." But she can have her important character say so without any significant threat to her own equilibrium. And since all the arguments of the "olde wyf" are irrefutable, the young knight, caught irretrievably, can only submit: "I put me in youre wise governance." With joy she forces him to acknowledge her sovereignty—"Thanne have I gete of yow maistrie"— and rewards him by her wonderful transformation:

"Kys me," quod she, "we be no lenger wrothe;
For, by my trouthe, I wol be to yow bothe,
This is to seyn, ye, bothe fair and good.
I prey to God that I moote sterven wood,
But I to yow be also good and trewe
As evere was wyf, syn that the world was newe.
And but I be to-morn as fair to seene
As any lady, emperice, or queene,
That is bitwixe the est and eke the west,
Dooth with my lyf and deth right as yow lest.
Cast up the curtyn, looke how that it is."
(III, 1239-1249)

Mastery the Wife of Bath may want in marriage and this she has been able to have, though at great cost, but love and continuing youth and beauty, "gentilesse" and "synlessnesse," have been the imponderable impossibles. The tale she has chosen to tell defines the conditions for the happiness she has not had; it has come out of some deep reservoir of "idealism" that all the talk about authority and experience, and all the cheerfully realistic acceptance of the lusting and lecherous nature that she knows hers to be, has not successfully covered. And it also defines the conditions under which she would be "good and trewe." That such wishful thinking as is embodied in her tale about marriage between a handsome young knight and an elderly hag who is transformed into beauty at the end is possible in the mind of a woman so beset by unhappiness in marriage—this is one of the reasons for the richness of the comedy in Chaucer's creation of her. That the whole tale is, in fact, a celebration of the fact of marriage and is, in effect, almost a plea for the sixth husband, whoever he may be, reaffirms one of the most essential elements of her nature: her joyous endurance in the face of what are really impossible odds, her refusal to be daunted by "life as it is." "Jhesu Crist us sende," she concludes, "Housbondes meeke, yonge, and fressh abedde,/ And grace t'overbyde hem that we wedde;/ And eek I praye Jhesu shorte hir lyves/ That wol nat be governed by hir wyves;/ And olde and angry nygardes of dispence,/ God sende hem soone verray pestilence!" (III, 1258-1264).

THE CLERK'S TALE

It is not surprising that the Wife of Bath's assertion that happiness in marriage is insured only when the woman has the mastery over the man arouses response from an audience predominantly male. Nor is it surprising that the first of the pilgrims to respond is the Clerk. The "holwe" and sober student from Oxford stands in sharp contrast to the robust and large Alisoun from "biside Bathe." But more importantly, her generalizations about the inevitable misogyny of clerks cannot have failed to have caught his ear. Her fifth husband, after all, was also a clerk and it was his nightly occupation of reading to her of "wikked wyves" that led to her explosive fury and brought from him the blow that made her deaf:

> "He knew of [wyves] mo legendes and lyves
> Than been of goode wyves in the Bible.
> For trusteth wel, it is an impossible
> That any clerk wol speke good of wyves
> But if it be of hooly seintes lyves,
> Ne of noon oother womman never the mo.
> Who peyntede the leon, tel me who?
> By God! if wommen hadde writen stories,
> As clerkes han withinne hire oratories,
> They wolde han writen of men moore wikkednesse

> Than al the mark of Adam may redresse.
>
> .   .   .   .
>
> . . . no womman of no clerk is preysed.
> The clerk, whan he is oold, and may noght do
> Of Venus werkes worth his olde sho,
> Thanne sit he doun, and writ in his dotage
> That wommen kan nat kepe hir mariage!"
>
> > (III, 686-696; 706-710)

The Clerk's choice of a tale, which he says he got from "Franceys Petrak," is a carefully made one, for many reasons. Ostensibly it is one selected to "gladly teche" the pilgrims all about the happiness given as reward for long-suffering and patient endurance. It is, upon cursory reading, a tale much like that of the Man of Law, except that it has nothing to say about the punishment given to the wicked. Walter's cruel testing of Griselda's obedience and love comes in for little condemnation by the Clerk; it is, indeed, necessary to point up his allegory:

> This storie is seyd, nat for that wyves sholde
> Folwen Grisilde as in humylitee,
> For it were inportable, though they wolde;
> But for that every wight, in his degree,
> Sholde be constant in adversitee
> As was Grisilde; therfore Petrak writeth
> This storie, which with heigh stile he enditeth.
>
> For, sith a womman was so pacient
> Unto a mortal man, wel moore us oghte
> Receyven al in gree that God us sent;
> For greet skile is, he preeve that he wroghte.
> But he ne tempteth no man that he boghte,
> As seith Seint Jame, if ye his pistel rede;
> He preeveth folk al day, it is ne drede,
>
> And suffreth us as for oure exercise,
> With sharpe scourges of adversitee
> Ful ofte to be bete in sondry wise;
> Nat for to knowe oure wyl, for certes he,
> Er we were born, knew al oure freletee;
> And for oure beste is al his governaunce.
> Lat us thanne lyve in vertuous suffraunce.
>
> > (IV, 1142-1162)

Griselda as the personification of "the soul" is tried even as Job was. "Men speke of Job, and moost for his humblesse," remarks the Clerk, but, agreeing with the Wife of Bath, he adds:

> ... as in soothfastnesse,
> Though clerkes preise wommen but a lite,
> Ther kan no man in humblesse hym acquite
> As womman kan, ne kan been half so trewe
> As wommen been, but it be falle of newe.
>   (IV, 932-938)

Like Constance and the reward finally given her perseverance, Griselda for her incredible sufferance is made happy at the end:

> And whan this Walter saugh hire pacience
> Hir glade chiere, and no malice at al,
> And he so ofte had doon to hire offence,
> And she ay sad and constant as a wal,
> Continuynge evere hire innocence overal,
> This sturdy markys gan his herte dresse
> To rewen upon hire wyfly stedfastnesse.
>
> "This is ynogh, Grisilde myn," quod he;
> "Be now namoore agast ne yvele apayed.
> I have thy feith and thy benyngnytee,
> As wel as evere womman was, assayed.
> In greet estaat, and povreliche arrayed.
> Now knowe I, dere wyf, thy stedfastnesse,"—
> And hire in armes took and gan hire kesse.
>   (IV, 1044-1057)

So whatever else the Clerk's tale of the patient Griselda may do, it does have the explicit intention of teaching a lesson not unlike those taught by the other pilgrims: happiness is reserved for those who endure injustice and poverty and indignity with resignation and faith. It is a narrative quite suitable for the scholarly and serious Clerk. But it is not until it is seen how the tale, in almost every word, in almost every situation, both implicitly and explicitly attacks the Wife of Bath, that it and its narrator become a vital part of the essential comedy of *The Canterbury Tales*.

The moral of the story is directed at all the pilgrims; the admonishing finger is pointed at Alisoun. Griselda, the model of wifely obedience and womanly virtue, is in every way what Alisoun is not. From the moment the Clerk introduces her as the bride who is to be chosen by the "lord . . . of the lond," she is in significant ways the opposite of the Wife:

> But for to speke of vertuous beautee,
> Thanne was she oon the faireste under sonne;
> For povreliche yfrostred up was she.
> (IV, 211-213)

There is no mistaking the object of the reference in the next lines; from a man who had the reputation of speaking "noght o word . . . moore than was neede," it has little relevance for the description of his heroine but a great deal for the Wife of Bath:

> No likerous lust was thurgh hire herte yronne.
> Wel ofter of the welle than of the tonne
> She drank, and for she wolde vertu plese,
> She knew wel labour, but noon ydel ese.
> (IV, 214-217)

This "tendre mayden," fostering with 'greet reverence and charitee/ Hir olde povre fader" and a "fewe sheep," is perfect in "obeisaunce and diligence" long before Walter puts her to the cruelty of his tests, and is ready to accept with quiet humbleness the conditions he makes as he asks for her in marriage:

> "I seye this, be ye redy with good herte
> To al my lust, and that I frely may,
> As me best thynketh, do yow laughe or smerte,
> And nevere ye to grucche it, nyght ne day?
> And eek whan I say, 'ye,' ne say nat 'nay,'
> Neither by word ne frownyng contenance?
> Swere this, and heere I swere oure alliance."
>
> Wondyrnge upon this word, quakynge for drede,
> She seyde, "Lord, undigne and unworthy
> Am I to thilke honour that ye me beede,
> But as ye wole youreself, right so wol I.
> And heere I swere that nevere willyngly,
> In werk ne thoght, I nyl yow disobeye,
> For to be deed, though me were looth to deye."
> (IV, 351-364)

Temporarily, Griselda is rewarded for her submission. Her virtue and gentleness increase after her marriage and with pointed definiteness the Clerk describes the happy results:

> Ther nas discord, rancour, ne hevynesse
> In al that land, that she ne koude apese,
> And wisely brynge hem alle in reste and ese.
>
> (IV, 432-434)

Her marriage was not barren, he says, with surely something like a glance in the direction of the five-times wedded yet apparently childless Wife: "She shewed wel, for no worldly unreste/ A wyf as of hirself, nothing ne sholde/ Wille in effect, but as hir housbonde wolde." And when, as the next to the final test of her obedience, Walter casts her from his house, she asks to be returned to her father's cottage, as poor as she had come, she makes a vow that she will lead there a life as "a wydwe clene in body, herte, and al," her last words strike directly at the joyous lustfulness of the "goode Wyf":

> "For sith I yaf to yow my maydenhede,
> And am youre trewe wyf, it is no drede,
> God shilde swich a lordes wyf to take
> Another man to housbonde or to make!"
>
> (IV, 837-840)

The figure of the virtuous Griselda is designed in every way to point up the vices of Alisoun; the tale that relates the woe she undergoes in marriage seems designed to prove the contrary of the Wife's thesis that sovereignty in the hands of the woman is necessary before married peace can be assured. But what the Clerk's tale does, in its elaborate and detailed way, is finally to corroborate Alisoun's view of the nature of women and the fact of female domination, and corroborate it not in a joyous but in a somewhat cynical and sardonic way.

As allegory, the story of Walter's exploitation of his wife's obedient submission is acceptable; as psychological reality it is not, unless, of course, one is willing to consider unobjectionable the premise that a good marriage depends upon the power of a sadist over a willing and conscious masochist. It is clear in the course of the narration that the Clerk does not entirely accept the psychological possibility of Walter. He admits his question about the persistent cruelty of his hero at least twice and can only answer it by asserting that "ther been folk of swich condicion" that when they make up their minds to do something "they kan nat stynte of hire entencion,/ But, right as they were bounden to a stake,/ They wol nat of that firste purpos slake" (IV, 701-705). As a result, the whole elaborate story about marriage is, in the end, really a fairy tale, and Griselda is declared by the Clerk to be not only "inportable" but so rare in her goodness as to be non-existent. The whole tale is about something that could not be, even as the *Wife of Bath's Tale*, in spite of its fantasy, is about a relationship that could be, given, of course, certain conditions which though not within the realm of possibility are somehow within the realm of probability.

The Clerk makes it explicit at the end that he has no more believed in Griselda as a person than we have. His allegorical meaning clearly explained, he finds he cannot leave the tale without a final reference to his heroine. "But o word, lordynges, herkneth er I go:/ It were ful hard to fynde now-a-dayes/ In al a toun Grisildis thre or two," he says, and directly looking at the Wife of Bath he adds:

> For if that they were put to swich assayes,
> The gold of hem hath so badde alayes
> With bras, that thogh the coyne be fair at ye,
> It wolde rather breste a-two than plye.
>
> For which heere, for the Wyves love of Bathe—
> Whos lyf and al hire secte God mayntene
> In heigh maistrie, and elles were it scathe—
> I wol with lusty herte, fressh and grene,
> Seyn yow a song to glade yow, I wene;
> And lat us stynte of ernestful matere.
> Herkneth my song that seith in this manere.
>   (IV, 1166-1176)

The song that concludes his tale mounts in sarcastic vigor. It seems to sound forth as the voice of the Wife of Bath's fifth husband must have, as it read aloud night after night to her "of wikked wyves." Its sarcastic extolling of the virago and the shrew betrays the Clerk's essential misogny and confirms not only Alisoun's conclusions about "clerkes . . . withinne hire oratories" but her assumptions about the nature of women and the conditions of "peaceful" márriage as well:

> O noble wyves, ful of heigh prudence,
> Lat noon humylitee youre tonge naille,
> Ne lat no clerk have cause or diligence
> To write of yow a storie of swich mervaille
> As of Grisildis pacient and kynde,
> Lest Chichevache yow swelwe in hire entraille!

Folweth Ekko, that holdeth no silence,
But evere answereth at the countretaille.
Beth nat bidaffed for youre innocence,
But sharply taak on yow the governaille.
Emprenteth wel this lessoun in youre mynde,
For commune profit sith it may availle.

Ye archewyves, stondeth at defense,
Syn ye be strong as is a greet camaille;
Ne suffreth nat that men yow doon offense.
And sklendre wyves, fieble as in bataille,
Beth egre as is a tygre yond in Ynde;
Ay clappeth as a mille, I yow consaille.

Ne dreed hem nat, doth hem no reverence,
For though thyn housebonde armed be in maille,
The arwes of thy crabbed eloquence
Shal perce his brest, and eek his aventaille.
In jalousie I rede eek thou hym bynde,
And thou shalt make hym couche as doth a quaille.

If thou be fair, ther folk been in presence,
Shewe thou thy visage and thyn apparaille;
If thou be foul, be fre of thy dispence;
To gete thee freendes ay do thy travaille;
Be ay of chiere as light as leef on lynde,
And lat hym care, and wepe, and wrynge, and waille!
                                        (IV, 1183-1212)

Thus the *Clerk's Tale*, for all its pious exhortation, effects a negation of all the values the Wife of Bath in her monologue and in her tale has charged with vital affirmation: love, sex, marriage, "gentilesse," and the joy of living in the midst of hostile forces. But all his dislike of her and "her secte" does not "quit" her nor her thesis about life. Though the irony of his corroboration of her conclusions may be intended to diminish her large and lusty presence, it does not do so. On the contrary, as his cynicism becomes more evident, so her zest becomes greater. In the contest of attitudes the Clerk may not lose, but neither does he win.

THE MERCHANT'S TALE

The response to the story of patient Griselda is immediate. The Host is enchanted by visions of female submissiveness: "By Goddes bones,/ Me were levere than a barel ale/ My wyf at hoom had herd this legende ones!" But it is the Merchant who has caught the cynicism of the Envoy and who has clearly seen what it is the Clerk has really proved about women and marriage. "Wepyng and waylyng, care and oother sorwe/ I knowe ynogh, on even and a-morwe," he says, quoting the last words of the Clerk's "song." And passionately embittered by his experience with the "wo that is in mariage," he tells what is perhaps Chaucer's most thoroughly cynical tale and becomes one of Chaucer's most complex characters.

By itself, and out of dramatic and thematic context, the tale of the marriage between the elderly January and the youthful May and of her ingenious cuckolding of her "olde housebonde" is comic only in the most coarse and obvious way. It has all the characteristics of the "dirty story"— sex, impotent old age, female cunning—that its countless analogues betray. Stories such as this one go on being told from age to age with a persistence so inevitable that one is inclined to think they are archetypal. There is no reason for Chaucer not to have included a "dirty story" among his comedies, of course. In addition to the snicker it raises, it has a kind of poetic justice that gives comic pleasure on another level, even as its spleenful misogyny arouses laughter no matter what the age or the audience; certainly the pilgrims (and Chaucer's contemporaries), who accepted the thesis that woman is "man's woe" and "all his confusion," would have delighted in this clear illustration of so cherished a doctrine.

But the true brilliance of the comedy, when it is seen in its context, is more noteworthy than this. If the Clerk has, by his negation of the vital joy of the Wife of Bath, made more rare the joy of her nature, the Merchant's sardonic and irascible hatred, that encompasses more than marriage or the relations between the sexes, makes her acceptance of all of life—whether characterized by indignity, or the coming of age, or the constant threat of Church and Society—a great affirmation indeed. The Clerk's misogyny is as much a professional attitude as it is a temperamental one; the Merchant's anguished bitterness that subsumes the whole universe, men and gods, nature animate and inanimate, has come from experience and has all the emotional absolutism of profound disillusion:

> "I have a wyf, the worste that may be;
> For thogh the feend to hire ycoupled were,
> She wolde hym overmacche, I dar wel swere.
> What sholde I yow reherce in special
> Hir hye malice? She is a shrewe in al.
>
> .   .   .   .
>
> A! goode sire Hoost, I have ywedded bee

> This monthes two, and moore nat, pardee;
> And yet, I trowe, he that al his lyve
> Wyflees hath been, though that men wolde hym ryve
> Unto the herte, ne koude in no manere
> Tellen so muchel sorwe as I now heere
> Koude tellen of my wyves cursednesse!"
>   (IV, 1218-1222; 1233-1239)

The degree of his bitter unhappiness that is almost complete despair is, it seems, so great that he will not consciously give into it by doing what the Wife of Bath has done. To the Host's plea that he tell on, he replies "Gladly, . . . but of myn owene soore,/ For soory herte, I telle may namoore." His is to be no autobiographical monologue, but a tale much like that just told by the Clerk. His very rejection of the invitation to speak directly of his own experience is a way of containing his wretchedness.

The tale he chooses begins in a way that echoes the two first stanzas of the story told by the Clerk: "Whilom ther was dwellynge in Lumbardye/ A worthy knyght, that born was of Pavye,/ In which he lyved in greet prosperitee." And for the first moments of the tale there are reminiscences of the opening scene of the story of Walter and the patient Griselda, for this "worthy knyght," too, is about to select a wife. But at this point the echoes fade; what had begun as fiction begins to sound suspiciously like fact. The "olde Knyght" of the *Merchant's Tale*, "sixty yeer a wyflees man," profligate and lecherous all his life, who decides to get himself a young wife and an heir, is quite unlike the noble "markys," Walter. Indeed, it is he who must persuade his counsellors to let him wed. The tale is not twenty lines told before the tone conveys disgust and bitterness, and it is clear that, though the pretense of fiction is being maintained, it is being maintained in spite of the emotional involvement that increases with almost every line. The Merchant's hero is a fool, and his decision to marry "whan that he was passed sixty yeer" may have been made "for hoolynesse," but more likely "for dotage,"—"I kan hat seye." His way of finding a wife is "t'espien" about the village among the young girls:

> Preyinge oure Lord to graunten him that he
> Mighte ones knowe of thilke blisful lyf
> That is bitwixe an housbonde and his wyf,
> And for to lyve under that hooly boond
> With which that first God man and womman bond.
>   (IV, 1258-1262)

The Merchant's cynical irony is unmistakable in the rationalization he gives his hero:

> "Noon oother lyf," sayde he, "is worth a bene;
> For wedlock is so esy and so clene,
> That in this world it is a paradys."
> Thus seyde this olde knyght, that was so wys.
> (IV, 1263-1266)

The ideal marriage between Walter and the gentle maiden, Griselda, is turned into an illusion at the end; the knight of this tale clearly cultivates the illusion to begin with. The foolish rationalizations of his aging lust make him both a repulsive and a pitiable figure from the beginning.

The tale that follows is made up of two parodies, one of *The Prologue and Tale of the Wife of Bath* and one of *The Clerk's Tale*. And his resorting to rhetorical forms now and then tells us that he has also listened to the Man of Law with care. But the Clerk of Oxford and Alisoun dominate his mind for they have touched most vitally upon his "owene soore." Like Walter, January finds a young wife from among the common people; his search for the right woman becomes a parody of Walter's for Griselda. Unlike the Wife of Bath, the relish he feels for the physical conveys not joy and a sense of vitality but a disgust and a lustfulness. "Heigh fantasye and curious bisynesse/ Fro day to day gan in the soule impresse/ Of Januarie about his mariage," and so he looks over the girls with lecherous eye. Until at last "apoynted hym on oon":

> And whan that he was in his bed ybroght
> He purtreyed in his herte and in his thoght
> Hir fresshe beautee and hir age tendre,
> Hir myddel smal, hire armes longe and sklendre,
> Hir wise governaunce, hir gentillesse,
> Hir womanly berynge, and hire sadnesse.
> (IV, 1599-1604)

Like Walter, January assumes that the word of the husband is law, that marriage unites perfectly into "o flessh" man and wife, "in wele and in distresse." "A wyf! a, Seinte Marie, *benedicite!*" he gloats:

> How myghte a man han any adversitee
> That hath a wyf? Certes, I kan nat seye.
> (IV, 1337-1339)

He determines to choose from among the poor because such a wife is bound to be frugal, kind, and obedient:

> Al that hire housbonde lust, hire liketh weel;
> She seith nat ones "nay," whan he seith "ye."
> "Do this," seith he; "Al redy, sire," seith she.
> O blisful ordre of wedlok precious,
> Thou art so murye, and eek so vertuous.
>   (IV, 1344-1348)

That the Merchant thinks his hero to be an idiot is clear, and the irony in his praise of the wedded state increases in sarcasm. "Every man that halt hym worth a leek," he says, ought to get on his knees and thank God he has a wife—and the irony sharpens into bitterness:

> Or elles preye to God hym for to sende
> A wyf, to laste unto his lyves ende.
> For thanne his lyf is set in sikernesse;
> He may nat be deceyved, as I gesse,
> So that he werke after his wyves reed.
> Thanne may he boldely beren up his heed,
> They been so trewe, and therwithal so wyse;
> For which, if thou wolt werken as the wyse,
> Do alwey so as wommen wol thee rede.
>   (IV, 1353-1361)

The transition from the Clerk's illusory view of marriage to the view held by the Wife of Bath he has made almost without pause. Though the Merchant has moved into his tale under the impetus of the Clerk's last words and a clear awareness of the absurdity of the portrait of the patient Griselda, he is clearly preoccupied with the Wife of Bath's view of marriage and the relation between the sexes. It is Alisoun, large and gat-toothed, lusty and joyous, defier of age and decay, who calls forth from him the embittered and cynical story of marriage, as if his agreement with her view that there is "wo in marriage" constitutes a masterly revenge upon her and all her sex.

There are many reasons for his need to have vengeance upon the Wife. Though we do not know the Merchant's age, it is not impossible to conclude that he, like his hero January, is "olde." The contrast between Alisoun's female sexuality, that is still in evidence despite her years, and his "cursednesse" is obvious to him as it is to anyone who hears him. The frankness of her sexuality generates much of the disgust— that is in large part surely envy—with which he describes the pathetic impotence of old age. The memory of his own unhappy marriage and his revulsion at Alisoun's account of the wedding between the "foul hag" and the young knight combine to give him the power to picture the union between January and May with undisguised ugliness. The vision of the old knight, stuffed with aphrodisiacs, in bed with the young May, is deliberately contrived in its mock-lyric tone to contrast with the moment in the Wife's Tale when she tells of the love that transforms age into youth, "foulness" into beauty, distress into joy:

> Parfourned hath the sonne his ark diurne;
> Ne lenger may the body of hym sojurne
> On the' orisonte, as in that latitude.
> Night with his mantel, that is derk and rude,
> Gan oversprede the hemysperie aboute;
> For which departed is this lusty route
> Fro Januarie, with thank on every syde.
> Hoom to hir houses lustily they ryde,
> Where as they doon hir thynges as hem leste,
> And whan they sye hir tyme, goon to reste.
> Soone after that, this hastif Januarie
> Wolde go to bedde, he wolde no lenger tarye.
> He drynketh ypocras, claree, and vernage
> Of spices hoot, t'encressen his corage;
> And many a letuarie hath he ful fyn,
> Swiche as the cursed monk, daun Constantyn,
> Hath writen in his book *De Coitu;*
> To eten hem alle he nas no thyng eschu.
> (IV, 1795-1812)

The details of the love-making that follow arouse in the reader a complex of response that is important for understanding some of the ways this tale is comic. The minuteness of the description of the sexual ugliness, the tone that reveals disgust, the quick glimpse of the impassive and enigmatic May, tell much about the Merchant's own awareness of his identification with January, but they also hint at how partial that awareness is. The Merchant seems to be sustaining the illusion of fiction only by the effort of will: he is both repelled by and attracted to the lecherous and old husband. As a result we see the "olde man" as both odious and pathetic, and for a moment we pity May, though we do not come near to liking her. There is here a preparation for the sense of justice the tale will give us at the end; the sense of relief that people as perverse and depraved as these do not go unpunished though that punishment is not administered by civil or ecclesiastical means. And

the figure of May, mute in bed—"But God woot what that May thoughte
in hir herte,/ Whan she hym saugh up sittynge in his sherte,/ In his
nyght-cappe, and with his nekke lene;/ She preyseth nat his pleyying
worth a bene" (IV, 1851-1854)—reminds us of the young Alisoun and her
first three good "old" husbands; and the reminder brings with it once
more, by the sharpness of the contrast, the sense of her joyous affirmation of the fact and act of marriage no matter what the woe.

For Alisoun the pilgrim, the Merchant has nothing but dislike. With
pointed emphasis he has had his hero say he wants only a young wife:

> "I wol noon oold wyf han in no manere.
> She shal nat passe twenty yeer, certayn;
> Oold fissh and yong flessh wolde I have ful fayn.
> Bet is," quod he, "a pyk than a pykerel,
> And bet than old boef is the tendre veel.
> I wol no womman thritty yeer of age;
> It is but bene-straw and greet forage."
>   (IV, 1416-1422)

Her prologue has clearly struck him as having been too full of learning,
and his January repeats "I wol noon oold wyf han right for this cause."
For Alisoun's vision of herself as the young wife of old husbands he has
furious hatred. He is all the old husbands in one; he is the cuckold, she
the cuckolder. May, lying, deceitful, lecherous, opportunistic, domineer-
ing in the final moments of his tale, is the fiction of which Alisoun is
the living fact. So aroused is he by the accuracy of her analysis of female
nature that at one moment in the tale he forgets he is narrating a story
and puts into the mouth of one of his characters a reference to the Wife.
Justinus, called in as one of the counsellors of January, knowing all the
objections to marriage sound hollow to the lustful eagerness of the "olde
knyght," repeats those words of the Wife of Bath that had defined her
consolation when she felt guilt at the way she was treating her fourth
husband, and elaborates upon them with sardonic glee:

> "Paraunter she may be youre purgatorie!
> She may be Goddes meene and Goddes whippe;
> Thanne shal youre soule up to hevene skippe
> Swifter than dooth an arwe out of a bowe.
> I hope to God, herafter shul ye knowe
> That ther nys no so greet felicitee
> In mariage, ne nevere mo shal bee,
> That yow shal lette of youre savacion,
> So that ye use, as skile is and reson,

> The lustes of youre wyf attemprely,
> And that he plese hire nat to amorously,
> And that ye kepe yow eek from oother synne.
> My tale is doon, for my wit is thynne.
> Beth nat agast herof, my brother deere,
> But lat us waden out of this mateere.
> The Wyf of Bathe, if ye han understonde,
> Of mariage, which ye have on honde,
> Declared hath ful wel in litel space.
> Fareth now wel, God have yow in his grace."
>   (IV, 1670-1688)

Indeed, the Wife of Bath's jovial hope that she has assured her husband's release from purgatory in the hereafter by providing it for him on earth haunts the Merchant and forms something of a unifying theme for his tale. January reveals from the beginning a concern with "bliss," with "paradys," with "purgatorie" as marriage ensures them. "Noon oother lyf," he says, "is worth a bene;/ For wedlok is so esy and so clene,/ That in this world it is a paradys." A wedded man lives a "lyf blisful and ordinaat,/ Under this yok of mariage ybounde." And Justinus' echo of Alisoun's words console him, for if, perchance, marriage is not "paradys" but "purgatorie," then he can rest assured that he is earning bliss and paradise in eternity.

But the reward granted in heaven for the suffering upon earth holds little real consolation for the Merchant. His cynical misogyny, his bitter disillusion, does not deny such reward its possibility nor its Christian validity. Indeed, his need to extend his unhappiness beyond the world of men is urgent, and the climax of his tale takes place among the gods as well as among his characters. Other pilgrims have brought in the supra-world of gods and fairies and so can he. In the garden that makes us think of the garden where roamed "Emelye the shene," in a world as fanciful as the world of the Loathly Lady—"Bright was the day, and blew the firmament;/ Phebus hath of gold his stremes doun ysent,/ To gladen every flour with his warmnesse" (IV, 2219-2221)—the copulation of May and Damyan in the pear tree is done, and the magical "unblinding" that awakens the old husband to "reality" is accomplished, though only momentarily. Pluto and Proserpine are present, though unseen by the human beings so busy about their own lust. Pluto, seated "upon a bench of turves, fressh and grene," takes up the old argument. "Experience . . . preveth every day," he says to Proserpine, that women are notable for "untrouthe and brotilnesse;" witness this old man who is about to be made a "cokewold." His sympathies are great and he has every determination to help the cuckolded and blind January:

"Now wol I graunten, of my magestee,
Unto this olde, blynde, worthy knyght
That he shal have ayen his eyen syght,
Whan that his wyf wold doon hym vileynye.
Thanne shal he knowen al hire harlotrye,
Bothe in repreve of hire and othere mo."
(IV, 2258-2263)

But the world of the gods, like the world of men, is ruled by the female. Proserpine, woman as well as goddess, has the last word as effectively as had Alisoun:

"Ye shal?" quod Proserpyne, "wol ye so?
Now by my moodres sires soule I swere
That I shal yeven hire suffisant answere,
And alle wommen after, for hir sake;
That, though they be in any gilt ytake,
With face boold they shulle hemself excuse,
And bere hem doun that wolden hem accuse.
For lak of answere noon of hem shal dyen.
Al hadde man seyn a thyng with bothe his yen,
Yit shul we wommen visage it hardily,
And wepe, and swere, and chyde subtilly,
So that ye men shul been as lewed as gees."
(IV, 2264-2275)

In a tone as authoritative as the Wife of Bath's, she casts scorn in the face of Pluto's "auctoritees," and in final exultation proclaims her affinity for all the Mays and all the Alisouns in the world:

"I sette right noght, of al the vileynye
That ye of wommen write, a boterflye!
I am a womman, nedes moot I speke,
Or elles swelle til myn herte breke."
(IV, 2303-2306)

"Madame," says Pluto, with all the resignation of all the men from Alisoun's five husbands to January, whose lesson is so soon to be learned, "be no lenger wrooth;/ I yeve it up!" Though aware of the futility of the gesture, he will, nevertheless, grant January his sight; at least one man may be given the chance to perceive the nature of illusion and may learn from the vision of reality.

The "olde, blynde man," once blinded by love, now blinded by age and the course of time, is given his moment of clear vision. "Allas, allas," says the old January, "For I am blynd!" But the miraculous restoration of sight is a devastating thing, for it reveals to him a totality of deception that proves to be more than he can bear:

> Up to the tree he caste his eyen two,
> And saugh that Damyan his wyf had dressed
> In swich manere it may nat been expressed,
> But if I wolde speke uncurteisly;
> And up he yaf a roryng and a cry,
> As dooth the mooder whan the child shal dye:
> "Out! help! allas! harrow!" he gan to crye,
> "O stronge lady stoore, what dostow?"
> (IV, 2360-2367)

May's answer, as Proserpine had promised, is ready: she did it to cure his blindness—besides the act of intercourse was all an illusion anyway: "Ye han som glynsyng, and no parfit sighte." With some reluctance but with no perseverance, January begins to be willing to be convinced and his retreat from truth is accompanied by evident relief. His "I se . . . as wel as evere I myghte" becomes "me thoughte he dide thee so," becomes

> "Now Dame . . . lat al passe out of mynde.
> Com doun, my lief, and if I have myssayd,
> God helpe me so, as I am yvele apayd.
> But, by my fader soule, I wende han seyn
> How that this Damyan hadde by thee leyn,
> And that thy smok hadde leyn upon his brest."
> (IV, 2390-2395)

It is May who speaks what is the Merchant's cynical conclusion about the whole business—the cuckolding of January, marriage, age, youth, truth, illusion:

> "Ye sire," quod she, "ye may wene as yow lest.
> But sire, a man that waketh out of his sleep,
> He may nat sodeynly wel taken keep
> Upon a thyng, ne seen it parfitly,
> Til that he be adawed verraily.
> Right so a man that longe hath blynd be,
> Ne may nat sodeynly so wel yse,
> First whan his sighte is newe come ageyn,
> As he that hath a day or two yseyn.

> Til that youre sighte ysatled be a while,
> Ther may ful many a sighte yow bigile.
> Beth war, I prey yow; for, by hevene kyng,
> Ful many a man weneth to seen a thyng,
> And it is al another than it semeth.
> He that mysconceyveth, he mysdemeth."
> And with that word she leep doun fro the tree.
>   (IV, 2396-2411)

There is in this final universalization of the Merchant's view of life what is almost a lessening of the emotional tension of the particular cynicism; in a way he has talked out his agony and has come to terms with his wretchedness in the telling of the tale. The bitterness is no less, but there is in the last lines a sense of recovered control over what is really a self-disgust:

> This Januarie, who is glad but he?
> He kisseth hire, and clippeth hire ful ofte,
> And on hire wombe he stroketh hire ful softe,
> And to his palays hoom he hath hire lad.
> Now, goode men, I pray yow to be glad.
> Thus endeth heere my tale of Januarie;
> God blesse us, and his mooder Seinte Marie!
>   (IV, 2412-2418)

He has learned the hard way to be resigned to what the Miller had said early in the pilgrimage: "An housbonde shal nat been inquisityf/ Of Goddes pryvetee, nor of his wyf./ So he may fynde Goddes foyson there,/ Of the remenant nedeth nat enquere" (I, 3163-3166).

The Merchant's Tale, out of context, is an ugly tale brilliantly told. Its unrelieved cynicism leaves a sour taste in the mouth; its bitterness is, for a moment, dismaying. As it parodies *The Wife of Bath's Prologue and Tale* and *The Clerk's Tale* it points up all their themes, underscores all their concerns in ways that strip away all complexity and reduce them to two simple statements about the relation between the sexes, and one simple statement about the nature of justice and truth: "Do alwey so as wommen wol thee rede," for there is nothing else you can do. There is no point in "seeing," for deception is the rule and the state of blindness is the only comfortable one. Besides, the old man got exactly what was coming to him, since, with stupid persistence he defied all warnings and went into the marriage "with open eyes." It is a tale that strikes something like horror to the heart of the Host: "Ey! Goddes mercy! . . . Now swich a wyf I pray God kepe me fro!" Even his wife, shrew that she is, cannot be compared to May. What keeps this tale within the comic mode is the Merchant's ultimate success in sustaining the fictional pretense, for though the tonal quality tells much about his emotional response to his story, he never really moves into auto-biography. Somehow he manages to maintain a kind of objectivity, even though it is seriously threatened at moments. Neither pathos nor fury completely dominate, and his equilibrium continues within the tension. The observer-pilgrim, Chaucer, had seen little indication of the conflict in his portrait of the Merchant; but, then, he could not have, for what rouses the "worthy man" from his "estatly . . . governaunce" has nothing to do with his appearance. It is possible to conjecture that had there been no Wife of Bath and no proposal about marriage to stir him into something approaching self-revelation, he would have spoken "ful solempnely,/ Sownynge alwey th'encrees of his wynnyng."

THE SQUIRE'S TALE

What Chaucer intended to do with the tale told by the Squire can be only tentatively suggested. That he expected to complete it seems clear from the praise given it by the Franklin:

> "In feith, Squier, thow hast thee wel yquit
> And gentilly. I preise wel thy wit,"
> Quod the Frankeleyn, "considerynge thy yowthe,
> So feelyngly thou spekest, sire, I allow the!
> As to my doom, ther is noon that is heere
> Of eloquence that shal by thy peere,
> If that thou lyve; God yeve thee good chaunce,
> And in vertu sende thee continuaunce!
> For of thy speche I have greet deyntee."
>   (V, 673-681)

There seems no hint of irony in the words, nor any indication that the Franklin has not heard the tale out to its conclusion.

It seems possible to conjecture that the tale as it exists is as close to a first draft as any tale in the Canterbury collection; that it is a hastily sketched outline of plot, theme, and characters that were, in time, to undergo reshaping and reforming. Why Chaucer did not return to it cannot, of course, be even a matter of guess. Although there are only 672 lines in it, it seems almost interminable in the reading. Neither Part One nor Part Two completes any incident initiated by the magical gifts made to Cambuscan or intimates any ways in which the stories might resolve, and the lines that outline the subject matter for the rest of the tale discourage any temptation to conjecture future development:

Thus lete I Canacee hir hauk kepyng;
I wol namoore as now speke of hir ryng,
Til it come eft to purpos for to seyn
How that this faucon gat hire love ageyn
Repentant, as the storie telleth us,
By mediacion of Cambalus,
The kynges sone, of which that I yow tolde.
But hennesforth I wol my proces holde
To speken of aventures and of batailles,
That nevere yet was herd so grete mervailles.
    First wol I telle yow of Cambyuskan,
That in his tyme many a citee wan;
And after wol I speke of Algarsif,
How that he wan Theodora to his wif,
For whom ful ofte in greet peril he was,
Ne hadde he ben holpen by the steede of bras;
And after wol I speke of Cambalo,
That faught in lystes with the bretheren two
For Canacee er that he myghte hire wynne.
And ther I lefte I wol ayagn bigaynne.
                 Explicit secunda pars.
                 Incipit pars tercia.
Appollo whirleth up his chaar so hye,
Til that the god Mercurius hous, the slye—
                 (V, 651-672)

Where from "Mercurius hous" the Squire, or Chaucer, was going, there is no way of guessing. It seems hardly likely that Chaucer has suddenly turned from the writing of tales that maintain the illusion of being contained within the narrative and dramatic framework of the pilgrimage and has decided to spin out, or have one of his characters spin out, a romance in the manner of the many metrical and prose writers of the day. Nor is there any reason to think that he intends to parody the metrical romances; at least nothing in the tone of the narration nor in the praise given it by the Franklin gives any evidence of this. As it stands, therefore, discursive, formless, awkward in narration, suggesting only in a minimal way any dramatic interest, it offers very little for the understanding of Chaucer's comedy. But it hints at the kind of person Chaucer may have meant to develop in a more complex fashion in the revision or reworking of the fragment, and such a person would in no way be a misfit among the pilgrims who, whatever their individualities, are, in the collective sense, recognizably consanguineous in Chaucer's comic world.

The fragment of the tale reveals a narrator who only in part seems like the Squire seen by the pilgrim-observer. The romantic fantasy of the tale, the imagination that is almost entirely literary, the enthusiasm for courtly festivity, the idealized heroine, Canacee, the interest in magic and adventure—all portray a narrator of youth and inexperience. In these ways the tale fits the Squire, "a lovyere and a lusty bachelor/ With lokkes crulle as they were leyd in presse;/ Of twenty yeer of age he was I gesse." But the embarrassed awkwardness with which the tale is told, the absence of a sense of order or form, the moments of dullness, do not fit the young man who "koude songes make and wel endite,/ Juste and eek daunce, and weel purtreye and write." It is possible, of course, that the discrepancy is intended as part of what might emerge as comic in the character of the Squire, but for this interpretation there is not the slightest hint in Chaucer's text. What the comic potential in the figure of the Squire and in the fragment of his tale is, it is possible to see. Although his view of life lacks a sense of order and seems unaware of the problem of justice, divine or otherwise, it is a view that promises to see human relationships with the mind of youth, "fressh" in its idealism, "curteis, lowely, and servysable"; the mind of one who had "born hym weel, as of so litel space,/ In hope to stonden in his lady grace." And the ideals he holds about faithfulness in love, about the "repentaunt" return of the faithless lover, about "gentilesse," about "pitee," about honor and bravery in "many batailles," though they are valued in the terms of a fairy tale, are the values raised to public view by the Wife of Bath, indirectly denied by the Clerk, and bitterly rejected by the Merchant. They are the ideals that will shortly be the concern of the Franklin, whose more complex and mature handling of them will transform them from the land of fairy to the world of possible reality. It is no wonder that Milton found the tale of "Cambuscan the bold" one worth meditating upon. And one is grateful to the tale for the way in which it breaks sharply with the mood of cynicism and bitterness created by the Merchant.

THE FRANKLIN'S TALE

"Thonked be God that is eterne on lyve" for the tale told by the Franklin! After the coarse and essentially cynical view of love and marriage revealed in all the fabliaux from the *Miller's Tale* through the *Merchant's*, after the romantic and sentimental view of the *Knight's Tale* and the tales of pious and impossible love, this view of marriage based upon mutual love, upon mutual trust, upon honesty, upon shared faith comes as a great relief. Its very uniqueness of view makes us unwilling to question it as improbable or impossible. If the *Merchant's Tale* is Chaucer's ugliest, the *Franklin's Tale* is his loveliest. Its unqualified belief in the possibility of human goodness makes palatable the tales of greater cynicism or of greater idealism, as they, in turn, help to transform its fantasy and ideality into reality. Without it the comic genius of Chaucer would be a lesser thing; with it, the sense of justice, the awareness of balance and order within and behind the nature of things, the belief in the ability of the human being to endure misfortune so variously illustrated in the other tales, receive convincing affirmation. It is in this tale that the many questions about the nature of human existence raised by the narrators of other tales become, for one dramatic and moving moment, the one great question—what is the nature of evil. The great black rocks that seem so useless and gratuitous a threat to the return of Dorigen's beloved husband become, in her meditative lament, the symbol that extends the questions asked by the other tales to the metaphysical; the answer, clearly Boethian in source, is Chaucer's answer and the answer of his kind of Comedy:

> "Eterne God, that thurgh thy purveiaunce
> Ledest the world by certein governaunce,
> In ydel, as men seyn, ye no thynge make.
> But, Lord, thise grisly feendly rokkes blake,
> That semen rather a foul confusion
> Of werk than any fair creacion
> Of swich a parfit wys God and a stable,
> Why han ye wroght this werk unresonable?
> For by this werk, south, north, ne west, ne eest,
> Ther nys yfostred man, ne bryd, ne beest;
> It dooth no good, to my wit, but anoyeth:"
>   (V, 865-875)

It is the tale that works out the answer, for what is good and what is evil, what is threatening and what is not, what is "wo" or what is "joye," depend upon the nature of the doer and the actor; in the words of Boethius' Philosophy, "al that evere is iknowe, it is rather comprehendid and knowen, nat aftir his strengthe and his nature, but aftir the faculte (*that is to seyn, the power and the nature*) of hem that knowen" (Book V, Prosa 4). God's plan, though not knowable, is good, and all things work toward the fulfilment of it, not automatically nor mechanically, but in full cooperation of the human will that has the power to act. In this tale, the human beings are conceived upon the premise that they are "good," but their actions, based upon partial sight, involve them in threats to happiness and to life itself. And although they are surrounded by illusions that they are controlled by forces that are deterministic, the Franklin makes it clear that these forces are "seemings" merely; the interrelated course of events is human-caused and human-caused only. Dorigen's conclusion that "al is for the beste,/ Though I ne kan the causes nat ynowe" is made by the complexity of the story that follows her lament, a tenable conclusion, still optimistic but no longer simply so.

Not only does *The Franklin's Tale* summarize and embody what is the essential view of life that is the source of Chaucer's comedy, it is also a significant part of the organism of *The Canterbury Tales* in obvious ways: it characterizes its teller in a way that makes him realizable as a member of the pilgrimage, and as a tale, it has the design or pattern of comedy—a happy ending after a threat of disaster.

The voice of the Franklin is heard only now and then as he tells his tale, but it is heard enough so that his presence is never forgotten. His attitude toward his story is one of objectivity; after the shrill voice of the Merchant, its quiet unemotionalism strikes the ear with relief and creates, in its clear simplicity, unquestioning acceptance for what it is telling.

The initial impression the Franklin gives as he begins his tale does little to confirm or deny the observer's portrait of him in the *General Prologue*. To the Host his words to the Squire seem to suggest he will be a person with pretensions toward solemnity and preachment. His comment at the end of the tale of "Cambuscan bold,/ Of Camball, and of Algarsif/ And who had Canacee to wife," which brings to mind for one brief second the figure of Shakespeare's Henry IV, intimates that he suffers helplessly the escapades of a dissolute and unruly son to whom the elegantly mannered and highly moral young Squire bears a sharp contrast:

> ". . . of thy speche I have greet deyntee.
> I have a sone, and by the Trinitee,
> I hadde levere than twenty pound worth lond,
> Though it right now were fallen in myn hond,
> He were a man of swich discrecioun
> As that ye been! Fy on possessioun,
> But if a man be vertuous withal!
> I have my sone snybbed, and yet shal,
> For he to vertu listeth nat entende;
> But for to pleye at dees, and to despende
> And lese al that he hath, is his usage.
> And he hath levere talken with a page
> Than to comune with any gentil wight
> Where he myghte lerne gentillesse aright."
>   (V, 681-694)

The Host, alarmed at the tone which seems to promise dreary moralizing, calls a halt to the Franklin's address: the order of comedy and mirth must be restored even at the cost of rudeness.

> "Straw for youre gentillesse!" quod oure Hoost.
> "What, Frankeleyn! pardee, sire, wel thou woost
> That ech of yow moot tellen atte leste
> A tale or two, or breken his biheste."
> (V, 695-698)

The Host's words recall not only the Franklin but all the pilgrims to the purpose of the "game," and rude though they may be, they restore to the pilgrimage its original perspective. The gradual loss of objectivity and of a sense of proportion from the Prologue of the Wife of Bath to the last bitter word of the Merchant is stopped. The perspective of the impersonal, of the narrative that has been threatened by the personal involvement and by the indulgence in autobiography, is re-established. The Franklin, fond of delight himself—"wel loved he by the morwe a sop in wyn;/ To lyven in delit was evere his wone,/ For he was Epicurus owene sone,/ That heeld opinioun that pleyn delit/ Was verray felicitee parfit"—is quite willing to comply:

> "That knowe I wel, sire," quod the Frankeleyn.
> I prey yow, haveth me nat in desdeyn,
> Though to this man I speke a word or two."
> "Telle on thy tale withouten wordes mo."
> "Gladly, sire Hoost," quod he, "I wole obeye
> Unto your wyl; now herkneth what I seye.
> I wol yow nat contrarien in no wyse
> As fer as that my wittes wol suffyse.
> I prey to God that it may plesen yow;
> Thanne woot I wel that it is good ynow."
> (V, 699-708)

That the Franklin is a man of honest, almost transparent simplicity is borne out in the brief apologia that precedes his tale and in the kinds of comments he makes in the course of telling it. Like the Clerk, he is careful to announce his source, a Breton lay; but he is anxious to acknowledge that he has not the learning some of the other pilgrims have shown—he must speak in a simple way, because he is a "burel man," "rude" of speech, untaught in "rethorik." "Thyng that I speke, it moot be bare and pleyn./ I sleep nevere on the Mount of Pernaso,/ Ne lerned Marcus Tullius Scithero" (V, 720-722). And while his tale reveals that though he does indeed know how to use "heigh style" when he wants to, his description of his powers is a true one: the style, "bare and pleyn" is the first of the several devices he uses to create belief in the story he tells.

Never once in the course of his tale does he close the distance between himself and his characters that his initial attitude establishes. Nor does he ever remove himself so far from the action, from the concern the tale embodies, that he becomes merely a re-teller as the Second Nun has. He is, more importantly, always conscious of his audience, aware that some things in his story need explanation or comment, even that some of the "rhetoric" he uses needs some translation into plainer terms. So he describes the departure of the rest of the guests who have been with Aurelius at the party:

> Tho coome hir othere freendes many oon,
> And in the aleyes romeden up and doun,
> And nothyng wiste of this conclusioun,
> But sodeynly bigonne revel newe
> Til that the brighte sonne loste his hewe;
> For th'orisonte hath reft the sonne his lyght,—
> This is as much to seye as it was nyght!
> (V, 1012-1018)

He is aware that there are some details in his story that are for obvious reasons, disturbing, but respectful of his source he will not alter them. It is somewhat a matter of distress for him that Aurelius (like "hende Nicholas" in *The Miller's Tale*), in the course of trying to win Dorigen from her husband, turns to astrology and to magic— "swich folye/ As in our dayes is nat worth a flye,—/ For hooly chirches feith in oure bileve/ Ne suffreth noon illusion us to greve" (V, 1131-1134). Indeed, so little respect has he for "swich a supersticious cursednesse" that he takes great pains to ascribe all the magician creates to illusion. His explicit concern with the nature of "diverse apparences," his repetition of the words "semed" and "apparence," result in separating clearly the illusion from the reality, and make it unquestionable that all happens in this tale happens because of the human beings, not because of any magical or supernatural intervention. What Aurelius "saugh" in the house of the magician was what he was led to see, not what was really magically produced. And since the Franklin has felt it necessary to attribute the magic he has found in his source to the artful creation of an illusion by the learned "tragetour," so he finds it important to comment upon the decision of Arveragus to send Dorigen into the arms of the squire Aurelius. "Paraventure an heep of yow, ywis," he says, "wol holden hym a lewed man in this/ That he wol putte his wyf in jupartie" (V, 1493-1495). Because he knows that the story is to end happily, he cannot resist intimating so to his listeners, aware that they too may question the moral rightness of the decision: "Herkneth the tale er ye upon hire crie./ She may have bettre fortune than yow semeth;/ And whan that ye han herd the tale, demeth" (V, 1496-1498).

"Colours ne knowe I none, withouten drede,/ But swich colours as growen in the mede" he has proclaimed at the beginning of his narrative, and so he reveals. His response to nature is as direct and as "pleyn" as his response to his characters is, and the moments when he describes setting or weather constitute another way in which he creates belief in what he is telling. Dorigen also walks in a garden where she is met by the romantic approaches of the young squire Aurelius. The garden in which Emelye "the shene" wandered had all the stylized elegance of tapestry; the garden in the Merchant's tale, whose beauty rivaled even that in *The Romance of the Rose*, was a silently ironic comment on the ugliness of the lechery and dissension in the world of both men and gods. This garden has qualities of actuality even as it reflects the essential goodness and harmony in those who enter it:

> So on a day, right in the morwe-tyde,
> Unto a gardyn that was ther bisyde,
> In which that they hadde maad hir ordinaunce
> Of vitaille and of oother purveiaunce,
> They goon and pleye hem al the longe day.
> And this was on the sixte morwe of May,
> Which May hadde peynted with his softe shoures
> This gardyn ful of leves and of floures;
> And craft of mannes hand so curiously
> Arrayed hadde this gardyn, trewely,
> That nevere was ther gardyn of swich prys,
> But if it were the verray paradys.
> The odour of floures and the fresshe sighte
> Wolde han maked any herte lighte
> That evere was born, but if to greet siknesse,
> Or to greet sorwe, helde it in distresse;
> So ful it was of beautee with plesaunce.
>   (V, 901-917)

Aurelius' attempt to meet Dorigen's task is made in December, and though in a way the brief description of the weather comments upon the threat he is about to offer to Dorigen's happiness, it conveys so exactly the sense of winter that in its union of rhetoric with "pleyn speche" it becomes almost lyrical:

> And this was, as thise bookes me remembre
> The colde, frosty seson of Decembre.
>   Phebus wax old, and hewed lyk laton,
> That in his hoote declynacion
> Shoon as the burned gold with stremes brighte;
> But now in Capricorn adoun he lighte,
> Where as he shoon ful pale, I dar wel seyn.
> The bittre frostes, with the sleet and reyn,
> Destroyed hath the grene in every yerd.
> Janus sit by the fyr, with double berd,
> And drynketh of his bugle horn the wyn;
> Biforn hym stant brawen of the tusked swyn,
> And "Nowel" crieth every lusty man.
>   (V, 1243-1255)

But what the Franklin most importantly reveals about himself in his tale is his awareness that social and moral values not only test human beings but are tested by them, that their concrete reality is realizable only when the human beings who are tested by them are, at the same time, defined in their essential natures. The values he has heard talked about in the interchange of tales are translated from their abstraction into particular actuality. The Wife of Bath's thesis that sovereignty in the hands of the woman is the condition for happiness in marriage is transformed in his tale to the thesis that mutual faith and trust make the question of "maistrye" irrelevant, except in so far as it is a practical necessity in the course of large action. The obedience and subservient love exhibited by Griselda become in this tale a love that by its very nature motivates the supreme act of obedience, even as the demand for obedience proves the degree of love it is based on. And the triangle situation that makes from the cynical conclusion of *The Merchant's Tale* a statement about human nature that is unmitigated in its despair, puts to the test, in this tale, the goodness of the people involved in it and results in a triumphant affirmation of that goodness.

From the beginning of his tale the Franklin is concerned with defining the nature of the love between Dorigen and Arveragus since this love is what is to be tested even as its testing is, in turn, to define the essential quality of the characters. Unlike the marriage between the Loathly Lady and the young knight, or between Walter and Griselda, or between January and May, this marriage is one of mutual attraction and agreement, entered into realistically as well as romantically, in "pleyn" terms as well as in courtly. The wooing of Dorigen by Arveragus, begun in all the lyrical ideality of Courtly Love, ends in the practical reality of mutually acceptable personalities. "Atte laste she, for his worthynesse,/ And namely for his meke obeysaunce,/ Hath swich a pitee caught of his penaunce/ That pryvely she fil of his accord/ To take hym for hir housbonde and hir lord,/ Of swich lordshipe as men han over hir wyves" (V, 738-743). Between these two, as between Walter and Griselda, as between the foul hag and her young husband, there is an explicit understanding about the nature of their relationship; but the difference is significant. The marriage between Dorigen and Arveragus is made in terms of a relationship freely and openly assented to, the inevitable question of mastery faced openly and answered by mutual agreement before it is necessary to face it in fact:

> And for to lede the moore in blisse hir lyves,
> Of his free wyl he swoor hire as a knyght
> That nevere in al his lyf he, day ne nyght,
> Ne sholde upon hym take no maistrie
> Agayn hir wyl, ne kithe hire jalousie,
> But hire obeye, and folwe hir wyl in al,
> As any lovere to his lady shal,
> Save that the name of soveraynetee,
> That wolde he have for shame of his degree.
> (V, 744-752)

His promise takes into consideration so many aspects of reality, the social and the psychological, that Dorigen's answer cannot be other than favorable. It, too, takes cognizance of the realities that must face any human relationship:

> She thanked hym, and with ful greet humblesse
> She seyde, "Sire, sith of youre gentillesse
> Ye profre me to have so large a reyne,
> Ne wolde nevere God bitwixe us tweyne,
> As in my gilt, were outher werre or stryf.
> Sire, I wol be youre humble trewe wyf,
> Have heer my thouthe, til that myn herte breste."
> Thus been they bothe in quiete and in reste.
> (V, 753-759)

At this moment the Franklin interrupts his own tale, his mind full of the accounts of the unhappy marriages so recently described. "Love," he says, looking surely at the Wife of Bath, "wol nat been constreyned by maistrye;/ Whan maistrie comth, the God of Love anon/ Beteth his wynges and farewel, he is gon!" (V, 764-766). He is perfectly willing to agree with her that women desire "libertee," "and nat to constreyned as a thral"; but he reminds her "so doon men, if I sooth seyn shal." With what can be said to be a kind of gentleness, he turns to the Clerk. "Looke who that is moost pacient in love,/ He is at his avantage al above." He, too, respects the virtue of patience, and his definition of it at one and the same time admonishes the Clerk for his impossible view of it, points out quietly the futility and wrongness of contention and revenge, and reveals an attitude that is, in a sense, Boethian:

> Pacience is an heigh vertu, certeyn,
> For it venquysseth, as thise clerkes seyn,
> Thynges that rigour sholde nevere atteyne.
> For every word men may nat chide or pleyne.
> Lerneth to suffre, or elles, so moot I goon,
> Ye shul it lerne, wher so ye wole or noon;
> For in this world, certain, ther no wight is
> That he ne dooth or seith somtyme amys.
> Ire, siknesse, or constellacioun
> Wyn, wo, or chaungynge of complexioun
> Causeth ful ofte to doon amys or speken.
> On every wrong a man may nat be wreken.
> After the tyme moste be temperaunce
> To every wight that kan on governaunce.
>   (V, 773-786)

The Franklin's idealism is not a matter of sentimentality or of in-experience. Alone among the pilgrims he is one who, apparently, has not known "the wo that is in mariage." His awareness of the difficulties in any human relationship erases any criticism that he is oversimplifying. The agreement between Dorigen and Arveragus, their "humble, wys accord," depends for its effectiveness upon their recognition of a neces-sary shifting of roles. "Thus hath she take hir servant and hir Lord,—/ Servant in love, and lord in mariage./ Thanne was he bothe in lord-shipe and servage./ Servage? nay, but in lordshipe above,/ Sith he hath bothe his lady and his love" (V, 792-795). That such married joy is possible he affirms from his own experience:

> Who koude telle, but he hadde wedded be,
> The joye, the ese, and the prosperitee
> That is bitwixe an housbonde and his wyf?
>   (V, 803-805)

It is not until he has left no question as to the nature of the love and trust between Dorigen and Arveragus that the Franklin tells of the testing of that love. Before he shows the right action of his characters, he has made such right action possible, though not necessarily inevitable. The sequence of happenings in his tale makes it clear that goodness does not predetermine happiness, nor does it guarantee right action. The suspense he creates is never the suspense of action alone; it is made up of the tension that comes when the possibilities for right action are constantly tested and gradually realized through the force of complexly interrelated circumstances. In this tale it is always possible for a wrong step to be taken; it is always possible for the tragic or the cynical view of human nature to take over. Even after Dorigen rejects the possibility of suicide that she has contemplated as a way to end her involvement with Aurelius, an act that she could conceivably have done, an act that would have turned the tale into pathos if not tragedy, and instead reveals to her husband the story of her promise to the young Squire, there is the suspense in the question of how Arveragus will act. And after his grief-stricken recognition that he must see to it that she honors her pledge, there is the question as to what Aurelius will do. His generous renunciation of her raises the question about his own fate at the hands of the magician to whom he is sadly in debt. Lest the intricately interdependent yet dependent series of right action seems reducible to some pat formula, to some banal oversimplification, the Franklin leaves his whole tale upon a question, as the analogues which hint at his source have not done in their eagerness to round off the whole tale. Where they claim that it is the last person to forgive who is the most generous, the Franklin will not make so simple a judgment:

> Lordynges, this question, thanne, wol I aske now,
> Which was the mooste fre, as thynketh yow?
> Now telleth me, er that ye ferther wende.
> I kan namoore; my tale is at an ende.
>   (V, 1621-1624)

Though he has agreed with the Host that he will not preach about the quality of "gentillesse," he has, by the end of his tale, defined it completely.

It is good to see how the Franklin corroborates the Wife of Bath's thesis about the nature of "gentillesse." His whole tale is based upon an agreement with her statement that "he is gentil that dooth gentil dedis," and it is as a kind of gesture toward joining forces with her against the Clerk and the Merchant, even as it is perhaps a mark of his respect for the Squire on the pilgrimage, that he puts his own words about it into the mouth of the young Aurelius. The capacity to do the "gentil deed," says the Wife of Bath, comes from God. The Franklin makes it clear that it is made possible by the grace of compassion, by the gift of an imagination that will project into the unhappiness of others. Aurelius, aware of the suffering he has caused both Dorigen and her husband, recognizing the quality of the generosity in the action of both of them who act to meet the test of "trouthe" even at the cost of their own sorrow, "in his herte . . . caughte of this greet routhe":

> Considerynge the beste on every syde,
> That fro his lust yet were hym levere abyde
> Than doon so heigh a cherlyssh wrecchednesse
> Agayns franchise and alle gentillesse;
> For which in fewe wordes seyde he thus:
>   "Madame, seyth to youre lord Arveragus,
> That sith I se his grete gentillesse
> To yow, and eek I se wel youre distresse,
> That him were levere han shame (and that were routhe)
> Than ye to me sholde breke thus youre trouthe,
> I have wel levere evere to suffre wo
> Than I departe the love bitwix yow two.
> I yow release, madame, into youre hond
> Quyt every serement and every bond
> That ye han maad to me as heerbiforn,
> Sith thilke tyme which that ye were born.
> My trouthe I plighte, I shal yow never repreve
> Of no biheste, and heere I take my leve,
> As of the treweste and the beste wyf
> That evere yet I knew in al my lyf."
> But every wyf be far of hire biheeste!
> On Dorigen remembreth, atte leeste.
> Thus kan a squire doon a gentil dede
> As wel as kan a knyght, withouten drede.
>   (V, 1521-1544)

Because he recognizes what Dorigen and Arveragus are, he is able to act in a way he had not hitherto suspected himself capable of acting. And in thus bringing into definition the quality of his own nature, he engenders "gentillesse" in the person of the magician. As the tale draws near its end, the repetition of the word "fre," as it describes both the cause and the quality of the doing of "gentil dedes," sounds forth with insistent emphasis. To the magician, Aurelius explains why he has not won his lady: of her sorrow he had "so greet pitee;/ And right as frely

as he sente hire me,/ As frely sente I hire to hym ageyn." And the
magician responds:

> . . . "Leeve brother,
> Everich of yow dide gentilly til oother.
> Thou art a squier, and he is a knyght;
> But God forbede, for his blisful myght,
> But if a clerk koude doon a gentil dede
> As wel as any of yow, it is no drede!
>   Sire, I releesse thee thy thousand pound,
> As thou right now were cropen out of the ground,
> Ne nevere er now ne haddest knowen me.
> For, sire, I wol nat taken a peny of thee
> For al my craft, ne noght for my travaille.
> Thou hast ypayed wel for my vitaille.
> It is ynogh, and farewel, have good day."
>
> (V, 1607-1619)

These two people act to renounce what they have held dear because
they are moved by the greater renunciation that has, for a moment,
promised them success. But Dorigen and Arveragus act out of the very
degree of the love they have. It is the love, with its freely accepted
obligations and responsibilities, its mutual trust and faith, that generates
the threat; and the threat in turn tests and reaffirms the validity of the
love. Again, it is the sequence in which the Franklin relates the incidents
in his tale that convinces of the reality of his characters who could so
easily, with the slightest variation or alteration in the sequence, have
been impossible to accept. Because it is clear what their love is at the
beginning of their marriage, the degree of Dorigen's grief in the absence
of Arveragus is believable. Her sad loneliness, her "desir of his presence,"
is made credible by the efforts of her friends to console her, and by the
psychologically valid way in which she finally responds: "She may nat
duren in swich rage." Since it is not possible to sustain immoderate grief
forever, she agrees to join her companions and to make at least a
pretense of joy. Because her sorrow is so deep and her anxiety about the
dangerous coastal rocks so acute, she is moved to make her unwise and
ominous bargain with the pleading Aurelius. True, she rejects his offer of
love, for she will "nevere been untrewe wyf/ In word ne werk, as fer as
I have wit"; but once that is understood, she can promise him "in pleye"
to give him her love if he removes "alle the rokkes, stoon by stoon" from
the coast "of Britayne." It is a promise, a bargain that, by the apparent
improbability of its condition, seems safe enough. In a rather moving
way it measures the degree of her loneliness and woe. "Is ther noon

oother grace in yow?" asks Aurelius. "No, by that Lord . . . that maked me!" she replies. And she sends him away with a gentle reproach:

> "For wel I woot that it shal never bityde.
> Lat swiche folies out of youre herte slyde.
> What deyntee sholde a man han in his lyf
> For to go love another mannes wyf.
> That hath hir body whan so that hym liketh?"
>
> (V, 1001-1005)

But wise though she may be in the understanding of her love for her absent husband, Dorigen is, as Aurelius comes to recognize innocent about "apparence or jogelrye" and the power of illusion. Caught in her own "trappe," her shock upon hearing that the "rokkes been aweye" measures the degree of her innocence in making the bargain:

> He taketh his leve, and she astoned stood;
> In al hir face nas a drope of blood.
> She wende nevere han come in swich a trappe.
> "Allas," quod she, "that evere this sholde happe!
> For wende I nevere by possibilitee
> That swich a monstre of merveille myghte be!
> It is agayns the proces of nature."
> And hoom she goth a sorweful creature;
> For verray feere unnethe may she go.
>
> (V, 1339-1347)

At this moment the story arrives at the point where its outcome could have been tragic. The Dorigen who meditates seriously the possibility of committing suicide, as other women have done to preserve their chastity and faithfulness, is the same Dorigen who had contemplated the "blakke rokkes" and who had refused the overtones of Aurelius. But the Dorigen who decides finally to tell her husband of her pledge to the young suitor is the same woman who had exchanged vows of mutual love so candidly and freely at the beginning. It is her confession to Arveragus that creates the greatest test for them both. Even as her willingness to reveal her plight to her husband attests to her innocence and her love, so his reception of her story proves his faith in her honesty, and measures, ironically, the magnitude of his love, which insists that she assume full responsibility for her folly. At first reading, the action of Arveragus shocks us, as it has the Franklin. But careful examination reveals that the Franklin respects both Arveragus' belief that she has not been untrue to him in fact, and the pain of his grief. "Is ther oght elles, Dorigen, but this?" he asks, "with glad chiere, in freendly wyse." Assured by her "Nay, nay," he makes her see that she must keep her part of the bargain; and then, says the Franklin, "with that word he brast anon to wepe" (V, 1480). "Trouthe is" indeed "the hyeste thyng that man may kepe," and the cost of keeping it, whether it be in respect to love, or in respect to any other relationship entered into freely, may well cause a man "to wepe." The "wo that is in mariage" for Arveragus and Dorigen is made up out of the threat to their great "joye," and the yielding up of his wife to Aurelius is an acknowledgement of the terrible cost of responsible action. The Franklin knows that all will come out well; Arveragus does not, nor does Dorigen, who goes to meet the squire "half as she were mad." The risk is great; that it is rewarded so happily does not in any way bring its greatness into question, for its joyous resolution depends precariously upon the "trouthe" of another human being that can only be known in the testing.

It is true that good women are far outnumbered by the bad, that Chichevache, the cow, will starve on her diet of "patient wives"—at least in the world of the pilgrims; but one Dorigen "atte leeste" almost counterbalances many Mays, and one marriage that survives the testing put to it provides one radiant moment among many that are dismal. The *Franklin's Tale*, by its insistence upon "gentillesse," makes all the questions of the other tales urgent only when "gentillesse" is absent. Like the black rocks, injustice, suffering, and contention are threats to happiness not in themselves but as they are made so by the free action of men. So dependent is the final joy of the characters upon the initial premise that each is "gentil" in heart, a premise that is made valid in the tale itself, that its essential rareness is never denied. And because it is so clearly an isolated moment when the possibility of human goodness is proclaimed, it is, in its idealism, as much a part of Chaucer's realistically comic vision as are the other tales of marriage. One need only pause to contemplate what might have been the effect of another sequence of the tales to rejoice that *The Franklin's Tale* is the last in the manuscript grouping.

chapteR 6

COMEDY'S UNMASKING OF VICE:
THE FRIAR'S TALE
THE SUMMONER'S TALE
THE PARDONER'S TALE

The three tales grouped together in this chapter have to do with hypocrisy and its unmasking. If the word "evil" were not too portentous for comedy, and for Chaucer's comedy in particular, it might be said that in these tales Chaucer most clearly singles out the characteristic that in human nature most arouses his moral condemnation.

For Chaucer, as, of course, for many other writers of comedy, hypocrisy was the cardinal sin. It was, and is, comedy's version of *hubris,* a vice to be disclosed and mocked. The hypocrite is always a threat to those around him. If his conscious pretensions and affectations, if his machinations are successfully concealed until too late, he is the villain of tragedy where "knavery's plain face is never seen till used." Iago's destructive power is made possible by the fatal innocence of most of those around him, his cleverness effecting its ends because those who should see, cannot, blinded as they are by their own passions. But if the hypocrite's affectations are plainly visible, he is ultimately a threat only to himself. No matter how clever his machinations may be, they but lead him to his own downfall. The conditions that ensure the visibility of his hypocrisy are, of course, many, and all are attended by comic joy. But the most intense comic joy is experienced when the collapse of pretensions follows upon a high degree of felt threat. The hypocrite-rogue is richly comic in that he forms one of the most hostile forces human beings must face, while at the same time, in becoming so satisfyingly his own victim, he is a joyous reminder that sometimes poetic

182

justice does exist. Since, in the course of enacting his own wickedness, he has used for his own ends beliefs and values treasured by the society he moves among, the hypocrite-rogue also enacts society's wish to punish him. His failure becomes a vindication of the values he sought to manipulate.

In *The Friar's Tale* and *The Summoner's Tale* the hypocrites are actors in the narratives, characters devised by the tellers as instruments for attack upon each other. Neither the summoner of *The Friar's Tale* nor the friar of *The Summoner's Tale* is a portrait of either of the pilgrims among the "nyne and twenty." They are portraits of what each pilgrim thinks the other to be. The Pardoner, however, is present in the company of travellers. In the almost disarmingly open hypocrisy of his prologue and in the power of his tale to spellbind pilgrim and reader, he becomes, for the moments he speaks, the rogue of Chaucer's comedy, a potential threat to the harmony and to the mirthful coexistence of the pilgrims themselves. The hypocrites in the tales of the Friar and the Summoner are unmasked by other characters in the tales; the hypocrisy of the Pardoner, blatantly proclaimed from the instant he says "Lordynges," affects its own astonished punishment, and affirms in the course of its enactment the morality it has threatened. In this fact lies some of Chaucer's richest mirth.

There is evidence that the Friar and the Summoner have been spoiling for an argument before either one is permitted to speak. Their mutual dislike seems to be personal as well as professional. "Lo . . . Goddes armes two!" says the Summoner, as he objects to the Friar's interruption of the Wife of Bath at the end of her prologue, "A frere wol entremette hym everemo./ Lo, goode men, a flye and eek a frere/ Wol falle in every dyssh and eek mateere." The hostility he feels is ill-disguised by his jovial tone: "What! amble, or trotte, or pees, or go sit doun! /Thou lettest oure disport in this manere" (III, 834-839). True, he is eager to hear Alisoun's tale, but his relish in admonishing the Friar is unmistakable.

The Friar is not slow to respond in kind. His quick retort, promising retaliation, threatens for the first time since the quarrel between the Reeve and the Miller to upset the "disport" of the pilgrimage. Once more the "quiting" principle of the first fragment activates dynamically and dramatically the journey of the pilgrims. Where the Miller, however, seems to have been innocent of the intention of arousing the Reeve to anger, the Friar is quite explicit in his purpose. He is willing to wait for his moment until the Wife of Bath has told her tale, but not before he has promised to "telle of a somonour swich a tale or two,/ That alle the folk shal laughen in this place" (III, 841-843). The Summoner, not to be outdone, swears to tell tales "two or thre" that "shal make thyn

herte for to morne" (III, 844-849). The Host's cry for "pees" holds off
the threatening contention until Alisoun's story of the Loathly Lady is
told, but the suspense is sustained until the altercation between the two
is resolved into the verbal blows of their respective tales.

It is not unlikely that the Wife of Bath has added to the Friar's irritation with the Summoner. Her comments on the Church and upon
"auctoritee" cannot have gone unnoticed. His chiding of her "prechyng"
is somewhat less than genial. But it is Summoners in general who arouse
his real ire—"ye may wel knowe by the name/That of a somonour may
no good be sayd"—and it is this summoner in particular, this "gentil
harlot" with his "fyr-reed cherubynnes face . . . hoot and lecherous as a
sparwe," he frankly detests. "A! sire," cries the Host, mindful of his
function as the keeper of the peace as well as umpire of the "game,"
and he reminds the Friar of the decorum expected of one of his "estaat."
Recalling to him the rules of the pilgrimage—"In compaignye we wol
have no debaat"—he wards off any open argument, either verbal or
physical (III, 1286-1289). The Summoner is willing to bide his time,
gathering together all the scurrility that is his for his counterattack.

> "Nay," quod the Somonour, "lat hym seye to me
> What so hym list; whan it comth to my lot,
> By God! I shal hym quiten every grot.
> I shal hym tellen which a greet honour
> It is to be a flaterynge lymytour;
> And eek of many another manere cryme
> Which nedeth nat rehercen at this tyme;
> And his office I shal hym telle, ywis."
>   (III, 1290-1297)

Only when the Host once more cries "Pees, namoore of this!" does the
tension in the atmosphere somewhat relax.

The tales that keep the "debaat" between the Friar and the Summoner
from becoming an open fight translate their mutual hostility into something resembling a verbal boxing match where the opponents are equal
in strength, though different in techniques. The match clearly ends in a
draw; no one wins and no one loses. But in the course of the combat,
lying, deception, and the methods of hypocrisy are described, defined,
and properly punished. Mirth does indeed here serve the ends of
Morality for the characters in the tales who bear the burden of the
animosity of the tellers bring about their own downfall. They become
their own condemners of the passions that have motivated them, even as
they reveal, obliquely, the worst faults of the narrators for all the
pilgrims to see.

The Friar's Tale is an anecdote, its economy and brevity accounting for much of its effectiveness as an attack upon summoners at large and upon this Summoner in particular. Avoiding elaboration, ignoring interpretive comment, Huberd's tale of the summoner who emerges as proud of being more ruthless, more unscrupulous than the emissary of the devil, delivers a concentrated and powerful blow to his opponent. It is no wonder that the Summoner is put into a livid and quivering fury at its conclusion, a fury so intense that he stood "hye" in his "Styropes" and "lyk an aspen leef he quook . . ." (III, 1665-1667).

The Summoner's rage is not only aroused by the concluding prayer of the Friar, which he could only have taken as sarcasm, no matter how the Friar intended it to be understood, but is intensified by the accumulative effect of the whole tale where he is portrayed as completely unregenerate. The Friar makes the contrast between his summoner and the "foul feend" clear from the first moment he brings them together. The fiend, in the guise of a yeoman, gaily and honestly going about his business of winning souls for the devil, is open and frank about his profession. But the summoner "dorste nat, for verray filthe and shame/ Seye he was a somonour, for the name," proud though he may be of his villainous skill:

> "I spare nat to taken, God it woot,
> But if it be to hevy or to hoot.
> What I may gete in conseil prively
> No maner conscience of that have I."
>
> (III, 1435-1438)

Boasting that he has neither "stomak ne conscience," he provokes some amusement from the "yeman" who has only to wait for such arrogance to damn itself. The Friar has a sure sense of narrative movement, of the ways to create economical dialogue and to portray dramatic confrontation. His tale moves swiftly to its climax as the summoner, of his own free will, closes the door of his own trap upon himself. The fiend simply waits, hands off, until the summoner sends himself to Hell. His damnation, self-induced, reveals once more Chaucer's relish in the possibility of poetic justice. Angry at the "olde wydwe" for her refusal to give him "twelf pens" to buy her way out of a false accusation of adultery, he, all unwittingly, delivers himself into the hands of his fiend-companion: "'Nay thanne,' quod he, 'the foule feend me fecche/ If I th'excuse, though thou shul be spilt!'" (III, 1609-1610). Her fury as she curses him simply reinforces the effectiveness of his own self-damnation, placing his soul securely in the power of the courteous and gentlemanly fiend who is quietly witnessing the scene. "Unto the devel blak and rough of hewe/

Yeve I thy body and my panne also," she cries. The summoner has the
chance to repent, but nothing could be further from his mind: "That is
nat myn entente . . . for to repente me," he boasts. The fiend, now fully
assured that he is entitled to the soul of his companion, reminds him of
the bargain they had made as "brothers" and makes off with him to Hell.
The Friar's voice, suave, controlled, "curteys," becomes prayerful as he
draws his tale to its pious and generalized conclusion:

> But for to kepe us fro that cursed place,
> Waketh, and preyeth Jhesu for his grace
> So kepe us fro the temptour Sathanas.
> Herketh this word! beth war, as in this cas:
> "The leoun sit in his awayt alway
> To sle the innocent, if that he may."
> Disposeth ay youre hertes to withstonde
> The feend, that yow wolde make thral and bonde.
> He may nat tempte yow over youre myght,
> For Crist wol be youre champion and knyght.
> And prayeth that thise somonours hem repente
> Of hir mysdedes, er that the feend hem hente!
>   (III, 1653-1664)

THE SUMMONER'S TALE

The Friar, conscious of his "estaat" and of his audience, has
attempted in his attack upon the Summoner of the pilgrimage to include
a condemnation of a general sort. The Summoner, whatever his general
opinion about friars may be, is clearly intent upon delivering a counterattack upon this Friar in the most personal way he can devise. Picking
up from the Friar's concluding words what he could well take to be
hypocritical cant, he retaliates in his tale by drawing a devastatingly
effective portrait of hypocrisy.

It is no surprise that the Summoner's tale depends for much of its
comedy upon coarse and open vulgarity. The observer-reporter, Chaucer,
had seen what manner of man he was. Diseased, drunken, foul-smelling,
blasphemous, illiterate, roaring out the burden to the song sung by the
Pardoner, he is the most obviously repulsive pilgrim—"Of his visage
children were aferd." Although the Middle Ages had less delicacy about
referring to bodily functions than later generations, the vulgarity of
The Summoner's Tale certainly had its shock value and could be considered even by the pilgrims (and Chaucer's audience) a questionable
violation of taste and manners. Admitting, as one must, that such
vulgarity has had and will always have certain comic value, it is not
what makes the tale one of Chaucer's most hilarious. Rather, it is because

its vulgarity measures so effectively the degree of vice possible in hypocrisy, because its coarseness so unequivocally condemns what it illustrates, because its physical concreteness so exactly awards tit-for-tat justice to the abstract wickedness, that it is one of Chaucer's most morally mirthful tales.

Many of the themes that have emerged as characteristic of Chaucer's poetry come here into gleeful focus: that man is responsible for his own downfall, freely chosen and willed; that there is justice which administers precise punishment; that wickedness will be found out; and that goodness (in this instance, ingenuity in combatting wickedness) will be rewarded. The climactic moments of the tale satisfy in ways that are both comic and moral. The "gift" made to the friar is almost punishment enough for the degree of hypocrisy the Summoner has portrayed in him. Because of it, the friar falls into all the sins he has so piously condemned. But it is the transforming of that "gift" from the apparently impossible fantasy into the possible reality that constitutes the real joy of this tale, for it translates moral condemnation into comic practicality. The young Squire, who so ingeniously solved the problem of the distribution of the "gift," is indeed deserving of the "newe gowne" he is given at the end. The Summoner's relish as he arrives at the final climax of his tale reveals the intensity of his pleasure in the revenge he is taking upon his adversary, the Friar. The mock solemnity of his Squire, and the professorial, scholarly tone the Summoner gives him as he outlines his solution to the problem of effecting the distribution of the "gift" according to the wishes of "olde, sike" Thomas, the giver, underscore the preposterously comic ridicule finally turned upon the sanctimonious friar of the tale. Given the nature of the teller, given the detailed explicitness of the hypocrisy described, it is difficult to see how the general approval of all those at the manor house who hear the young squire's proposal is not also our approval:

> The lord, the lady, and ech man, save the frere,
> Seyd that Jankyn spak, in this matere,
> As wel as Euclide dide or Ptholomee.
> Touchynge the cherl, they seyde, subtiltee
> And heigh wit made hym speken as he spak;
> He nys no fool, ne no demonyak.
> (III, 2287-2292)

It is the Summoner's effectiveness in portraying the hypocrisy of the "frere" to be so rudely "rewarded" by the gift of a fart that creates a willing suspension of judgment as to the vulgarity of his tale. He has drawn a friar who well deserves the punishment meted out to him. Only a small section of the tale contains any action; most of it is devoted to

a minute drawing of its main character. And the Summoner proves himself from the beginning a master of characterization, inspired into brilliance, perhaps, by his aroused hostility. His friar is made to appear before
us as upon a stage. His appearance is not described but we know him well
before he has been long before us. His bodily movements, his voice, are
all we need. To the aged and bedridden man whose house he enters with
bold familiarity he speaks "curteisly and softe." With a gesture that
reveals his arrogant presumption to ownership of all he sees "fro the
bench he droof awey the cat,/ And leyde adoun his potente and his
hat,/ And eek his scrippe, and sette hym softe adoun." "O Thomas,
Thomas; O Thomas, Thomas," the name sweet and "softe" on his
unctuous tongue, iterates and reiterates throughout the scene, the Latin
and French affectations coating in honey the pious cant they preface.

Thomas has little chance to speak, but the silence he is forced to maintain in the room that echoes with the hypocritically sweet concern of the
friar grows more and more eloquent. We hear with his ears the friar's
words to the wife, a woman worried about her husband's persistent
illness and bad temper, and saddened by the recent death of her child.
With the greatest of ease the friar makes the transition from lecturing
Thomas on the sin of ire to a request for food—food humble and simple
to befit his calling, perhaps but the liver of a capon and a "shyvere . . .
of youre softe breed" and then a "rosted pigges heed—/ But that I nolde
no beest for me were deed"—to the pious consolation for her recent
sorrow. Between the tone that had voiced the humbleness of his needs
and the tone that comforts the mother there is no change of quality.
"Er that half an hour" after the death of the child, he says, "I saugh
hym born to blysse. . . . And up I roos, and al oure covent eke,/ With
many a teere trillyng on my cheke, . . . *Te Deum* was oure song, and
nothyng elles,/ Save that to Crist I seyde an orison,/ Thankynge hym
of his revelacion" (III, 1856-1868). The Summoner, his dislike of his
fellow pilgrim calling to mind his hatred of all friars, cannot let a good
thing alone. With repulsive oiliness the voice of his friar slides into
generalities that plainly italicize the degree of hypocrisy he manifests:

> "For, sire and dame, trusteth me right weel,
> Oure orisons been moore effectueel,
> And moore we seen of Cristes secree thynges,
> Than burel folk, although they weren kynges.
> We lyve in poverte and in abstinence,
> And burell folk in richesse and despence
> Of mete and drynke, and in hir foul delit.
> We han this worldes lust al in despit.
>
> .   .   .   .

> We fare as seith th'apostle; clooth and foode
> Suffisen us, though they be nat ful goode.
> The clennesse and the fastynge of us freres
> Maketh that Crist accepteth oure preyeres."
>
> (III, 1869-1884)

We are ready to cry out our rejection of his "dissymulacioun" long before Thomas is; and our sense of what must be the "olde" man's growing fury becomes more and more acute as we also listen to the elaborate sermon against anger and vengeance. "Thomas! Thomas! so moote I ryde or go/ . . . Nere thou oure brother, sholdestou nat thryve." "Your inconstance is youre confusion," he points out, remonstrating with the old man for giving money to others of the clergy. "What," he asks, "is a ferthyng worth parted in twelve?" as the Summoner gleefully predicts the end of his tale. "What nedeth yow, Thomas, to maken stryf? . . . Ire is a synne, oon of the grete of sevene,/ Abhomynable unto the God of hevene." "Now, Thomas, leeve brother, lef thyn ire," he requests, and speaking more than he can know, he concludes "Thou shalt me fynde as just as is a squyre."

At the end of the scene, climaxing in sanctimony as the friar kneels at the bedside of Thomas in his final plea for money, there comes enormous release from the tension of indignation for the reader as well as for Thomas in the violent and vulgar act of the sick man that gives into the grasping and groping hand of the friar the "gift" he has earned. It is not just that hypocrisy has been marked out for what it is—worth but a fart; it is also that the hypocrite has called down his punishment upon himself. And the "gift" that so enrages him reveals clearly for all to see the fulness of his pretension, sending him in furious ire from the house to the manor of the lord of the village. It is no wonder that the ingenuity of that "burel man," Thomas, fills the members of the noble household with awe:

> The lady of the hous ay stille sat
> Til she had herd what the frere sayde.
> "Ey, Goddes mooder," quod she, "Blisful mayde!
> Is ther oght elles? telle me feithfully."
> "Madame," quod he, "How thynke ye herby?"
> "How that me thynketh?" quod she," so God me speede,
> I seye, a cherl hath doon a cherles dede.
> What shold I seye? God lat hym nevere thee!
> His sike heed is ful of vanytee;
> I holde hym in a manere frenesye."
>
> (III, 2200-2209)

Her words are in the nature of a right judgment of the tale (and, ironically, of the teller), but they are not the final ones. Her husband is far more unqualified in his admiration of the whole story. It is his view that makes the final comment upon the tale; it is the comment that gathers unto itself all the kinds of laughter the tale sets going:

> The lord sat stille as he were in a traunce,
> And in his herte he rolled up and doun,
> "How hadde this cherl ymaginacioun
> To shewe swich a problem to the frere?
> Nevere erst er now herde I of swich mateere.
> I trowe the devel putte it in his mynde."
>
> (III, 2216-2221)

The "cherl hath doon a cherles dede" and a "cherl" has told a "cherles" tale. Scurrilous the Summoner on the pilgrimage may be, but he has told a moral tale without once violating the consistency of his own character. What the Friar's reaction to the tale was we are not told. It hardly seems relevant. Ironically, for all his intention of attacking his adversary in his portrait of the hypocritical friar, the Summoner has ended by attacking Hypocrisy; the character he has created out of personal venom has become an impersonal figura for allegory.

THE PARDONER'S TALE

The hypocrite threatens society and its members because he depends for his existence upon perverting certain deeply treasured values. A key adjective for the Pardoner is "perverted." Rascal and rogue, he is one of Chaucer's most compelling achievements, moral and comic. Physically and spiritually perverse, he becomes for a few moments in his brilliant vanity something of a real threat to the harmony and the well-being of the pilgrims. It is his brilliant vanity, however, that ultimately saves the pilgrimage from disruption, for it blinds him to the fact that what he is is clear for all to see. It is his vanity that finally makes him the agent of his own unmasking, that renders ineffective his openly proclaimed hypocrisy. The comic and the moral force of the portrait of the Pardoner and of the dramatic moments his presence creates, depend for their degree upon the quality of the rascality he betrays. And the quality of the rascality depends upon the degree to which he seems, at least momentarily, to pervert successfully some of man's most important values. An unscrupulous rascal in a profession dealing with the souls of men is a potentially terrifying threat in any age, though the generation since Freud speaks of the psyche instead of the soul. And the more he is felt in all his brilliant fascination, the greater is the relief that is effected by being released from the possibility of his temporary mastery. The Pardoner is patently a rogue, yet so persuasive and so seductive are his powers that one is momentarily apprehensive that roguery might, for once, win out. The question, "Will the pilgrims be taken in in spite of themselves?" accounts in large measure for the suspense that attends the reading of his tale. So, when in fury the Host responds with coarse vulgarity to the tale and its arrogant conclusion, he releases into unabashed laughter our tension, confirming for us our deep-rooted wish that wickedness will not be allowed to succeed.

Justice is of many kinds in this tale and its dramatic context. That his hypocrisy is made impotent by the Host's explosive vulgarity shocks the Pardoner's vanity and is worldly punishment enough. Like the friar in *The Summoner's Tale* he is made to feel the degree of his rascality and presumption in a way no argument by reason could achieve. But the punishment his own arrogant blasphemy ironically threatens to involve him in, is more significant than the threat of the Host's knife. Like the summoner in *The Friar's Tale* he utters his own damnation in the eloquent last lines of his sermon-tale, and a lament that ironically states his own case:

> O cursed synne of alle cursednesse!
> O traytours homycide, O wikkednesse!
> O glotonye, luxurie, and hasardrye!
> Thou blasphemour of Crist with vileynye
> And othes grete, of usage and of pride!
> Allas! mankynde, how may it bitide
> That to thy creatour, which that the wroghte,
> And with his precious herte-blood thee boghte,
> Thou art so fals and so unkynde, allas?
>
> (VI, 895-903)

To claim, as some critics do, that this vainglorious egoist undergoes even for a moment a shudder of repentance seems to me to read out of context and to be deaf to tone. It is to make sentimental what is comic and moral in its vision of justice. The words he addresses directly to the pilgrims—"And lo, sires, thus I preche"—proclaim his delight in his powers as "a noble ecclesiaste" even as they reveal his admiration for the blasphemy he has admitted to from the beginning. "And Jhesu Crist, that is oure soules leche,/ So graunte yow his pardoun to receyve,/ For that is best" are words that do not "deceyve" no matter how skilled the deceiver, but they do not indicate a change of heart in the deceiver. That he speaks doctrinal and religious truths in no sense hints that he is giving thought to reforming, any more than his utterance of such truths in any way affects their validity. His final reference to Christ is his climactic gesture to the pilgrims, his trump card, his most calculated appeal since it contains his most incontrovertible truth. To show that the buying of indulgences, which could in some measure help toward remission of punishment for sins, is here available, is his main purpose. "But, sires, o word forgat I in my tale," he concludes, impudently confident that he has made his companions "his apes" as surely as the unlearned people of the villages he frequents. His vanity is here at its most evident, trusting as it does to his power to win him money in spite of his having just openly and joyously detailed that he has "relikes and pardoun in my male,/ As faire as any man in Engelond,/ Which were me yeven by the popes hond." Sure that his tale has won his listeners in spite of his openly advertised charlatanism, he asks in anticipation:

> If any of yow wole, of devocion,
> Offren, and han myn absolucion,
> Com forth anon, and kneleth heere adoun,
> And mekely receyveth my pardoun;
> Or elles taketh pardoun as ye wende,
> Al newe and fressh at every miles ende,
> So that ye offren, alwey newe and newe,
> Nobles or pens, which that be goode and trewe.
> (VI, 923-930)

The moment is one of suspense as one waits to see how the pilgrims, clearly aware of the falsity of his "relikes"—his "longe cristal stones,/ Ycrammed ful of cloutes and of bones"—yet perhaps under the spell of his compelling tale, will respond. With jovial irony that will almost immediately backfire on himself, the Pardoner speaks directly to the Host as one most "envoluped in synne." That he should choose Harry Bailly as the first of his victims among the pilgrims has, of course, its obvious comedy. But it is more than a gesture for comic effect. It reminds us once more of the vital interaction of those travelling together on the road to Canterbury. It takes but a moment to remember that shortly before being invited to take his turn in the telling of tales, the "gentil Pardoner" had observed the Host's emotional response to the Physician's sad tale of Virginia and Virginius— "Wel I woot," the Host had said, "thou doost myn herte to erme,/ That I almoost have caught a cardynacle." The Pardoner's logic is inevitable. Given his magnificent ego, given his alertness for a ready customer, given his awareness for what in his audience can best be exploited, he can be presumed to expect the Host to have been "envoluped" in the terrors of his tale.

The concluding moments between the Pardoner and the Host are like a small drama. Moving from the sermonizing oratory of his *exemplum* to the explicit application of his thesis that he directs—with dramatic force—at the one pilgrim he has singled out as the most ready victim, the Pardoner turns his monologue into a scene charged with tension. "It is an honour to everich that is heer," his noxiously cheerful voice points out, "that ye mowe have a suffisant pardoneer/ T'assoille yow, in contree as ye ryde,/ For aventures whiche that may bityde." His assumption is clear: all who have heard him have been taken in by the power of his eloquence. And so he turns his "glarynge eyen" upon "oure Hoost" as he speaks:

> "Com forth, sire Hoost, and offre first anon,
> And thou shalt kisse the relikes everychon,
> Ye, for a grote! Unbokele anon thy purs."
> (VI, 943-945)

The Host's rage reflects, of course, his indignation at being so singled out. The vulgarity of his swift counterattack measures the degree to which he has, for the moment, lost his usual genial control of himself. But it also measures the degree of his scorn for all the Pardoner openly represents.

> "Nay, nay!" quod he, "thanne have I Cristes curs!
> Lat be," quod he, "it shal nat be, so theech!
> Thou woldest make me kisse thyn olde breech,
> And swere it were a relyk of a seint,
> Though it were with thy fundement depeint!
> But, by the croys which that Seint Eleyne fond,
> I wolde I hadde thy coillons in myn hond
> In stide of relikes or of seintuarie.
> Lat kutte hem of, I wol thee helpe hem carie;
> They shul be shryned in an hogges toord!"
> (VI, 946-955)

The Pardoner, his vanity inoperative for the moment, "answerede nat a word;/ So wrooth he was, no word ne wolde he seye" (VI, 956-957). The Host's final comment—"I wol no lenger pleye/With thee, ne with noon oother angry man"—though it seems to be making an attempt to return the pilgrimage to harmonious balance, reveals that he is still seething. It is the Knight who steps in to re-establish the perspective necessary for the resumption of "mirth." "Namoore of this, for it is right ynough!" he admonishes. And the wise and worthy man asks:

> "Sire Pardoner, be glad and myrie of cheere;
> And ye, sire Hoost, that been to me so deere,
> I prey yow that ye kisse the Pardoner.
> And Pardoner, I prey thee, drawe thee neer,
> And, as we diden, lat us laughe and pleye."
>
> (VI, 963-967)

The two antagonists renounce enmity with a kiss and the disorder that has threatened the pilgrimage is resolved into order; comic equilibrium is once more restored and the "game" resumed.

Chaucer's election of the Knight as the significant actor in this scene recalls two interesting facts: that the portrait of the Knight has been the first in the *General Prologue* as that of the Pardoner has been the last; and that the tale told by the Knight, as the first of all the Tales, has outlined in a simple and clear way the presence of such values in life as order, and justice, and "pitee." He becomes, in this dramatic moment, as I have suggested earlier, almost a symbol of Order, restoring into harmonious coexistence the elements that threaten disorder, a function he assumes also in the Fragment that contains *The Monk's Tale*.

In a sense, therefore, the Pardoner can be seen as Chaucer's symbol of Disorder, and the situation he creates so dramatically can be read as a metaphor for the total infection disorder can bring. The wickedness he so openly professes is plain for all to see. He, like the Knight, is exactly what he appears to be. But the virtues the Knight practices are the virtues the Pardoner deliberately perverts, and his perversions seem, for the moment, to proclaim the rule of Disorder. Honesty and candor are used to flaunt his own self-professed charlatanism; he must have a "draughte of corny ale" before he can tell "som moral thyn." He is most profitably eloquent about the sin he most assiduously cultivates—"radix malorum est cupiditas" has been the theme that has brought him "monie, wolle, chese, and whete" as satisfactorally as his selling of false relics. And the undoubted brilliance of the tale he is "wont to preche for to wynne" attests to the perversion of his training as a "noble ecclesiaste."

It is his tale with its chillingly effective portrayal of the wages of avarice that forms the actual threat to the pilgrims. In spite of the fact that the Pardoner has boasted of his trickery in vivid detail, in spite of the fact that he has advertised himself to his companions as "a ful vicious man," he clearly assumes that the tale he tells will, by its moral force and its narrative power, create in his audience a willing suspension of all that they know about him. Presumption has seldom been higher than this. There seems to be no question in his mind whatsoever that the pilgrims will respond to the illusion he is creating in spite of their knowledge of the reality and that he can make the force of evil win out even though he has explicitly described his intentions. Comic though his presumption may be, it has enough potential for success to create moral tension. And when that tension is broken by the coarse words of the Host, both comic and moral ends are served. The Pardoner of the "confessional" prologue offers no threat to the pilgrims; the Pardoner, as entertaining narrator of the tale, almost does. The vanity that characterizes his monologue renders his wickedness powerless; the *hubris* that motivates him to seduce the pilgrims with his powers as a creator of sermons proves to be his downfall. Thus, in the very fulness of his viciousness, he becomes a comic joy.

It is hardly necessary to examine in any detail the artistry of the Pardoner's tale for it has long been acknowledged. The "wel affile(d) . . . tonge" is a master of narrative pace. The Pardoner's ear for dialogue, his eye for the precisely vivid descriptive detail, his ability to create suspense, the gusto and relish that evidences in every word his "joye" in his "bisynesse" compel fixed attention and ask for an almost completely uncritical involvement on the part of his audience. The small drama that is the heart of his "sermon" is made to take place in our imaginations with almost hypnotic power. The story of the search of the three drunken rioters for Death, which becomes a reality in their violent struggle over the gold at the foot of the tree, is indeed "som moral thyng" in many ways that are clearly intentional. But it is moral in a way he does not suspect, for it delineates its narrator's essence—rejoicing in his cupidity to the point where it becomes its own destruction. The tale ostensibly about *Cupiditas* is also about Death.

In a way, for all his gleeful energy, the Pardoner has been on the side of Death from the beginning. It is possible to see some symbolic significance in the fact that he is the one among the pilgrims to interrupt the Wife of Bath as she begins her monologue. Chaucer has made it clear in the *General Prologue* that the Pardoner's sexual vitality is questionable. The comic irony of his words to the sexually robust Wife is, therefore, obvious. "Ye been a noble prechour in this cas," he says to her, and adds, gratuitously, "I was aboute to wedde a wyf, allas!/ What sholde I bye it on my flessh so deere?/ Yet hadde I levere wedde no wyf to-yeere" (III, 165-168). But this apparent sexual sterility is more significant than this. It is a reflection of his spiritual sterility, of the negation in his very being of values both physical and moral. The figure of the "oold man" who directs the three rioters to the gold and thus to their deaths in his tale becomes, in retrospect, a morally admonitory comment upon the Pardoner. As Life-in-Death, or Death-in-Life, he points ironically towards his narrator's avowed goal in life—to preach "of no thyng but for coveityse"—a goal that is of the self, for the self, and from the self, and can only be self-destructive.

What it is that is continually moving about this figure in his tale almost defies analysis, but surely one reason may be that his words define the true lot of the perverter of Life, though the Pardoner is not conscious that they do so. "I ne kan nat fynde/A man, though that I walked into Ynde,/ Neither in citee ne in no village,/ That wolde chaunge his youthe for myn age; /And therfore moot I han myn age stille,/ As longe tyme as it is Goddes wille," we hear the old man reply to the rude questioning of "the proudeste of thise riotoures three." And the shrill voice of the Pardoner cannot hide the poignancy of the lines:

> "Ne Deeth, allas! ne wol nat han my lyf.
> Thus walke I, lyk a restelees kaityf,
> And on the ground, which is my moodres gate,
> I knokke with my staf, bothe erly and late,
> And seye 'Leeve mooder, leet me in!
> Lo how I vanysshe, flessh, and blood, and skyn!
> Allas! whan shul my bones been at reste?
> Mooder, with yow wolde I chaunge my cheste
> That in my chambre longe tyme hath be,
> Ye, for an heyre clowt to wrappe in me!'
> But yet to me she wol nat do that grace
> For which ful pale and welked is my face."
>   (VI, 721-738)

So it is that the Pardoner, intent upon the brilliant performance he is giving the pilgrims, describes, unknown to himself, his own true nature. In spite of his powers to make most people his "apes," on this pilgrimage he will not be able to do so. Though rudely jolted back to the actuality of the journey to Canterbury he remains, as far as we are able to see, unregenerate. Within the context of the present moment he has been punished and, we can assume, continues on the journey, still the "gentil Pardoner of Rouncevale" though now made impotent by his own over-weening ego. Whatever his future condemnation may be, Chaucer would be the last to say. He, too, is included among the sinners who may win Christ's mercy in the Parson's Tale that ends the pilgrimage. But the perversion of values he boasts of remains clearly delineated, affirming by their rendered inefficacy the real existence of such values.

chapter 7

SOME TALES IN FRAGMENT VII —
COMEDY PREDOMINANTLY
PHILOSOPHICAL:

SIR THOPAS, THE TALE OF MELIBEE
THE MONK'S TALE
THE NUN'S PRIEST'S TALE

Six tales with their various connective links comprise *Fragment VIII;* two of them, *The Shipman's Tale* conjecturally once intended for the Wife of Bath, and *The Prioress' Tale* have been looked at elsewhere in this book. The four tales left from the group, Chaucer's two tales, the *Monk's Tale,* and the *Nun's Priest's,* demand attention in the light of each other.

Much that is revealing of Chaucer's Comedy goes on in this fragment: in some ways it contains the climax of his comic statement about life. Thus, for want of a better word, I have called them "philosophic," for they dramatically formulate what has consistently been of fundamental concern to him: the nature of human existence in the world, the question of justice, the problem of free will, the role of Fortune, and the evidence of meaningful order in life. In addition, the comic action of the pilgrimage is made more interesting because Chaucer, the pilgrim, takes part, and the Host, hitherto so sure of his capability as interpreter of men and as peacemaker, is seen to be as fallible as the rest of men. Dissension and the possibility of contention still exist, and the human need to retaliate by some form of "quiting" again gives rise to a tale. The marriage question rises once more, though not as a major concern, and the Knight, in a return to his role as peacemaker and restorer of order gives us Chaucer's definition of Comedy. It is even true that in the Nun's Priest's story of Chauntecleer and Pertelote a comic eye is cast backwards to the tragedy of *Troilus and Criseyde.*

Not the least of the comic riches in this fragment is the *Tale of Sir Thopas* told by Chaucer, the pilgrim. It follows directly upon the sad and pious little tale of the Prioress' little "clergeon," and its jog-trot doggerel effectively breaks the somewhat melancholy religiosity that threatens to preclude any more mirth among the pilgrims. Its farcical hilarity, its brilliance as parody, is in such sharp contrast to the gentle soberness of the tale just heard that it leaves that tale intact in its innocent intrusion upon the comic mode; the spirit of game and mirth and play returns to the pilgrimage in a way that is wonderfully tactful.

The Host is, fittingly, the one who initiates the return to the "myrthe" that seems, in the mood of the moment, irretrievable. Hopefully he turns to Chaucer, who looks as if he surely could "telle us a tale of myrthe." He speaks still under the spell of the Prioress, in the solemn and formal stanza of her tale, the "Troilus stanza":

> Whan seyd was al this miracle, every man
> As sobre was that wonder was to se,
> Til that oure Hooste japen tho bigan,
> And thanne at erst he looked upon me,
> And seyde thus, "What man artow?" quod he;
> "Thou lookest as thou woldest fynde an hare,
> For evere upon the ground I se thee stare.
>
> "Approche neer, and looke up murily.
> Now war yow, sires, and lat this man have place!
> He in the waast is shape as wel as I;
> This were a popet in an arm t'enbrace
> For any womman, smal and fair of face.
> He semeth elvyssh by his contenaunce,
> For unto no wight dooth he daliaunce."
>   (VII, 691-705)

And to the Host's request, "Sey now somwhat, syn oother folk han seyd," Chaucer modestly replies:

> "Hooste," quod I, "ne beth nat yvele apayd,
> For oother tale certes kan I noon,
> But of a rym I lerned longe agoon."
>   (VII, 707-709)

"Ye, that is good," says the Host, and speaks for us all: "Now shul we heere/ Som deyntee thyng, me thynketh by his cheere." He has not yet really guessed wrong, not really failed to interpret from the "cheere" of any one of the pilgrims the kind of tale he will draw forth: even the Pardoner has told a "moral tale" and the Franklin's story of "gentillesse" has not really been a "prechyng."

That all of us are fooled along with the Host makes us for a moment the butt of the joke so that when his explosive interruption comes it is doubly welcome: we are spared more of the jigging monotony of the tale and we rejoice in the boldness of our "umpire." But we are also pleased that we are, in a sense, more appreciative than the Host is of the very good quality of the parody Chaucer, the poet, is creating in his tale of the "doghty swayn"; it is one of the few times in Chaucer when the reader is allowed to feel superior to any of his characters, to see himself, in Meredith's words, as "a citizen of the selecter world."

For the *Tale of Sir Thopas* is noteworthy parody. Like all good parodies it burlesques its subject both in form and spirit. In this instance high fun is made of the metrical romances that were popular in Chaucer's day. There is the possibility that something more particularly topical may have been in his mind, because of his care in pointing out that his hero was born "in fer contree,/ In Flaundres, al biyonde the see,/ At Poperyng, in the place." Whatever the object of the satire, it seems perfectly clear that Chaucer had no intention of devoting much of his time to the attack, nor, from the brevity of the Tale, does he seem to be interested in seriously ridiculing the genre. He burlesques most of its characteristics in short order, his satiric and comic purposes are served, and he quickly passes to something more important.

Sir Thopas is the mechanical man of the Middle Ages, or, to use Bergson's words, "something mechanical encrusted on the living." He is the "hero" who acts out the part tradition and convention have assigned to him, an automaton, a genial soul without motivation or design. He is a hero because he is a hero and since he is a hero he must do everything heroes are supposed to do. He is chaste in spite of being much loved by "ful many a mayde, bright in bour"; he is brave and therefore must go out in search of adventures. He is blissfully unaware that his world is a very tame and bourgeois one indeed. The wild beasts in the forest are the buck and the hare; the forest of wild impenetrability is a forest of herbs and flowers; the mysterious and wonderful sounds he hears upon his journey are the songs of birds—"The sparhauk and the papejay," the "thrustelcok" and the "wodedowve upon the spray." Adventures for such as Sir Thopas were usually encountered as the hero was in search for his lady-love, or as he was sent by her to accomplish some dangerous task.

Sir Thopas has no lady-love; but no matter. He falls in "love-longynge" anyway, when "he herde the thrustel synge."

> And pryked as he were wood.
> His faire steede in his prikynge
> So swatte that men myghte him wrynge;
>   His sydes were al blood.
>
>   Sire Thopas eek so wery was
> For prikyng on the softe gras,
>   So fiers was his corage,
> That doun he leyde him in that plas
> To make his steede som solas,
>   And yaf hym good forage.
>   (VII, 774-783)

Although the jog-trot never lets up, nothing in the poem seems to move. Chaucer has caught exactly that curious effect created by the metrical romances of an enormous stasis that dulls the mind no matter how exciting the adventures may be.

> "O seinte Marie, *benedicite!*
> What eyleth this love at me
>   To bynde me so soore?
> Me dremed al this nyght, pardee,
> An elf-queene shal my lemman be
>   And slepe under my goore.
>
>   "An elf-queene wol I love, ywis,
> For in this world no womman is
>   Worthy to be my make
>   In towne;
>   Alle othere wommen I forsake,
> And to an elf-queene I me take
>   By dale and eek by downe!"
>   (VII, 784-796)

Following the path to the "contree of Fairye" worn smooth by the heroes he is imitating, he meets, of course, a giant, "Sir Olifaunt" by name, and a fight is arranged for. If one is to fight with a giant, one must be armed properly, according to ceremony and ritual. With minstrels and wine, with mead and gingerbread, he is made ready for battle, dressed in layer upon layer of garment:

> His sheeld was al of gold so reed,
> And therinne was a bores heed,
>   A charbocle bisyde;
> And there he swoor on ale and breed
> How that the geaunt shal be deed,
>   Bityde what bityde!
> > (VII, 869-874)

The voice of the narrator keeps doggedly on matching absurdity of tale with metrical inanity, never wavering from the rhythmical pattern prescribed by the genre. The second "fit" that is only allowed to go for four stanzas hints at no conclusion in any foreseeable future. That there are to be almost countless adventures goes without saying, for Thopas seems determined to imitate as many heroes as he can. The Host's outburst comes at exactly the moment when it really seems impossible to bear any more of this dead-pan nonsense. "Namoore of this, for Goddes dignitee," he cries out:

> . . . "for thou makest me
> So wery of thy verray lewednesse
> That, also wisly God my soule blesse,
> Myne eres aken of thy drasty speche.
> Now swich a rym the devel I biteche!
> This may wel be rym dogeral." . . .
> > (VII, 919-925)

We shall never know what happened to Sir Thopas, but we shall not forget the last vision of him and are grateful that the Host's interruption did not come until we had seen "sir Thopas" on his "goode steede," dressed in his armor, with a helmet to outshine all helmets; for "upon his creest he bar a tour,/ And therinne stiked a lilie flour." "God," indeed, "shilde his cors fro shonde!"

Chaucer's bewilderment at the words of the Host plays out the game of literary buffoon. "Why so?" he asks, and makes the protest that no one of the other pilgrims has been interrupted: this is, after all, the "beste rym" he knows. The Host, still growling in disappointment and chagrin at having erred so in reading Chaucer's "cheere," replies:

> "By God, . . . for pleynly, at a word,
> Thy drasty rymyng is nat worth a toord!
> Thou doost noght elles but despendest tyme.
> Sire, at o word, thou shalt no lenger ryme.
> Lat se wher thou kanst tellen aught in geeste,

> Or telle in prose somwhat, at the leeste,
> In which ther be som murthe or som doctryne."
>   (VII, 929-935)

"Gladly," responds Chaucer, and tells the *Tale of Melibee*.

To formulate hypotheses to account for the image of self Chaucer is deliberately creating is, of course, possible. But they will always be hypotheses and as such, interesting, though not really illuminating about his art. Chaucer, the naïve and youthfully imperceptive narrator, first made his appearance in *The Book of the Duchess;* Chaucer, the corpulent and unwilling companion of the Eagle, muttered his uncommunicative "Yis" in the *House of Fame;* Chaucer, the impartial observer was in the crush of birds in *The Parliament of Fowls;* Chaucer, the "translator" of the tragedy of *Troilus and Criseyde*, admitted his helplessness in face of the fact of Criseyde's treachery; Chaucer, the pilgrim, looked about him at the company gathered at the Tabard Inn and described, in the posture of objectivity, what he saw. From the beginning he has taken pains to cultivate an image of himself as a not very good poet or "maker," though one who hopes to be "in processe of tyme"; or one whose work has been futile or unrewarded, whose "bookys, songes, dytees,/ In ryme, or elles in cadence" have been made in spite of the fact that "in thy hed ful lyte is." Perhaps he was wary of the vagaries of Fame, conscious of all the warnings issued against her mutability and illogic, yet taking care to keep his figure always in her gaze. Whatever the possible explanations, what ultimately matters is the effect his particular kind of self-image has in the situation where it appears.

Chaucer, the buffoon, has obvious possibilities for comedy. His inept bumbling in reciting the *Tale of Sir Thopas* does not contradict the impression he has given us in the *General Prologue* of being perfectly able to observe the human beings around him and to report clearly and accurately what he sees. That he is a good reporter does not mean that he is also a good poet. And, after all, he is making no pretense at creating his own narrative; he is merely reciting "a rym" he "lerned longe agoon." The pilgrim, Chaucer, is not responsible for the rhyme's monotony or the story's absurdity. That he should tell the dullest and the most boring of all the tales is clearly, broad Socratic irony. The audience of listeners or of readers that was his first must have enjoyed the joke as much as all generations of audiences have since then. The disappointment of the Host is funny. He was entitled to his expectations: the richer the expectation, the more dramatically comic the reversal of that expectation, and the indignation of the Host is both justifiable and infectious. And the choice of the buffoon as the narrator of a metrical romance makes even more telling the attack on the inanities of the genre than if made by someone consciously satirizing.

Some characterizing of the pilgrim, Chaucer, was necessary if Chaucer, the poet, was to sustain the illusion of an observer-reporter who was also a participant in "the game and the pleye." It is not difficult to see what important problems are solved by making his pilgrim-self less skillful at narration than any of the others. As part of the background, as a minor figure among those created to take the center of the stage, he could not tell a tale better than theirs, nor outdo in narrative power the "best" Chaucer, the poet, has already done. Both comic high spirits and aesthetic ends are gained in the figure of this genial, rotund dolt of a pilgrim.

It is also possible to suggest that he gave to himself the "rym doggeral" of Sir Thopas in order to disabuse the pilgrims and us as much as possible from expecting him to show any narrative skill whatsoever, so that when he speaks discursively, as he will in *The Tale of Melibee*, there will be little possibility for a critical rejection of it. That he moved from *The Tale of Sir Thopas* to the lengthy, prose treatise on the misfortunes of Melibeus with the intention of substituting one kind of boredom for another does not seem to me to be a tenable thesis. If the evident respect he shows for his source, the French condensation of the thirteenth-century Latin *Liber Consolationis et Consilii* by Albertanus of Brescia, is to be questioned as proof of the seriousness of his intent, the respect his listeners show for his tale cannot be. Not unless we are suddenly supposed to believe that in their regard for the treatise, the Host and the pilgrims are the butt of a joke they are not aware of. As far as I have been able to see, Chaucer never plays jokes on his characters that are not clearly recognized by someone for what they are. A pilgrim may contest with a pilgrim, a pilgrim may upset the expectations of other pilgrims, but the poet is never obscure nor ambiguous in creating the situation. And he never joins forces with the audience against his own characters. The Host has interrupted the monotony of *Sir Thopas* and he will rejoice in the Knight's interruption of the Monk; he listens to this long prose tale of Melibee with complete patience. His response at the end, a response that takes us and the pilgrims back once more into the dramatic and dynamic world of the pilgrimage, and back in a boisterous way, to the world of comedy, in no way hints at disapproval or ennui:

> Whan ended was my tale of Melibee,
> And of Prudence and hire benignytee,
> Oure Hooste seyde, "As I am feithful man,
> And by that precious corpus Madrian,
> I hadde levere than a barel ale

> That Goodelief, my wyf, hadde herd this tale!
> For she nys no thyng of swich pacience
> As was this Melibeus wyf Prudence.
>   (VII, 1889-1896)

Her advice to him is quite the opposite of that Melibeus' wife gives to persuade him from seeking revenge for his injuries; Goodelief, on the contrary, roars against his timidity. "Slee the dogges everichoon,/ And brek hem, bothe bak and every boon! . . . Allas! . . . that evere I was shape/ To wedden a milksop, or a coward ape,/ That wol been overlad with every wight!/ Thou darst nat stonden by thy wyves right!" "This is my lif," says the Host, "but if that I wol fighte."

The kind of tale Chaucer chooses when halted in his attempt at rhyming, moreover, has been somewhat asked for by the Host. "Lat se wher thou kanst tellen aught in geeste,/ Or telle in prose somwhat, at the leeste,/ In which ther be some murthe or som doctryne." Chaucer's description of his "moral tale vertuous" as "a litel thyng in prose" and "this litel tretys heere" in view of the very long treatise that follows is ironic, but only functional as it continues for a little while the illusion of a rather stupid narrator, not as it makes a joke out of the tale so inaccurately described. That Chaucer should think of the "tale I write" in terms not adequate to describe it, seems to me quite in keeping with the Chaucer who bungled so laughably the invitation to tell "som deyntee thyng." *The Tale of Melibeus* can be taken seriously without forcing a contradiction on the already defined nature of the narrator. The transition from farce and burlesque and comic high jinks to the high seriousness of a moral treatise is a difficult one to make; it is made here with a minimal of awkwardness. Dolt though he may be, the pilgrim, Chaucer, is aware the tale he is about to tell may be more serious than the pilgrims want:

> "Therfore, lordynges alle, I yow biseche,
> If that yow thynke I varie as in my speche,
> As thus, though that I telle somwhat moore
> Of proverbes than ye han herd bifoore
> Comprehended in this litel tretys heere,
> To enforce with th'effect of my mateere,
> And though I nat the same wordes seye
> As ye han herd, yet to yow alle I preye
> Blameth me nat; for, as in my sentence,
> Shul ye nowher fynden difference
> Fro the sentence of this tretye lyte
> After the which this murye tale I write.

> And therfore herkneth what that I shal seye,
> And lat me tellen al my tale, I preye."
> (VII, 953-966)

Thus by the time the treatise-tale is under way, pilgrims and readers are led to attend it with respect. Chaucer's characters and his audience, accustomed to moral treatises of far greater length and of far less narrative artistry than this one, needed less persuasion to accept the "tretys" as "litel" than we do. And it is surely literal-minded to say that Chaucer is violating the illusion of realism he has sought to establish in creating tales that can be told while the narrators are riding on the road to Canterbury. *The Tale of Melibee* no more shakes the "willing suspension of disbelief" than does *The Knight's Tale.*

It is easy to see why Chaucer selected the account of the trial and testing of Melibeus for his alter ego to tell. Like *The Franklin's Tale* it contained almost all of the concerns that had interested him throughout his literary life. It is, like *The Consolation of Boethius,* made up of a dialogue between a wise woman and a man intent upon solving the problem of suffering. In form, thus, it is agonistic even as in subject matter. The specific question in this prose allegory is one of right action: should Melibeus exact revenge for his injuries or not. In moral and philosophic terms Chaucer is here examining the very principle by which many of *The Canterbury Tales* have been generated: the principle of contention, of giving tit for tat, of seeing to it that some kind of justice is done for injury received. And in the course of the dialogue there arise, inevitably, questions about the true nature of patience, about the best way to choose and depend upon the advice of others, about the relations between husband and wife, about the physical and spiritual danger of giving in to anger, about the nature of Fortune, and, ultimately, about "gentillesse" and "the gentil dede." It is not only the kinds of issues raised in this moral treatise that interested the poet, Chaucer; it is also the wise serenity, the common sense, the reasonableness of the whole that must have appealed to him. In the end, *The Tale of Melibee* is truly a "murye" one, though not a humorous one.

There is no point in looking for psychological reality in this story of Melibeus and his wife Prudence. Neither for Chaucer nor for his audience would the question have been relevant. It is an allegory and therefore cannot afford to distract from its lesson by making the personalities more interesting in their complexities than the issues they are portraying. Melibeus is Man—man blessed by God in many ways:

> "Thy name is Melibee, this is to seyn, 'a man that drynketh hony.'/ Thou hast ydronke so muchel hony of sweete tem-

poreel richesses, and delices and honours of this world,/
that thou art dronken, and hast forgeten Jhesu Crist thy
creatour./ Thou ne hast nat doon to hym swich honour and
reverence as thee oughte."

(VII, 1409-1411)

Sophie, the daughter of Melibeus and Prudence, who has been injured
because of his self-indulgence, is his "soul," or "spiritual nature," its
well-being impaired by the "three enemys of mankynde, that is to seyn,
the flessh, the feend, and the world" (VII, 1419-1422). Prudence, the
wife, is Good Judgment; all that she says makes her almost an extended
definition of the true nature of right action and of the best kind of
common sense. As she and Melibeus argue in their prosaic fashion, we
are reminded of the prickly marriage question so much more dynamically
and dramatically treated in the earlier group of tales. Melibeus, like
the other husbands, will not be guided by her counsels, for if he is, other
men will hold him "thanne a fool." As stoutly as Jankyn, he maintains
that women are "alle . . . wikke" and not to be trusted with "maistrie"—
"And Salomon seith: 'Nevere in thy lyf to thy wyf, ne to thy child, ne
to thy freend, ne yeve no power over thyself' " (VII, 1058-1060). But
the battle of the sexes is not the major concern of the dialogue: it is
the question of battle itself—of contention, of revenge, of force against
force. "Werre! werre!" cry his advisers, and it is with great reluctance
that he heeds the prudent words of his wife. Wrong does not cure wrong,
she says, and thus comments ironically upon the principle of dramatic
action of *The Canterbury Tales*, "For certes, wikkednesse is nat contrarie
to wikkednesse, ne vengeance to vengeaunce . . . but everich of hem
encreesceth and aggreggeth oother" are words that point directly to the
hostilities and contentions among the pilgrims (VII, 1285). But, Melibeus
insists, such contentions and their attendant suffering exist. Why must
this be so, he asks. Why must pain and injustice be the lot of man. In
short, he asks the question Boethius asked, the question that Dorigen
asked, that Chaucer himself asks both implicitly and explicitly throughout
all his work: why does a good and benevolent God allow evil in all its
forms. And Prudence replies:

"Now, sire, if men wolde axe me why that God suffred men
to do yow this vileyne, certes, I kan nat wel answere, as for
no soothfastnesse./ For th'apostle seith that 'the sciences
and the juggementz of oure Lord God almyghty been ful
depe;/ ther may no man comprehende ne serchen hem suf-
fisantly.'/ Nathelees, by certeyne presumpciouns and con-
jectynges, I holde and bileeve/ that God, which that is ful

of justice and of rightwisnesse, hath suffred this bityde by
just cause resonable."
(VII, 1405 ff).

That Melibeus has brought his own trouble upon himself is a secondary
explanation; why the just and good God allows man to be his own worst
enemy is the primary question. Prudence can only advise acceptance of
the fact and can only suggest the adoption of an attitude that will make
the condition of man endurable. "The tribulaciouns of this world but
litel while endure, and soone passed been and goon" she reminds him.
The joy of God is everlasting, and patience and unwavering faith in
God's goodness and justice are the conditions for attaining that joy.
For the particular comfort of Melibeus in his present woe, Prudence
reminds him that justice exists in the world of men and is sometimes
happily in evidence. But he must also acknowledge his own "vileynye,"
his own responsibility for the suffering that has come upon him. Warning him that excessive self-punishment is wrong for it is "agayn resoun
and out of mesure," she makes clear that towards himself as well as toward his enemies he must have mercy "to the effect and entente that God
Almighty have mercy on yow in his laste juggement./ For Seint Jame
seith in his Epistle: 'Juggement withouten mercy shal be doon to hym
that hath no mercy of another wight!' "

Finally won over to the counsels of his wife, Melibeus, like the squire
and the magician in *The Franklin's Tale*, is able to perform "the gentil
dede." Grateful to God for having sent him "a wyf of so greet discrecioun," he calls in his adversaries and renounces revenge (VII, 1882 ff.).
The whole tale ends on a prayer of quiet joy, its protagonist willing to
submit to measure and reason, to accept the trials of life with patience,
judgment, and perspective; and to trust that "oure Lord God . . . so
free and so merciable/ that he wole foryeven us oure giltes,/ and
bryngen us to the blisse that nevere hath ende. Amen"

In retelling the *Livre de Melibee et de Dame Prudence*, Chaucer, the
pilgrim, makes no attempt to alter the allegorical mode of the original.
It is a tale that depends primarily upon the clearly defined and limited
figura for making its point: abstractions are turned into approximate
personifications and the story exists for the illustration of the general
philosophical and moral thesis. As pilgrim, he may not be an effective
creator of narrative prose, but he has an orderly and a clear mind,
and his prose, as prose goes in the Middle Ages, is lucid and articulate,
only at times pedestrian. The teller who comes directly after him betrays
no such orderly and lucid a mind. Perhaps this is because the problem
the Monk attempts to deal with, the relation of man to Fortune or
Destiny, lends itself to greater confusion than the "problem of evil

per se" that had been the pilgrim Chaucer's concern. In any case, the Monk, in his effort to deal with abstractions, creates chaos and poses somewhat of a threat to the "mirth" of the whole company once more.

THE MONK'S TALE

There are several important ways in which the collection of anecdotes the Monk tells as his Tale fulfil a comic function in *The Canterbury Tales*. The situation in its dramatic realization is amusing. His definition of "tragedie" leads to the Knight's (and Chaucer's) definition of comedy. His somewhat confused handling of the question of Fortune and its relation to the course of human events prefaces *The Nun's Priest's Tale* with its brilliant presentation of the complexities inherent in the question. And the boredom he seems to arouse threatens the "myrth" of the pilgrimage as it, momentarily at least, seems to suggest disorder and irrationality in the affairs of men. Its "hevynesse" is caused not only by its constant emphasis upon "tragedie" but also by its apparent denial of reasonable cause and effect, a denial which, though not to be taken as intentional on the part of the Monk, suggests the existence of chaos that endangers both mirth and morality.

The situational comedy is the most obvious. Once more Chaucer is reminding us that appearances are deceptive only when misread. From what the Monk so clearly appears to be, a "manly man," a "lord ful fat and in good poynt," it is not unreasonable to expect him to tell a tale in harmony with his non-ascetical aspect. It is the expectation obviously held by the Host whose coarsely vulgar invitation openly proclaims his anticlericalism while, at the same time, asking the Monk to corroborate his assumption. What the Host gets, of course, is a series of dreary tragedies, unimaginatively and prosaically narrated. Our sense of the comic surprise is not released until the Knight does it for us. His interruption, "Hoo . . . good sire, namoore of this!/ That ye han seyd is ryght ynough, ywis,/ And muchel moore" (VII, 2767-2769), confirms our right to feel somewhat irked at what promises to be an unending succession of sad tales. And our feeling is released into laughter by the Host's quick follow-up. "Ye," he says to the Knight, "by seint Poules belle!/ Ye seye right sooth; this Monk he clappeth lowde."

> "Sire Monk, namoore of this, so God yow blesse!
> Youre tale anoyeth al this compaignye.
> Swich talkyng is nat worth a boterflye,
> For therinne is ther no desport ne game.
> Wherfore, sire Monk, or daun Piers by youre name,
> I pray yow hertely telle us somwhat elles;
> For sikerly, nere clynkyng of youre belles,

That on youre bridel hange on every syde,
By hevene kyng, that for us alle dyde,
I sholde er this han fallen doun for sleep,
Althogh the slough had never been so deep;
Thanne hadde your tale al be toold in veyn."

(VII, 2788-2799)

Freed from our own boredom, we laugh with Harry Bailly, but we also laugh at him. Once more he has been proved fallible. His misreading of the appearance of the Monk has been almost as humiliating to his robust arrogance as has his misreading of the appearance of Chaucer, the pilgrim. For a moment we are granted a modicum of superiority over him, the guide and the umpire. But even in the second of laughing at the Host we laugh at ourselves, for our expectations also have been somewhat disappointed. We, too, have erred in reading appearances. Some comic pleasure comes also from a sense of justice done, for the boredom that the Host suffers is in a way a kind of reprimand for his jocularly vulgar anticlericalism. The Host in his turn, has been "quited."

What, of course, the Host and "al this compaignye" fail to guess from the appearance of the Monk is that he is likely to tell exactly the kind of tale he does. He is clearly a busy and effective administrator. Though fond of hunting and good living, he seems capable in the performance of his duties. That we (and the Host) have been tempted to read more than we should into the observer-reporter's description of him is a joke on us all. The statement that he was "a fair for the maistrie,/ An outridere, that loved venerie,/ A manly man, to been an abbot able" seems to be quite literally so, intended to suggest that his community has profited by his presence, materially if not spiritually, and intended to suggest nothing else. Though worldly, he is unquestionably a religious, and self-conscious of his importance as a religious. That he should tell a solemn tale, that he should not be skilled in the arts of narration, is thus, even more likely than that he should tell one of bawdy.

"Daun Piers" is explicit about the kind of tale he will tell. Taking, as Chaucer tells us, the Host's references to his apparent sexual vigor "al in pacience," he promises in words of dignified restraint that he will do all his "diligence,/ As fer as sowneth into honestee,/ To telle yow a tale, or two, or three" (VII, 1966-1968). Though not given to studying "in cloystre," he has an acquaintance with the kinds of stories that might have been found in any monk's community—legends of saints, historical anecdotes, stories of antiquity—all useful for "oure doctrine." That he chooses to tell "tragedies" is not, upon reflection, surprising. Since they are stories "as olde bookes maken us memorie,/ Of hym that stood in greet prosperitee,/ And is yfallen out of heigh degree/

Into myserie, and endeth wrecchedly," they serve both moral and spiritual ends, pointing out, as they do, the instability and woe that is in this present life. His understanding of tragedy (an understanding that was also Chaucer's) has come from Trivet's comment on Boethius and is a brief but respectable simplification of Aristotle's. To illustrate it he draws upon many notable writers, among whom was Boccaccio, whose *De Casibus Virorum Illustrium* he acknowledges as he announces his tale.

A sad tale of serious moral import need not preclude mirth. Other pilgrims have told and will tell such tales and do not suffer interruption. It is not the matter in the Monk's "tragedies" that threatens the mirthful spirit of the pilgrimage but the discomfort that begins to increase as his recitation of anecdote after anecdote, in monotonous succession, reveals that he does not really comprehend the complexity of his theme. Though his tales do not specifically deny the existence of a meaningful relation between Fortune and man's sufferings nor propose to question assumptions of Order, they, in effect, during the length of time it takes to tell them, suggest that confusion and chaos may exist. Such a suggestion is disquieting in a world ruled by the principles of the "game." So it is significant that it is the Knight who puts a stop to the Monk's voice. If the "worthy man" is a symbol of Order, as I have suggested in the case of his establishing peace between the Pardoner and the Host, his interference once more attests to his symbolic role. Objecting to the unrelieved "hevynesse" of the accumulated effect of the stories, the Knight explains that "it is a greet disese,/ Whereas men han been in greet welthe and ese,/ To heeren of hire sodeyn fal, allas!" He reminds the Monk that the pilgrimage was to be full of mirth, and counters the definition of tragedy that preceded the narration with a definition of comedy, though he does not call it such:

> "And the contrarie is joye and greet solas,
> As whan a man hath been in povre estaat,
> And clymbeth up and wexeth fortunat,
> And there abideth in prosperitee.
> Swich thyng is gladsom, as it thynketh me,
> And of swich thyng were goodly for to telle."
>
> (VII, 2769-2779)

Thus he voices Chaucer's concept of comedy, a concept that, in spite of its apparent unsophisticated simplicity, says as much in definition as need be said.

The Monk has openly confessed to his lack of skill as a narrator, admitting before he has begun his tales that he will tell them in no special order—"But tellen hem som bifore and some bihynde,/ As it now comth unto my remembraunce" (VII, 1983-1990). But it is not until the second or the third "ensample" of his governing thesis—"whan that Fortune list to flee,/ Ther may no man the cours of hire withholde" (VII, 1991-1992)—that it becomes clear he has little concern for causal order, a fact that is potentially much more disturbing than his inability to arrange his stories in some meaningful way. Drawing his illustrations from the Old Testament, from Greek mythology, from Latin history, from Dante, from Boccaccio, he conveys the sense of an existential absurdity. What happens to man is sometimes caused by that man's own crime, but sometimes not; sometimes it is caused by "wikked wyves," sometimes by the machinations of others who go unpunished; sometimes misfortune results simply because of Fortune's unpredictable whim. There is little perceptible justice; and any concept of moral responsibility seems irrelevant. His portrayal of Fortune is much like Chaucer's vivid picturization of Fame in the third book of *The House of Fame*, fickle, arbitrary, whimsical, as often just as unjust, as often reasonable and meaningful as unreasonable and meaningful. That Fame should be so is not disturbing; that Fortune (in this tale a synonym for Fate) should be so is disturbing, for the world that Chaucer's art proclaims in content and in form is one of rational meaning, not one of irrational absurdity. The Monk has learned many examples of how Fortune and Man relate, but he has not made himself "wood" by puzzling out the inherent complexities within his theme. He is not a contemplative, but a businessman. And he is neither by training, by temperament, nor by inclination a teller of tales. It is not surprising that he refuses to go on with "the game," and replies to the Host's request to "sey somwhat of huntyng": "I have no lust to pleye./ Now lat another telle, as I have toold." The tone has sounds of disgruntlement in it and a sufficient note of finality to preclude coaxing so that the Host turns to the Nun's Priest, in whose tale the concept so confusedly handled by the Monk becomes brilliantly coherent and meaningful.

THE NUN'S PRIEST'S TALE

The Monk's concern with Fortune is also the concern of the Nun's Priest, but his statement of it indicates clearly that he, unlike his predecessor, understands something necessary to its action. The last words the Monk is allowed to say, "Fortune that alwey wole assaille/ With unwar strook the regnes that been proude," are, in effect the thesis of the Priest's tale of Pertelote and Chantecleer.

Chaucer, the pilgrim-observer, has given no detail about the Nun's Priest's appearance, nor, other than listing him as one of the "preestes thre" accompanying the Prioress, has he given any hint of his ecclesiastical function as a member of her entourage. It has been, therefore, for some readers of *The Canterbury Tales*, an irresistible temptation to fill in the portrait Chaucer neglected to supply, describing him in ways as oppositely varied as genial and large, or waspish and thin. The references the Host makes to his brawn have been taken literally or ironically, his narrative as subtle retaliation upon the Prioress for her feminine power over him, or as an attack upon the higher clergy in the person of the Monk. The Host's joyous gratification for the tale the priest tells reveals his characteristic anticlericalism and coarseness and comments upon the happy effect of the tale. It clearly evidences Harry Bailly's relief at expectation fulfilled, but its descriptive details do little to create a visual image of the teller. Only his voice that seems genial and amiable in his acceptance of the Host's invitation to speak provides a tonal clue to his personality.

Why Chaucer gave to a pilgrim so sketchily described this "murie tale of Chauntecleer" that has been justly acclaimed as one of his great tales, can only be guessed. The suggestion that he at one time intended to tell this story himself, assigning it to the priest when he decided on the Thopas-Melibee tales as his, is a tribute to the narrative and comic powers, to the moral significance of the adventure of the cock and the fox; it does not answer the question of the attribution, though it does confirm the thesis that Chaucer, the pilgrim, was not to rival nor surpass his fellow pilgrims in the telling of his tale. What seems to me to be the important effect of giving this tale to a pilgrim who has not been portrayed in the *General Prologue* is that it is the tale itself that ultimately matters and not the teller. Here the themes allegorically portrayed in the story of Melibeus are dramatically vitalized by a cock, a hen, and a fox; here the relation between the individual and disaster, between man and Fortune, chaotically described by the Monk, is made philosophically and psychologically meaningful; here all the themes central to the fragment are given comic perspective and clarity of focus.

All this is not to say that the narrator's voice is not heard; it is. But the fact that it both communicates an attitude toward and establishes a distance from the action it is narrating is of greater significance than what it conveys of the personality of the teller. "But ye that holden this tale a folye,/ As of a fox, or of a cok and hen,/ Taketh the moralite, goode men./ For seint Paul seith that al that writen is,/ To oure doctrine it is ywrite, ywis;/ Taketh the fruyt, and lat the chaf be stille" (VII, 3438-3443), his voice concludes. His amused detachment from his story has been so consistently maintained that it is indeed up to his hearers to "taketh the fruyt," for he gives no guidance. Is the "fruyt" of the tale the lesson that women's counsels are not to be trusted? Is it that flatterers are to be avoided? Is it that disaster is fated? Is it that Fortune is fickle? Is it that lust and pride bring their own punishment? Is it that wit matched against wit ensures survival? It is all these, but not in any simple way. And the narrator will not by word or gesture simplify them into one "moralite."

What *The Nun's Priest's Tale* is, in effect, is a translation into mock epic terms of what seems to have been for Chaucer an important thesis in Boethius. It is a thesis that is comic in essence for it proposes an attitude toward the trials of life that makes those trials endurable: "For it is set in your hand (*as who seith, it lyth in your power*) what fortune yow is levest (*that is to seyn, good or yvel*); for alle fortune that semeth scharp or aspre, yif it ne exercise nat the goode folk ne chastiseth the wikkede folk, it punysseth" (Book IV, prosa 7). Fortune, whether ill or good, is a manner of speaking only; it is a figura created to corporealize the known and the unknown forces that both shape and are shaped by man. To blame it as the cause of joy or wretchedness is, in effect, to question the degree to which the human being has moral responsibility or free will and choice. Man's happiness depends finally upon his own capacity to climb into Fortune's favor, or to hang on until her Wheel makes its upward turn. Chantecleer's near-disaster comes upon him because of his own fault; his survival and triumph are insured when he makes use of that "sapience" that lies within his power, when he chooses to make use of that very power which in his ill-use of it, had threatened him.

To argue that *The Nun's Priest's Tale* is in any sense a comic transliteration of Boethius is, of course, absurd. The world of the "povre wydwe" and her farmyard that is the large frame that encloses the small but dramatic action of the cock's world is not the universe of God that encompasses the world of men. But it is a way of contrasting two worlds, one of which is contained within the other, both of which coexist. And it is one way of showing how the smaller, and in this instance, the more important world has its own being in its own terms, uninfluenced by the larger, encompassing one. The bare and cheerful farmyard that is by the "narwe cotage,/ biside a grove, stondynge in a dale" that belongs to "a povre wydwe, somdeel stape in age" is the stage for heroism, for near tragedy, and for final comedy. It is a stage modest and humble in its setting, potentially happy in the intention and design of the human being who created it. "This wydwe," says the Nun's Priest, "in pacience ladde a ful symple lyf,/ For litel was hir catel and hir rente."

> By housbondrie of swich as God hire sente
> She foond hirself and eek hir doghtren two.
> Thre large sowes hadde she, and namo,
> Three keen, and eek a sheep that highte Malle.
> (VII, 2828-2831)

Temperance and joy characterize her small world, moderation and "hertes suffisaunce" her humble life. This is the only close-up we have of the human world that frames the drama of the cock-world until at the end, widow and daughters, friends and neighbors, are joined by bird, beast, and bee in the wild pursuit of the fox who is making away with Chantecleer:

> So hydous was the noyse, a, *benedicitee!*
> Certes, he Jakke Strawe and his meynee
> He made nevere shoutes half so shrille
> Whan that they wolden any Flemyng kille,
> As thilke day was maad upon the fox.
> Of bras they broghten bemes, and of box,
> Of horn, of boon, in whiche they blewe and powped,
> And therwithal they shriked and they howped.
> It semed as that hevene sholde falle.
>   (VII, 3393-3401)

All to no avail. It is not the "powping" and the howping," not the shrieking and the yelling, not the mad chase of the fox that saves Chantecleer; it is his own ingenious employment of his own "sapience" that makes good out of his evil "fortune."

Within this humble farmyard is the royal demesne of Chantecleer, the cock. No matter in what version of the popular *Roman de Renart* the Nun's Priest found his hero, there is no cock like his. He is neither anthropomorphic bird nor avian man, but he is *Homo Sapiens* and *Rara Avis* at one and the same time. Before he is anything else he is a cock:

> In al the land, of crowyng nas his peer.
> His voys was murier than the murie orgon
> On messe-dayes that in the chirche gon.
> Wel sikerer was his crowyng in his logge
> Than is a clokke or an abbey orlogge.
> By nature he knew ech ascencioun
> Of the equynoxial in thilke toun;
> For whan degrees fiftene weren ascended,
> Thanne crew he, that it myghte nat been amended.
>   (VII, 2850-2858)

In the drab farmyard he shines in brilliant glory:

> His coomb was redder than the fyn coral,
> And batailled as it were a castel wal;

His byle was blak, and as the jeet it shoon;
Lyk asure were his legges and his toon;
His nayles whitter than the lylye flour,
And lyk the burned gold was his colour.
(VII, 2859-2864)

Like Melibeus, like the heroes and the heroines of the *Monk's Tale*, Chantecleer is, at the beginning of his story, wonderfully favored by Fortune. He is one who has indeed "ydronke so muchel hony of sweete temporeel richesses, and delices and honours of this world" that like Melibeus, he almost invites disaster. Courtly and uxorious, lover and husband, he rejoices in his seven hens and especially in his favorite, Pertelote:

Curteys she was, discreet, and debonaire,
And compaignable, and bar hyrself so faire,
Syn thilke day that she was seven nyght oold,
That trewely she hath the herte in hoold
Of Chauntecleer, loken in every lith;
He loved hire so that wel was hym therwith.
(VII, 2872-2877)

With genial "governaunce" he rules his world—"swich a joye was it to here hem synge,/ Whan that the brighte sonne gan to sprynge,/ In sweete accord, 'My lief is faren in londe!' " For, the Nun's Priest reminds us, in "thilke tyme, as I have understonde,/ Beestes and briddes koude speke and synge." For we are not to be allowed to forget that what he is telling is a fable, lest in losing the illusion of the cock-world we miss the mockery it directs at the world of human beings.

Chantecleer has clear warning that danger is about to threaten him, that happiness is about to be changed into woe. The dream he has, that alarms him and sets him to groaning on his perch, shows him exactly what he must fear from a "beest/ Was lyk an hound." Pertelote's practical common sense that lays his "vision" to indigestion has nothing to do with his failure to recognize the col-fox for what he is when he falls prey to flattery. Her advice that he "taak som laxatyf . . . that bothe of colere and of malencolye/ Ye purge yow" is no more the solution than was Criseyde's plan to return to Troy within ten days. This the imaginative cock knows, as did Troilus. "Digestyves/ . . . Of lawriol, centaure, and fumetere,/ Or elles of ellebor, that groweth there,/ Of katapuce, or of gaitrys beryis,/ Of herbe yve, growyng in oure yeerd, ther mery is" (VII, 2962-2966) will not help him, for he is full of his own well-being and happy in his physical prowess. And at this moment when he is most blind in his pride he is nearest to disaster:

Bifel that Chauntecleer in al his pryde,
His sevene wyves walkynge by his syde,
Caste up his eyen to the brighte sonne,
That in the signe of Taurus hadde yronne
Twenty degrees and oon, and somwhat moore,
And knewe by kynde, and by noon oother loore,
That it was pryme, and crew with blisful stevene.
"The sonne," he seyde, "is clomben up on hevene
Fourty degrees and oon, and moore ywis.
Madame Pertelote, my worldes blis,
Herkneth thise blisful briddes how they synge,
And se the fresshe floures how they sprynge;
Ful is myn herte of revel and solas!"
But sodeynly hym fil a sorweful cas,
For evere the latter ende of joye is wo.
God woot that worldly joye is soone ago.
(VII, 3191-3206)

The fox appears, and with the instinct of his "kynde" to flee his "con-trarie," Chantecleer cries out in alarm: " 'Cok! cok!' and up he sterte,/ As man that was affrayed in his herte." Nature warns him of danger, confirming the dream; his pride quiets his fear and brings him close to "tragedy." It is not that the fox flatters him that is the cause of his near-downfall; it is that in praising Chantecleer's singing, the fox is praising the very source and manifestation of his cock-hood, that which is the emblem of all his pride and happiness.

This Chauntecleer, whan he gan hym espye,
He wolde han fled, but that the fox anon
Seyde, "Gentil sire, allas! wher wol ye gon?
Be ye affrayed of me that am youre freend?
Now, certes, I were worse than a feend,
If I to yow wolde harm or vileynye!
I am nat come youre conseil for t'espye,
But trewely, the cause of my comynge
Was oonly for to herkne how that ye synge.
For trewely, ye have as myrie a stevene
As any aungel hath that is in hevene.
Therwith ye han in musyk moore feelynge
Than hadde Boece, or any that kan synge.
My lord youre fader—God his soule blesse!—
And eek youre mooder, of hire gentillesse,
Han in myn hous ybeen to my greet ese;
And certes, sire, ful fayn wolde I yow plese.

> But, for men speke of syngyng, I wol seye,—
> So moote I brouke wel myne eyen tweye,—
> Save yow, I herde nevere man so synge
> As dide youre fader in the morwenynge.
> Certes, it was of herte, al that he song."
>
> (VII, 3282-3303)

"This Chauntecleer," says the Nun's Priest, "his wynges gan to bete,/ As man that koude his traysoun nat espie,/ So was he ravysshed with his flaterie." And he "stood hye upon his toos,/ Strecchynge his nekke, and heeld his eyen cloos,/ And gan to crowe loude for the nones" (VII, 3322-3324).

It is at the moment of imminent disaster that the Nun's Priest pauses to meditate upon the reason for the fate that seems to be in store for Chantecleer, his words solemnly elevating his cock to the grandeur of the epic hero. "O false mordrour, lurkynge in thy den!/ O newe Scariot, newe Genylon,/ False dissymulour, o Greek Synon,/ That broghtest Troye al outrely to sorwe," his voice takes on the mock heroic tone, for the questions it is to pose are significant ones, whether asked about cock or man. The amused perspective from which he has viewed and related the action in the farmyard becomes now a perspective that embraces mankind. What Philosophy had called "a prykke at regard of the gretnesse of hevene," this earth, is at this moment of mock elevation made at one and the same time to include more than cock and to become smaller in size. "And ye thanne, that ben envyrouned and closed withynne the leeste prykke of thilke prykke, thynken ye to manyfesten or pub-lisschen your renoun and doon yowr name for to be born forth?" she asks Boethius. And though that is not the question explicitly asked by the Nun's Priest, the mock epic moment that prepares for the climax of the action suggests it.

The question the narrator puts rhetorically to the world at large is the one asked by Troilus as he lamented the coming loss of Criseyde: is Chantecleer's end to be one that has been predetermined, is it that "what . . . God forwoot moot nedes bee?" Does his hero act from free choice or from "symple necessitee" or "by necessitee condicionel?" With these philosophical questions left unanswered—"I wol nat han to do of swich mateere"—he suddenly moves from the "high style" and the meta-physical moment to the tale and its particular concern:

> My tale is of a cok, as ye may heere,
> That tok his conseil of his wyf, with sorwe,
> To walken in the yerd upon that morwe
> That he hadde met that dreem that I yow tolde.
>
> (VII, 3252-3255)

For a moment the Nun's Priest becomes again an actor in the dramatic situation of the pilgrimage. Unobtrusive as he seems to have been, it is evident that he had heard the Wife of Bath and has been a silent witness to the contest aroused by her marriage thesis. He is also reminding his audience of the counsels given Melibee by Prudence, those abstractions he is translating into concretely vivid characters even as his mock heroic version makes humorously ironic comment on Chaucer's solemn tale. The marriage question is made to echo once more, though the Nun's Priest skillfully evades giving it his answer. Where he stands on questions of love, or of lust, or of women, is left undefined. But his hero's artless mistranslation of the Latin phrase he speaks to Pertelote is pointedly ironic; it reveals something of Chantecleer's pretension to learning as, at the same time, it keeps safe the ambiguity of the Nun's Priest's attitude. "For al so siker as *In principio, Mulier est hominis confusio,—/* Madame, the sentence of this Latyn is,/ 'Womman is mannes joye and al his blis' " (VII, 3160-3166), says the royal cock, and sums up in one statement the views taken toward women by many of the narrators of *The Canterbury Tales.* Chantecleer may or may not know the correct translation of the Latin. The narrator of his story certainly does, though before he comes to the climactic moment of the tale, he makes it clear that knowing does not necessarily amount to agreeing with the full implications of the phrase. With genial concern that he be understood, the Priest remarks:

> Wommennes conseils been ful ofte colde;
> Wommannes conseil broghte us first to wo,
> And made Adam fro Paradys to go,
> Ther as he was ful myrie and wel at ese.
> But for I noot to whom it myght displese,
> If I conseil of wommen wolde blame,
> Passe over, for I seyde it in my game.
> Rede auctours, where they trete of swich mateere,
> And what they seyn of wommen ye may heere.
> This been the cokkes wordes, and nat myne;
> I kan noon harm of no womman divyne.
>
> (VII, 3256-3266)

Though obviously fending off any objection his words might evoke, the Nun's Priest is also directing his tale toward the essential question: who is, after all, to blame for what happens to the cock? And he is rejecting the easy answer suggested in some of the tragedies narrated by the Monk. Surely Pertelote is not the cause of Chantecleer's woe. Her scorn for his apprehension of the fearsome dream about the "beest/ Was lyk an hound" may have quieted his anxiety, but he has indignantly refused her advice to take "som laxatyves." Certainly Venus is not to be blamed; his loyal service is a well-known fact. Nor can Destiny be held responsible for his near fatal encounter with the col-fox; indeed, she had seen to it that he had ample and explicit warning in his dream. That cock (or man) can rightfully charge anyone or anything with the disasters that come upon him is a conclusion this pilgrim refuses to propose. It is Chantecleer himself who is to blame. It is his failure to translate dream into reality, to see clearly what is plainly before him, to read the appearance aright, to make use of the knowledge that has been given him. Saved in time by the recovery of that "sapience" he had almost lost, freed from the mouth of the fox by means of his own cleverness, Chantecleer admits his own responsibility:

> "... I shrewe us bothe two.
> And first I shrewe myself, bothe blood and bones,
> If thou bigyle me ofter than ones.
> Thou shalt namoore, thurgh thy flaterye,
> Do me to synge and wynke with myn ye;
> For he that wynketh, whan he sholde see,
> Al wilfully, God lat him nevere thee!"
>   (VII, 3426-3432)

He has learned from actual experience the lesson taught Melibeus by Prudence; though perhaps not over "alle thynges," at least over some things in the future he will do "his diligence" to keep his "persone and to warnerstoore [his] hous." All his knowledge about the nature of dreams, all his eloquent citation of authority and example, all his cocksureness have blinded him, just as "sweete temporeel richesses, and delices and honours of this world" had made Melibeus "dronken" and vulnerable to spiritual harm. The col-fox is but a catalytic agent for the woe that comes upon him because of his own great pride. "Ful of sly iniquitee" the fox may be, but he is no villain and no real threat to the regal cock until the cock "wynkes" when he should see. The fox, too, acts "accordaunt to kynde" and, in the final moment of tit for tat, suffers his own punishment for his own blindness. "Nay," he replies to Chantecleer's acknowledgment of fault, "but God yeve hym meschaunce/ That jangleth when he sholde holde his pees." The loud laments of the hens, the shrieking of Pertelote, the yelping of dogs, and the cacophony of the pursuit have not made him lose his prey; he has done it quite on his own. Tragedy might have ensued in this barnyard world, but it did not; and what threatened to be "yvel fortune" was turned into good, both protagonists emerging the wiser thereby. No wonder the Host cries "faire

chapter 8

THE LAST TALES AND THE
KNITTING UP "A GREET MATEERE":
THE CANON'S YEOMAN'S TALE
THE MANCIPLE'S TALE
THE PARSON'S TALE
AND THE *RETRACTION*

Fragments VIII, IX, and X containing *The Second Nun's Tale, The Canon's Yeoman's Tale, The Parson's Tale,* and Chaucer's *Retraction* are, according to all manuscript traditions the last of *The Canterbury Tales.* There is no question but that Chaucer intended to end the telling of tales with the prose treatise of the Parson; but there is some question whether he meant to place the tales in Fragments VIII and IX among the last to fulfil the initial plan of the pilgrimage, or in some other position and sequence. Though the *Parson's Prologue* contains a reference to the tale immediately preceding it as told by the Manciple, there is evidence that the word "manciple" was added by a scribe. The hint of an explanation for this is, of course, that Chaucer had at some time in the course of the years since he began upon his great plan changed it, perhaps forced to come to terms with the obvious difficulty of writing some 120 tales in the midst of a busy public life and in face of the inevitable lessening of physical and intellectual energy age brings.

Something other than position hints the beginning of the end. *The Second Nun's Tale* has the qualities of a sketched first draft or of a slightly revised second draft. *The Canon's Yeoman's Tale,* though it reveals that Chaucer has not lost his energy for inventiveness and his interest in trying new ways of varying familiar narrative techniques, has suffered somewhat a diminution in comic joy and zest: there is little that is "myrie" about the tale. *The Manciple's Tale* is in one way Chaucer's most unmerry, his most uncomic in all the senses used in this study. Indeed, its quality is so cynical and its thesis about life so negative that if it were not for its brilliance as narrative it would be difficult to recognize any familiar Chaucer tone in it at all. Cynics there have been among the pilgrims—the Reeve, the Merchant, the Pardoner, even the Clerk before he ceases to speak. But their cynicism has in one way or another not denied the possibility of the moral and spiritual values it may have questioned, and their bitterness has, as it has been seen in the comic framework of the pilgrimage, been full of vitality and zest. In this tale the cynic is a cynic and nothing more. His denial of values in no way and at no moment suggests doubt about the validity of the denial. To interpret this as evidence of cynicism in the now older Chaucer is not the point; but that he failed to make some comic use of this cynicism does suggest, perhaps, fatigue. And the Parson's religious treatise, so explicitly intended to "knytte up al this feeste," makes not even the small gesture at drama that *The Tale of Melibee* made. It is comedy, but in the theological sense, making a last statement about justice, about right action, and about the conditions for the eternally joyous ending. There is in these last tales not a falling off of literary powers but there is a moderating of high spirits and a lessening of vitality.

THE CANON'S YEOMAN'S TALE

There are many ways in which *The Canon's Yeoman's Tale* is remarkable, and all reveal that Chaucer has not lost interest in experimenting with methods of creating dramatic narrative. There has been no portrait of this narrator in the *General Prologue* for the simple reason that he was not among the pilgrims gathered at the Tabard on that April day. His rush upon the scene in the company with his master, the Canon, both their horses wet with sweat, surprises Chaucer as much as it does the others. Captured thus by his surprise and curiosity, we, too, become aware of the mystery that surrounds this nervous intrusion among familiar acquaintances. Instantly we too become observers, no more knowledgeable about the two new arrivals than Chaucer, not even as alert to the sinister in them as "oure Hoost," in his questioning of the Yeoman, seems to be. Neither Chaucer nor we can quite gather what is in Harry Bailly's mind, nor see or hear other than what Chaucer reports to us. The immediacy of the effect in this scene is unlike anything else Chaucer has done. Chaucer's eyes are our eyes as they see the approach of "a man that clothed was in clothes blake,/ And under-nethe he hadde a whyt surplys." The first impression is of somewhat frenzied haste. The "hakeney" of the one figure sweated so "that it wonder was to see," and the "hors that his yeman rood upon" was so covered with "foom" that it was "flekked as a pye" (VIII, 559-567). All we can know of the Canon and his Yeoman is how they "semed" to Chaucer, and we can only guess from their appearances what he guesses.

> Al light for somer rood this worthy man,
> And in myn herte wondren I began
> What that he was, til that I understood
> How that his cloke was sowed to his hood;
> For which, whan I hadde longe avysed me,
> I demed hym som chanoun for to be.
> His hat heeng at his bak doun by a laas,
> For he hadde riden moore than trot or paas;
> He hadde ay priked lik as he were wood.
> A clote-leef he hadde under his hood
> For swoot, and for to keep his heed from heete.
>
> (VIII, 568-578)

Our reporter's relish of the excitement and mystery of the two is infectious: ". . . it was joye for to seen hym swete!/ His forheed dropped as a stillatorie,/ Were ful of plantayne and of paritorie" (VIII, 579-581).

We can only watch what happens as Chaucer watches, and hear only what he hears. The Host, once more the leader of the pilgrims, asks the questions in ways that suggest he has more than a vague idea what they are. But the answers he gets are evasive and ambiguous and equivocal; they are the answers Chaucer hears. As far as the Host is concerned they are welcome to join the pilgrims, for, as he says to the Yeoman whom he is questioning, "certein it wolde seme/ Thy lord were wys, and so I may wel deme;/ He is ful jocunde also, dar I leye!" And he asks: "Can he oght telle a myrie tale or tweye,/ With which he glade may this compaignye?" "Who, sire? my lord? ye, ye, withouten lye," replies the Yeoman, and begins his series of answers that are undeniably ironic in meaning. "He kan of murthe and eek of jolitee/ Nat but ynough"—and there is something about the triple negative that alerts those of us who listen to double meaning in all that follows. "Also, sire, trusteth me,/ And ye hym knewe as wel as do I,/ Ye wolde wondre how wel and craftily/ He koude werke, and that in sondry wise." "If ye hym knewe," he repeats again, "it wolde be for youre prow;/ Ye wolde nat forgoon his aqueyntaunce." "He is a man of heigh discrecioun"; he says, and in a pun that hints at the Canon's imminent departure he warns "he is a passyng man" (VIII, 594 ff.).

The answer he gives to the Host's next question—"Is he a clerk, or noon? telle what he is"—is no more informative than his others have been:

> "Nay, he is gretter than a clerk, ywis,"
> Seyde this Yeman, "and in wordes fewe,
> Hoost, of his craft somwhat I wol yow shewe.
>   I seye, my lord kan swich subtilitee—
> But al his craft ye may nat wite at me,
> And somwhat helpe I yet to his wirkyng—
> That al this ground on which we been ridyng,
> Til that we come to Caunterbury toun,
> He koude al clene turne it up-so-doun,
> And pave it al of silver and of gold."
>   (VIII, 617-626)

The Host, clearly suspicious that what he has with him is the medieval equivalent of the confidence man, insists on drawing the Yeoman out, deliberately refusing to be satisfied with the equivocations he is getting as answers. "*Benedicitee!*" he remarks, it is marvelous that so clever a man looks so impoverished:

> "Why is thy lord so sluttish, I the preye,
> And is of power bettre clooth to beye,
> If that his dede accorde with thy speche?
> Telle me that, and that I thee biseche."
>   (VIII, 636-639)

With each answer the Yeoman's voice becomes less controlled, more strident, more clearly ironic in the ambiguities it utters.

> "Why?" quod this Yeman, "wherto axe ye me?
> God help me so, for he shal nevere thee!
> (But I wol nat avowe that I seye,
> And therfore keepe it secree, I yow preye.)
> He is to wys, in feith, as I bileeve.
> That that is overdoon, it wol nat preeve
> Aright, as clerkis seyn; it is a vice.
> Wherfore in that I holde hym lewed and nyce.
> For whan a man hath over-greet a wit,
> Ful oft hym happeth to mysusen it.
> So dooth my lord, and that me greveth soore;
> God it amende! I kan sey yow namoore."
>   (VII, 640-651)

The bitter recognition that his master is the victim of his own cleverness, too bright for his own good, leads the Yeoman, in his reply to the Host's next question—"Where dwelle ye"—to give the most concrete and specific detail he has yet given, and to almost a total loss of his barely sustained objectivity:

> "In the suburbes of a toun," quod he,
> "Lurkynge in hernes and in lanes blynde,
> Whereas thise robbours and thise theves by kynde
> Holden hir pryvee fereful residence,
> As they that dar nat shewen hir presence;
> So faren we, if I shal seye the sothe."
> (VIII, 657-662)

It is now clear to Chaucer and to us that these newcomers are alchemists and puffers, for such were the environs they were relegated to by law.

The Host's last question, "Why artow so discoloured of thy face?" sets free the tightly controlled fury and rage in the Yeoman, and the anguish of disillusionment pours forth in a torrent of words like "illusioun," "fals," "grope," "faille," an anguish that warns the Canon of more particular details to come and sends him away "for verray sorwe and shame," as "fot-hot" as he had come. There is, in the Yeoman's answer, no doubt left as to the dishonesty of their practice:

> "Peter!" quod he, "God yeve it harde grace,
> I am so used in the fyr to blowe
> That it hath chaunged my colour, I trowe.
> I am nat wont in no mirour to prie,
> But swynke soore and lerne multiplie.
> We blondren evere and pouren in the fir,
> And for al that we faille of oure desir,
> For evere we lakken oure conclusioun.
> To muchel folk we doon illusioun,
> And borwe gold, be it a pound or two,
> Or ten, or twelve, or manye sommes mo,
> And make hem wenen, at the leeste weye,
> That of a pound we koude make tweye.
> Yet it is fals, but ay we han good hope
> It for to doon, and after it we grope.
> But that science is so fer us biforn
> We mowen nat, although we hadde it sworn,
> It overtake, it slit awey so faste.
> It wole us maken beggers atte laste."
> (VIII, 665-683)

With the departure of his "lord," the Yeoman is free to tell his story—
"Al that I kan anon now wol I telle"—and this he does, with the fury of
one who has been victimized and has willingly allowed himself to be:
". . . for al my smert and al my grief,/ For al my sorwe, labour, and
meschief,/ I koude nevere leve it in no wise" (VIII, 704; 712-714).

The tale he tells—that is not a tale at all in the ordinary sense, but
is an anguished combining of autobiographical monologue and the
exemplum used in sermons to make concrete the subject of the "prechyng"
—becomes a working through of his rage. Emotions govern its organization; disillusionment, frustration, a never quite stilled desire to go on
and on, hope that is at the same time illusion, give place to each other
in rapid succession. It is a tale that is shaped by the very tensions that
have been created by its theme and it portrays its teller as one in the
act of sustaining equilibrium in the face of the constant threat of dis-
equilibrium. By the end of the tale some measure of calm, some modicum
of peace has come, though it is clear that both are temporal.

Many things have caused the rage within the Yeoman and it is impossible to tell what one rankles more than another. It is his long
apprenticeship that has resulted in nothing but financial and physical
impoverishment:

> With this Chanoun I dwelt have seven yeer,
> And of his science am I never the neer.
> Al that I hadde I have lost therby,
> And, God woot, so hath many mo than I.
> Ther I was wont to be right fressh and gay
> Of clothyng and of oother good array,
> Now may I were an hose upon myn heed;
> And wher my colour was bothe fresshe and reed,
> Now is it wan and of a leden hewe—
> Whoso it useth, soore shal he rewe!—
> And of my swynk yet blered is myn ye.
> Lo! which avantage is to multiplie!
> That slydynge science hath me maad so bare
> That I have no good, wher that evere I fare;
> And yet I am endetted so therby,
> Of gold that I have borwed, trewely,
> That whil I lyve I shal it quite nevere.
>   (VIII, 720-736)

It is his indignation, more righteous than moral, at the realization that
others have also been foolishly attracted to alchemy, "that slydyng
science." It is resentment that he has been given knowledge in quantity,

yet has never really comprehended that knowledge; and it is, at the same time, his pride in that knowledge. The terms of alchemy tumble out in their exact detail, but what they really mean, or how they can be worked into general concepts, he does not understand. "The elvysshe craft," for all his experience with it, remains a mystery, and he cannot forget that he is kept in real ignorance, a "lewed man." And it is his recognition that the search for the philosopher's stone is inevitably doomed to futility and yet at the same time is absolutely irresistible. More deeply anguishing than the failure to find that which will turn sick-ness into health, woe into joy, the fragilely mortal into the immortal, has been the urgent desire to uncover the quintessence that lies at the heart of "the diversity of thynges."

> A! nay! lat be; the philosophres stoon,
> Elixir clept, we sechen faste echoon;
> For hadde we hym, thanne were we siker ynow.
> But unto God of hevene I make avow,
> For al oure craft, whan we han al ydo,
> And al oure sleighte, he wol nat come us to.
> He hath ymaad us spenden muchel good,
> For sorwe of which almoost we wexen wood,
> But that good hope crepeth in oure herte,
> Supposynge evere, though we sore smerte,
> To be releeved by hym afterward.
> Swich supposyng and hope is sharp and hard;
> I warne yow wel, it is to seken evere.
> (VIII, 862-874)

His search has been like the search of men everywhere, in all times, for the impossible:

> That futur temps hath maad men to dissevere,
> In trust thereof, from al that evere they hadde.
> Yet of that art they kan nat wexen sadde,
> For unto hem it is a bitter sweete,—
> So semeth it,—for nadde they but a sheete,
> Which that they myghte wrappe hem inne a-nyght,
> And a brat to walken inne by daylyght,
> They wolde hem selle and spenden on this craft.
> They kan nat stynte til no thyng be laft.
> (VIII, 875-893)

The "hope" that "is sharp and hard," the terrible need to "seken evere,"

has destroyed not only his health and his purse, but has undermined
his whole sense of truth, his trust in his capacity to read reality aright:

> . . . I dar seye this,
> That we concluden evermoore amys.
> We faille of that which that we wolden have,
> And in oure madnesse evermoore we rave.
> And whan we been togidres everichoon,
> Every man semeth a Salomon.
> But al thyng which that shineth as the gold
> Nis nat gold, as that I have herd it told;
> Ne every appul that is fair at eye
> Ne is nat good, what so men clappe or crye.
> Right so, lo, fareth it amonges us:
> He that semeth the wiseste, by Jhesus!
> Is moost fool, whan it cometh to the preef;
> And he that semeth trewest is a theef.
> That shal ye knowe, er that I fro yow wende,
> By that I of my tale have maad an ende.
>
> (VIII, 956-971)

The embittered irony, the impassioned cynicism he reveals, is a way
of handling his disillusionment, but it is clear from the degree of passion
with which it is proclaimed that he has not fully yielded to his own
conclusion.

   The "Pars Secunda" of his tale, the *exemplum* he relates to prove his
bitter conclusion, describes the ways in which a "chanoun of religioun,"
by "sleightes and . . . infinite falsenesse" fools a greedy and stupid priest.
It is an illustration of how the racket works, how the tricks of the
trade are used in this particular confidence game, how hope for the easy
money makes victims of many men. Though he protests that he is not
speaking about "his canon" but about another, whose cleverness was
legendary, it is not hard to guess, from the degree of emotional involvement in his account, from the confusion of third person pronouns, that
he is indeed relating from actual experience the activity of his own
master, "the foule feend hym quelle!" "Al to symple is my tonge to
pronounce,/ As ministre of my wit, the doublenesse/ Of this chanoun,
roote of alle cursednesse!" he says, and the demonstrative pronouns join
with the personal to create an apparent ambiguity that points in reality
to the canon so lately fled from among the pilgrims:

> He semed freendly to hem that knewe hym noght,
> But he was feendly bothe in werk and thoght.

It weerieth me to telle of his falsnesse,
But nathelees yet wol I it expresse,
To th'entente that men may be war therby,
And for noon oother cause, trewely.
(VIII, 1302-1307)

It is the detailed description of the trickery practiced by this "chanoun," this "cursed man," this "roote of al trecherie," upon a priest who deserved no better than he got, that brings to the Yeoman some resolution of his rage, some quieting of his fury, some resignation to his frustration. By the end of the tale he can give voice to some pious maxims about the evils of money and can resign himself to remaining ignorant about "the secree of secrees" that God intends shall never be revealed to men. For the moment, at least, his personal anguish is stilled as he gives recognition to ancient and medieval wisdom, pagan and Christian, that conspire to calm as well as to frustrate the human being eternally questing for the answer to the mystery at the heart of things:

Thanne conclude I thus, sith that God of hevene
Ne wil nat that the philosophres nevene
How that a man shal come unto this stoon,
I rede, as for the beste, lete it goon.
For whoso maketh God his adversarie,
As for to werken any thyng in contrarie
Of his wil, certes, never shal he thryve,
Though that he multiplie terme of his lyve.
And there a poynt; for ended is my tale.
God sende every trewe man boote of his bale!
(VIII, 1472-1481)

THE MANCIPLE'S TALE

However cynical he may have become about his craft, the anguished tone suggests that the Canon's Yeoman is not really cynical about life. The truth he is in search of cannot be reached, but that does not necessarily deny the existence of other truths. For the Manciple, all truth is so difficult to be got at, so bitter in the search, that it is best not to try at all; any concept of its nature turns out to be illusory and what is "fals" and what is "trewe" becomes impossible to distinguish. "My sone, be war," his mother has taught him, "and be noon auctour newe/ Of tydynges, wheither they been fals or trewe;/ Wherso thou come, amonges hye or lowe,/ Kepe wel thy tonge, and thenk upon the crowe." Even the brief comic action that precedes the telling of his tale of "Phebus" betrays the essentially cold-bloodedness of the man, the cruelty of the true cynic. Because it is obvious that the Cook, delegated by the Host as the next to tell a tale, is far gone in wine, the Manciple takes it upon himself to "excuse" him "of his tale." "See how he ganeth, lo! this dronken wight,/ As though he wolde swolwe us anonright," he points out:

> "Hoold cloos thy mouth, man, by thy fader kyn!
> The devel of helle sette his foot therin!
> Thy cursed breeth infecte wole us alle.
> Fy, stynkyng swyn! fy, foule moote thee falle!
> A! taketh heede, sires, of this lusty man.
> Now, sweete sire, wol ye justen atte fan?
> Therto me thynketh ye been wel yshape!
> I trowe that ye dronken han wyn ape,
> And that is whan men pleyen with a straw."
>
> (IX, 37-45)

That the Cook's wrath is aroused is evident, but drink has made him helpless. With his thumping collapse upon the ground, it is clear to the Host that the Cook is indeed too drunk to speak—he has more than enough to do to stay upright on the horse they have restored him to. But, the Host warns the Manciple, though defenseless when drunk the Cook may not be so when sober. And the Manciple, wanting no contest, suggests the addition of more wine to the mouth already "stynkyng" with it:

> "Yet hadde I levere payen for the mare
> Which he rit on, than he sholde with me stryve.
> I wol nat wratthen hym, also moot I thryve!
> That that I spak, I seyde it in my bourde.
> And wite ye what? I have heer in a gourde
> A draghte of wyn, ye, of a ripe grape,
> And right anon ye shul seen a good jape.
> This Cook shal drynke thereof, if I may.
> Up peyne of deeth, he wol nat seye me nay."
>
> (IX, 78-86)

That Chaucer, the pilgrim, finds the Manciple's action unfunny is clear:

> And certeynly, to tellen as it was,
> Of this vessel the Cook drank faste, allas!
> What neded hym? he drank ynough biforn.
> And whan he hadde pouped in this horn,
> To the Manciple he took the gourde agayn;

> And of that drynke the Cook was wonder fayn,
> And thanked hym in swich wise as he koude.
>
> (IX, 87-93)

But the Host, relieved that the danger of contention is over, is overjoyed that mirth is once more ensured:

> Thanne gan oure Hooste to laughen wonder loude,
> And seyde, "I se wel it is necessarie,
> Where that we goon, good drynke with us carie;
> For that wol turne rancour and disese
> T'acord and love, and many a wrong apese.
>   O thou Bacus, yblessed be thy name,
> That so kanst turnen ernest into game!"
>
> (IX, 94-100)

The Manciple has learned well the lesson his mother has taught him. Advised by her against "muchel spekyng," he tells a tale so short and so taut that it is over almost before it has begun. Warned by her against assuming that a distinction can be made between what is "fals" and what is "trewe," he illustrates the accuracy of her thesis and, in the process, negates whatever values his story might seem to propose.

For his tale he chooses a story that tells how the crow became black. Though in many ways it resembles Ovid's account in the *Metamorphoses*, it is in no way a translation of the Latin; nor is there any analogue exactly like it, no version in which action and motivation are so inconsistent, so contradictory, nor the punishment given the crow so essentially unjust. "Phebus," though he is "the semelieste man . . . fulfild of gentillesse,/ Of honour, and of parfit worthynesse," kills his wife upon being told by his pet crow the truth about her infidelity. But no sooner was she dead than he turns upon the crow that was at that time "whit . . . as is a snow-whit swan" and punishes him for telling the truth. In spite of the fact that there has been no question about her betrayal, "Phebus" laments her death as if she were the purest and most faithful of wives:

> "O deere wyf! o gemme of lustiheed!
> That were to me so sad and eek so trewe,
> Now listow deed, with face pale of hewe,
> Ful giltelees, that dorste I swere, ywis!
> O rakel hand, to doon so foule amys!
> O trouble wit, o ire recchelees,
> That unavysed smyteth gilteles!
> O wantrust, ful of fals suspecion,
> Where was thy wit and thy discrecion?"
>
> (IX, 274-282)

"Traitour," he cries to the crow, "O false theef"

"I wol thee quite anon thy false tale.
Thou songe whilom lyk a nyghtyngale;
Now shaltow, false theef, thy song forgon,
And eek thy white fetheres everichon,
Ne nevere in al thy lyf ne shaltou speke.
Thus shal men on a traytour been awreke;
Thou and thyn ofspryng evere shul be blake,
Ne nevere sweete noyse shul ye make,
But evere crie agayn tempest and rayn,
In tokenynge that thurgh thee my wyf is slayn."

                                                    (IX, 293-302)

The Manciple's attitude toward Phoebus and the doting love he bore his wife is as contemptuously sardonic as it is toward the wisdom of the crow for not holding its tongue. Phoebus was jealous of her and tried to keep her away from other men. The vanity of that, intimates the Manciple, ought to be obvious. A good wife should not be kept apart, and a "shrewe" cannot be; besides, there is not much one can do about "a thyng which that nature/ Hath natureelly set in a creature." Put a bird in a cage, treat it kindly and generously, keep it "clenly as thou may," yet it will forever "doon his bisynesse" to escape. Take a cat and give him milk and "tendre flessh, and make his couche of silk," but let him see a mouse "go by the wal" and off he will run, scorning "milk and flessh and al." Men are, he admits, given to "newefangelnesse" as much, even more so, than women, but it is a woman who betrays his hero and, he hints, it is only to be expected as part of her nature as woman. He is jocosely ironical about the ways men have found to "name the deed"—betrayal is betrayal whether done by a lady or a peasant woman:

And so bifel, whan Phebus was absent,
His wyf anon for hir lemman sent.
Hir lemman? Certes, this is a knavyssh speche!
Foryeveth it me, and that I yow biseche.
    The wise Plato seith, as ye may rede,
The word moot nede accorde with the dede.
If men shal telle proprely a thyng,
The word moot cosyn be to the werkyng.
I am a boystrous man, right thus seye I,
Ther nys no difference, trewely,
Bitwixe a wyf that is of heigh degree,
If of hir body dishonest she bee,

And a povre wenche, oother than this—
If it so be they werke bothe amys—
But that the gentile, in estaat above,
She shal be cleped his lady, as in love;
And for that oother is a povre womman,
She shal be cleped his wenche or his lemman.
And, Got it woot, myn owene deere brother,
Men leyn that oon as lowe as lith that oother.

(IX, 203-221)

Mankind, he asserts, is no more reasonable, no more logical in its evalua-
tion of other "dedes"; there is no difference between a tyrant, an outlaw,
and a "theef erraunt" except that a tyrant, being mightier than others, is
"cleped capitayn." What men do, apparently, with any principle of
justice that may exist is to deprive it of any meaning. And, in any case,
the less one speaks about anything, the better. The Manciple repeats his
mother's advice almost as if it were a litany, its renunciation of the possibility of any vital communication between human beings underscoring
unmistakably his own wearied view of life:

Lordynges, by this ensample I yow preye,
Beth war, and taketh kep what that ye seye:
Ne telleth nevere no man in youre lyf
How that another man hath dight his wyf;
He wol yow haten mortally, certeyn.
Daun Salomon, as wise clerkes seyn,
Techeth a man to kepen his tonge weel.
But, as I seyde, I am noght textueel.
But nathelees, thus taughte me my dame:
"My sone, thenk on the crowe, a Goddes name!
My sone, keep wel thy tonge, and keep thy freend.
A wikked tonge is worse than a feend;
My sone, from a feend men may hem blesse.
My sone, God of his endelees goodnesse
Walled a tonge with teeth and lippes eke,
For man sholde hym avyse what he speeke.
My sone, ful ofte, for to muche speche
Hath many a man been spilt, as clerkes teche;
But for litel speche avysely
Is no man shent, to speke generally.
My sone, thy tonge sholdestow restreyne
At alle tymes, but whan thou doost thy peyne
To speke of God, in honour and preyere.

> The first vertu, sone, if thou wolt leere,
> Is to restreyne and kepe wel thy tonge;
> Thus lerne children whan that they been yonge.
> My sone, of muchel spekying yvele avysed,
> Ther lasse spekyng hadde ynough suffised,
> Comth muchel harm; thus was me toold and taught.
>
> .   .   .   .
>
> Thyng that is seyd is seyd, and forth it gooth,
> Though hym repente, or be hym nevere so looth.
> He is his thral to whom that he hath seyd
> A tale of which he is now yvele apayd.
> My sone, be war, and be noon auctour newe
> Of tidynges, wheither they been false or trewe.
> Whereso thou come, amonges hye or lowe,
> Kepe wel thy tonge, and thenk upon the crowe."
>   (IX, 309-337; 355-362)

It is not hard to discern in this unloquacious speaker the "gentil Manciple" of the *General Prologue* whose shrewdness quietly "set the cappe"
of the young lawyers "byynge of vitaille" he was in charge of.

THE PARSON'S TALE

To the Parson, the most idealized portrait in the *General
Prologue* the Host gives the task of making an end to the telling of tales.
"The sonne fro the south lyne was descended," it was four o'clock, the
shadows that foretell the end of day are gathering, and the pilgrims
are entering a "thropes ende." In a multitude of ways Chaucer announces
that *The Canterbury Tales* have almost all been narrated, that the pilgrimage is nearing its destination, though we have not been told
whether that destination is Canterbury or London. And the Host, in
eminent satisfaction, says to "oure joly compaignye":

> . . . "Lordynges everichoon,
> Now lakketh us no tales mo than oon.
> Fulfilled is my sentence and my decree;
> I trowe that we han herd of ech degree;
> Almoost fulfild is al myn ordinaunce."
>   (X, 15-19)

His words to the Parson tell us that the game is finished; no longer does
he want the spirit of play to dominate. ". . . Me thynketh by thy
cheere/ Thou sholdest knytte up wel a greet mateere," he comments
and concludes, "Telle us a fable anon, for cokkes bones!" The Parson has

no questions about the nature of his task. It has been his "bisynesse" to draw folk to heaven; it becomes his business now to translate the journey of the pilgrims into terms that will "shewe . . . the wey, in this viage./ Of thilke parfit glorious pilgrymage/ That highte Jerusalem celestial" (X, 48-51). The time for entertainment is past, now is the moment for "moralitee and vertuous mateere." "I kan nat geeste 'rum, ram, ruf,' by lettre," he announces, therefore, "I wol yow telle a myrie tale in prose/ To knytte up al this feeste, and make an ende." The pilgrims to a man assent.

> For, as it seemed, it was for to doone,
> To enden in som vertuous sentence,
> And for to yeve hym space and audience.
>
> .   .   .   .
>
> Oure Hoost hadde the wordes for us alle:
> "Sire preest," quod he, "now faire yow bifaille!
> Telleth," quod he, "youre meditacioun.
> But hasteth yow, the sonne wole adoun;
> Beth fructuous, and that in litel space,
> And to do wel God sende yow his grace!
> Sey what yow list, and we wol gladly heere."
>   (X, 62-64; 67-73)

Banter and joking, contention and strife, lusty joy and earthy gaiety are stilled, but "mirth" remains, for the Parson's "meditacioun," though it deals with sin, defines the conditions for forgiveness and ends with the promise of eternal happiness in God's infinite mercy and love. In this religious treatise the human comedy of the pilgrimage is not so much translated into a divine comedy as it is shown to be a way in which divine happiness can be gained. Sinful the pilgrims may be, yet the doctrine of the Parson shows the way sins can be made to work for good. Penitence, Confession and Satisfaction are available for anyone who will know himself well enough to recognize their power. *The Parson's Tale,* in spite of those critics who regret its lack of dramatic and narrative interest, is a fitting end to what is really a long narrative poem, no matter how dramatic in essence, no matter how theatrical in many of its moments. It makes a prose statement, abstract and theoretical, moral and religious, about the human nature that the tales have revealed in vital concreteness and in all the particularity of "accidence." Though *The Canterbury Tales* are not turned into allegory in the light of *The Parson's Tale,* they are, without losing any of their particularity, charged with a generality and a universality. The Parson's analysis of human nature is simply another way of understanding the "diversity" of men that has already been revealed in the action and interaction of the tales. It knits up the whole matter of *The Canterbury Tales,* reducing the complex reality to the simplicity of exposition, summarizing in non-dramatic form what Chaucer seems to have understood of the nature of human existence.

At the beginning of the tale, and throughout the greater part of it, Chaucer maintains his intention of letting the tale reveal the teller. Though the voice of the Parson is kept low and unobtrusive, though the revelation of personality is underplayed in order that there may be no distraction from the content of the tale itself, that voice is heard. The man who speaks is clearly the "povre Persoun of a toun," the pilgrim whom Chaucer has described in the *General Prologue*: "a goode man . . . riche . . . of hooly thoght and werk, . . . a shepherde and noght a mercenarie." Severe though he is in his discussion of sin, and uncompromising in his attitude toward it, he is never "despitous,/ ne of his speche daungerous ne digne,/ But in his techyng discreet and benynge." His essential message is "divinely myrie"—that despair has no place in the heart of man and wanhope is the most deadly of sins, since it denies the love and mercy of God and is, in effect, a refusal to admit that man himself is capable of loving God. No tale of all *The Canterbury Tales* ends on a more benignly happy note than this one as it promises, upon the condition of penance, the "endelees blisse of hevene." For the pilgrims who have just spent many days in contention and rivalry, in vital and joyous clash there is the reminder that in heaven there is "no contrarioustee of wo ne grevaunce; ther alle harmes been passed of this present lyf." The company there shall be "blisful," rejoicing not among the guests at the Tabard nor in bawdy tales nor even in fictional promises of earthly or divine reward, but "everich of otheres joye." And "ther as the body, that whilom was syk, freele, and fieble, and mortal is inmortal, and so strong and so hool that ther may no thyng apeyren it;/ . . . but every soule replenyssed with the sighte of the parfit knowynge of God" (X, 1075 ff).

The treatise, for which no known source has been discovered, is an effective illustration of the Parson's ability to "snybben sharply for the nonys." Waiting after "no pompe and reverence," he includes Monk, Prioress, Knight, Wife of Bath, Pardoner, Chaucer—all who have preceded him in the "game" of the pilgrimage—within his description of human nature. His opening lines, quoted from *Jeremiah 6*, set forth clearly the perspective from which we, in retrospect, are to view the pilgrimage:

> *State super vias, et videte, et interrogate de viis antiquis que sit via bona, et ambulate in ea; et inuenietis refrigerium ani-*

mabus vestris, etc. . . . . Stondeth upon the weyes, and seeth
and axeth of olde pathes (that is to seyn, of olde sentences)
which is the goode way,/ and walketh in that wey, and ye shal
fynde refresshynge for youre soules.

(X, 71 ff.)

And thus he translates the "wey" of the "nyne and twenty" into the
familiar image of the journey of life. "Of whiche weyes," the Parson
points out, "ther is a ful noble wey and a ful convenable, which may nat
fayle to man ne to womman that thurgh synne hath mysgoon fro the
righte wey of Jerusalem celestial." The "ful noble wey" is the way of
Penitence, the way of recognition and acknowledgement of sins per-
formed. And Penitence can not come unless the "thynges apertenen and
bihoven to Penitence" are known, and these "thynges" can be known
only when the nature of sin is understood.

His treatise, divided into three parts, has as its purpose the description and definition of those "thynges" that constitute "sin." Sober though
he may be and serious about his subject matter, the Parson moves in
his discussion of Penitence, Contrition, and the seven deadly sins with
their opposite virtues, always from sadness to joy. True penitence, he
says, wins for the penitent grace and joy: "For soothly oure sweete Lord
Jhesu Crist hath spared us so debonairly in oure folies, that if he ne hadde
pitee of mannes soule, a sory song we mygthen alle synge" (X, 312). With
words eloquent in faith, he concludes the section on Contrition by reminding his audience of God's love and of His reception of man's love.
And he ends his whole discourse with a plea against despair. No sin is
too evil for repentance, no relapse into sin too frequent, no moment too
late—"the mercy of Crist is alwey redy to receiven hym in mercy . . . if
him list" (X, 1070 ff.). The righting of the soul with God, the re-establishing of the "spiritual equilibrium," is for the Parson a matter of human
choice, even as the constant effort to keep in equilibrium the tensions
of human relations and the conflicts within the self was a matter of
choice and of personal responsibility for the pilgrims.

It is in the longest section—the third, given over to the delineation of
the seven deadly sins and their contrary virtues— that the Parson describes by indirection the natures of the pilgrims who have been with
him on the road to Canterbury. His order of listing the vices and virtues
is the one that seems to have been the most usual in the Middle Ages;
Pride and Humility, Envy and Charity, Anger and Patience (or "Debonairtee"), Wanhope and Fortitude, Avarice and Generosity (or "Pitee"), Gluttony and Abstinence, Lechery and Chastity. But the amount of
detail in his analyses is not equal. Arranged in order of weighted importance, the Parson's list suggests a corresponding hierarchy of con-

demnation. Anger, Pride, Lechery, Avarice, Wanhope, Envy, and Gluttony reveal by their sequence the degree of his concern with the
vices; Chastity, Patience, Charity, Pity, Fortitude, Humility, and Abstinence, his concern with the virtues. Neither Gluttony nor Abstinence
receive marked attention; Anger and Chastity do. And we are reminded
that man's contentious nature has been responsible for much of the
dramatic movement of the pilgrimage. "Accordaunt to knyde" the pilgrims have journeyed, in "sodeyn Ire . . . withouten avisement and
consentynge of resoun," sometimes full of "rancour" and pride "that
ay bloweth and encreesseth the fir by chidynge and wikked wordes,"
sometimes in open discord and "strif." The opposite of "Ire" is, of course,
"Debonairtee," and "eek another vertu that men callen Pacience or
suffrance." Contentious the pilgrims have been, but sufferance has been
imposed upon them and the "game" has been played out to the end.
There has been a Griselda, a Constance, a Cecilia, a Virginia, and a
Dorigen in the stories to stand as examples of sufferance. And there is
the narrator, the "povre Parson," whose voice is the last to be heard.
But in general, tolerable co-existence among the pilgrims has depended
upon the constant re-establishment of mutual sufferance, upon control
exerted by the Host, upon the following of rules which artificially set
limits upon all that was aggressive and hostile in those who agreed to
play "the game."

If there are any pilgrims who take offense at any of the words of the
last tale, it can only be because they recognize themselves as members
of the human race. The Parson directs no clearly specific condemnation
toward any one of the "nyne and twenty." In no sense have they been
allegorical devices or personifications of the vices and virtues, but complex embodiments of all the ingredients of human kind. Inevitably, however, certain pilgrims come vividly to mind as the Parson describes the
appearances of the sins.

The Pardoner emerges in retrospect as the one most "envoluped in
synne," as he himself had vaingloriously characterized himself, "a ful
vicious man." There is no one of the seven sins he does not fit into,
though the terms defining Pride most clearly suggest his nature. "No
man kan outrely telle the nombre of the twigges and of the harmes
that cometh of Pride," says the Parson, "yet wol I shewe a partie of hem,
as ye shal understonde." The "twigges" he lists read like an analysis of
the "noble ecclesiaste" and convey a last final moral judgment upon
him: "Inobedient is he that disobeyeth for despit to the commandementz
of God . . . ; Avauntour is he that bosteth of the harm . . . that he
hath doon; Ypocrite is he that hideth to shewe hym swich as he is, and
sheweth hym swich as he noght is; . . . Inpudent is he that for his
pride hath no shame of his synnes; swellynge of Herte is whan a man

rejoyseth hym of harm that he hath doon; . . . Inpacient is he that wol nat been ytaught ne undernome of his vice, and by strif werreieth trouthe wityngly, and deffendeth his folye" (X, 390 ff.). Like those given to Anger, he is guilty of spiritual manslaughter; and his text, *radix malorum est cupiditas*, unites him to those given over to Avarice, those whose dedication to the material have thus lost the comfort of God. The Glutton, given to "dronkenesse, that is the horrible sepulture of mannes resoun," calls up the voice of the Pardoner, shrill and arrogant with its "draughte of moyste and corny ale."

No other pilgrim so clearly manifests the combination of the sins the Parson describes. It is true that the Wife of Bath comes to mind most frequently when he is distinguishing certain qualities of Pride, or Envy, or Anger, or Lechery; but so do one or more of the other pilgrims. If Alisoun, in her pride, is guilty of "an outrageous array of clothyng," so are the Prioress, the Monk, the Friar, the Merchant, and the Squire. If her envy of other women and her contention with her husbands is being pointed out, so is the anger of the Miller, the Reeve, the Friar, the Summoner, the Manciple, the Cook, and the Host. And if her love of love is to be condemned as Lechery, at least her "corage" and her love have saved her from Wanhope. Patient she may not have been in her struggles with life's circumstances, but she has surely shown Fortitude, "this vertu" that makes "folk to undertake harde thynges and grevouse thynges, by hir owene wil, wisely and resonably." In her own terms she has withstood despair "by wit and by resoun and by discrecioun," and though by no means exempt from moral judgment, she can be viewed with understanding (X, 730 ff. and 930 ff.).

So the last tale, in its sober fashion, clearly joins together the real that is probable and the ideal that is possible in human nature. And in the whole gravely gentle document, the Wife of Bath, the Pardoner, the "nyne and twenty," are granted compassionate understanding and a promise that it is never too late to ensure "perdurable joy." For the pilgrims are of the human race and as such are the sons and daughters of Adam—" . . . of hym flesshly descended . . . and engendred of vile and corrupt mateere. . . . Witnesse on Seint Jame the Apostel, that seith that 'every wight is tempted in his owene concupiscence'; that is to seyn, that everich of us hath matere and occasioun to be tempted of the norissynge of synne that is in his body" (X, 330 ff.).

Chaucer, the "maker," like Chaucer, the pilgrim, is also sinner, for he, likewise, is descended from Adam. As the voice of the Parson fades into the fictional world it had finally dominated, the voice of the poet is heard, for he, too, is subject to the conditions of penitence. It is as a man, not as an artist, that Chaucer confesses his "literary sins" at the end of *The Canterbury Tales*:

> Now preye I to hem alle that herkne this litel tretys or rede, that if ther be any thyng in it that liketh hem, that therof they thanken oure Lord Jhesu Crist, of whom procedeth al wit and al goodnesse./ And if ther be any thyng that displese hem, I preye hem also that they arrette it to the defaute of myn unkonnynge, and nat to my wyl, that wolde ful fayn have seyd bettre if I hadde had konnynge./ For oure book seith "Al that is writen is writen for oure doctrine," and that is myn entente.
> (X, 1081 ff.).

The list he makes of the works he knows are "worldly" and are therefore to be freely acknowledged as not "hooly thynges," includes his "translacions and enditynges of worldly vanitees . . . as is the book of Troilus; the book also of Fame; the book of the xxv. Ladies; the book of the Duchesse; the book of Seint Valentynes day of the Parlement of Briddes; the tales of Caunterbury, thilke that sownen into synne;/ the book of the Leoun; and many another book, if they were in my remembrance, and many a song and many a leccherous lay; that Crist for his grete mercy foryeve me the synne."

Though he "revokes" thus the tales most readers, being also members of the human race, find most worthy to be praised, his revocation does not deny their creation. That he has written them is a fact, even as the committing of sin is a fact for the sinner, an act done and not to be undone, since it is a part of the doer. And though in many ways it is true that even sin and error can be turned to good account if the sinner is contrite and penitent—"al that writen is writen for oure doctrine"—a charitable and a holy deed is of great value in appraising the nature of the sinner. So Chaucer lists his "goode werkes" that "refreyne venial synne":

> But of the translacion of Boece de Consolacione, and othere bookes of legendes of seintes, and omelies, and moralitee, and devocioun,/ that thanke I oure Lord Jhesu Crist and his blisful Mooder, and alle the seintes of hevene,/ bisekynge hem that they from hennes forth unto my lyves ende sende me grace to biwayle my giltes, and to studie to the salvacioun of my soule, and graunte me grace of verray penitence, confessioun and satisfaccioun to doon in this present lyf,/ thurgh the benigne grace of hym that is kyng of kynges and preest over alle preestes, that boghte us with the precious blood of his herte;/ so that I may been oon of hem at the day of doom that shulle be saved. *Qui cum patre et Spiritu Sancto vivit et regnat Deus per omnia secula. Amen.*

The sense of encroaching old age and the awareness that death was not far off may or may not have led Chaucer to write the sober but not uncheerful *Parson's Tale* and to make his own "confessioun" publicly. But the view of man's life and his relation to God, here specifically religious and theological in statement, is the same view he has always had. It represents no "conversion" to an attitude and a belief that have not been his. To take it as such is to forget an essential fact about the Middle Ages; and it is to ignore an essential fact about the poetry of Chaucer—its intrinsic union of mirth and morality. The vision of life that finds its lucid summary in his last words is the vision that has informed his poetry from the beginning, the one that made him, in spite of his one venture into tragedy, the comic poet he was. It is clearly the source of the moral essence of his comedy.

Chaucer's "mirth" came into being almost as an attestation of his moral vision and is an exploration of the complex potential of that morality. What is "mirthful" in his poetry is so because his ways of making sense out of the world of human experience included the reality of human diversity, the facts of the mutability of things and the temporality of life as part of a larger moral order. Life is what all Chaucer's poetry affirms— perhaps the act of living is a more accurate way of putting it. His characters become vital in their contests to maintain the self, and the contests dramatize his moral and ethical values. Aspects of life that seem to be opposites are truly so; it is the larger reality their coexistent tensions create that is a hint of the nature of the whole. All oppositions vitalize each other, all are appearances reflecting in their necessary diversity the "both-and" of reality.

selecteɒ bibliogᴙaphy

The bibliography that follows is intended to be a general guide for those interested in reading some of the standard works on Chaucer and his poetry; in no way does it take note of the many specialized studies, for to have done so would have been to extend it many pages. The chronological arrangement is intended merely to indicate the continuing vitality of the study of Chaucer into this present century.

ANNOTATED EDITIONS

Robinson, F. N. *The Poetical Works of Chaucer*, second edition, Boston 1957

Donaldson, E. T. *Chaucer's Poetry: An Anthology for the Modern Reader*, New York 1958

WORKS OF GENERAL CRITICISM

Kittredge, G. L. *Chaucer and His Poetry*, Cambridge 1915

Manly, J. M. *Some New Light on Chaucer*, New York 1926

Lowes, J. L. *Geoffrey Chaucer*, Oxford 1934

Patch, H. R. *On Rereading Chaucer*, Cambridge 1939

Coghill, Nevill. *The Poet Chaucer*, Oxford 1949

Tatlock, J. S. P. *The Mind and Art of Chaucer*, Syracuse 1950

Speirs, John. *Chaucer the Maker*, London 1951

Malone, Kemp. *Chapters on Chaucer*, Baltimore 1951

Gerould, G. H. *Chaucerian Essays*, Princeton 1952

Muscatine, Charles. *Chaucer and the French Tradition*, Berkeley and Los Angeles 1957

Baum, Paull F. *Chaucer: A Critical Appreciation*, Durham 1958

Bronson, B. H. *In Search of Chaucer*, Toronto 1960

242

Robertson, D. W., Jr. *A Preface to Chaucer: Studies in Medieval Perspectives*, Princeton 1962

WORKS OF CRITICISM OF PARTICULAR POEMS

The Parliament of Fowls
Bennett, J. A. W. *The Parlement of Foules*, Oxford 1957
Troilus and Criseyde
Meech, Sanford B. *Design in Chaucer's Troilus*, Syracuse 1959
The Canterbury Tales
Bowden, Muriel A. *A Commentary on the General Prologue to the Canterbury Tales*, New York 1948
Lawrence, W. W. *Chaucer and the Canterbury Tales*, New York 1950
Baldwin, R. *The Unity of the Canterbury Tales*, Copenhagen 1955
Owen, Charles A. *Discussions of the Canterbury Tales*, Boston 1961
Brooks, H. F. *Chaucer's Pilgrims: the artistic order of the portraits*, London 1962

COLLECTIONS OF CRITICAL ESSAYS (paperback)

Wagenknecht, E. C. *Chaucer: Modern Essays in Criticism*, Oxford 1959
Schoeck, R. and Jerome Taylor. *Chaucer Criticism*. 2 vols., Notre Dame 1960-1961

MEDIEVAL PHILOSOPHY

Patch, H. R. *The Tradition of Boethius*, Oxford 1935
Hawkins, D. J. B. *A Sketch of Medieval Philosophy*, New York 1948
Gilson, Etienne. *History of Christian Philosophy in the Middle Ages*, New York 1955
Knowles, Dom David. *The Evolution of Medieval Thought*, London 1962

REFERENCE WORKS

Wells, J. E. *A Manual of Writings in Middle English*, New Haven 1916; subsequent supplements 1919, etc.
French, R. D. *A Chaucer Handbook*, New York and London, 1947

index